What others are saying about this book:

"This book is a must for those considering publishing as a business, for writers who want to investigate self-publishing, and is eminently useful for its new and old ideas to those who have already begun to do it. A fine and handy guide by a fine and successful publisher." - Small Press Review.

"Never before has this reviewer seen such accurate, concise information covering all the aspects of self-publishing as will be found in this helpful book." - Naples, Florida, Daily News.

"Poynter is at his best when discussing such specifics as starting one's own publishing house; dealing with printers; establishing discount, credit and return policies; promoting, advertising and selling a book; and order fulfillment." Publishers Weekly.

"Self-publishers: This how-to book and encyclopedia will be your most important investment. The subject matter is succinctly stated, well-organized with excellent illustrations, and particularly notable are the sections on how to gather and refine material for any nonfiction book, no matter who publishes it." - Teacher-Writer.

"A handy, concise and informative sourcebook...Expertly organized and chock full of hard facts, helpful hints, and pertinent illustrations...Recommended for all libraries..." - The Southeastern Librarian.

"The most comprehensive, readable, and informative book about self-publishing on the market today. None better. **If you can afford to buy only one book on self-publishing, buy this book.** *It is indispensable."* - John Kremer, Self-Publishing Book Review.

"The Self-Publishing Manual is by far the best on the market, and a fabulous addition to my library. More than that, it is a handbook, an encyclopedia, a friend, a companion, and a labor of love." - Paul E. Harris, Jr., Soccer For Americans, Inc.

The Self-Publishing Manual

How to write, print & sell your own book

Dan Poynter

Third edition, completely revised

 Para Publishing, Santa Barbara, California

THE SELF-PUBLISHING MANUAL

How To Write, Print & Sell Your Own Book

By Dan Poynter

Published by:

Para Publishing
Post Office Box 4232
Santa Barbara, CA 93103-0232, U.S.A.

Copyright © 1979 and 1984 by Daniel F. Poynter
    First Printing 1979
    Third Printing 1984 Completely Revised
    Printed in the United States of America

Library of Congress Cataloging in Publication Data.
Poynter, Daniel F.
    The Self-Publishing Manual
    How to Write, Print & Sell Your Own Book
    Bibliography: p.
    Includes index.
1. Self-Publishing—Handbooks, manuals, etc.
2. Publishers and Publishing—Handbooks, manuals, etc.
3. Printing, Practical—Handbooks, manuals, etc.
4. Authorship—Handbooks, manuals, etc.
I. Title
Z285.5.P69 1984 070.5'02'02 84-7632
ISBN 0-915516-37-3 Softcover

ABOUT THE AUTHOR

Dan Poynter fell into publishing. He spent eight years researching a labor of love. Realizing no publisher would be interested in a technical treatise on the parachute, he went direct to a printer and "self-published." The book sold, the orders poured in and he suddenly found he was a publisher himself.

In 1973, he became interested in a new aviation sport, couldn't find a book on the subject so he sat down and wrote one. After four months of writing and intense research which took him from coast to coast, he delivered the manuscript to the printer. So far, Hang Gliding has sold over 125,000 copies; a "best seller!"

Continuing to write, Dan has produced 16 books and some have been translated into Spanish, Japanese, Russian, and German. Over the years, Dan has developed a system of writing which makes it all so easy and fun. His books are loaded with facts and figures and contain detailed inside information. They are always up-to-date as he prints small quantities so they may be periodically revised. Dan has sold over a quarter million books including several best sellers for nearly two million dollars in sales. Many of his books sell at the rate of a steady 10,000 copies per year, every year.

Dan has become one of the most successful of the author/publishers. In fact, considering his volume, he is probably the world's largest one-person publishing company. As a one man show, an author/publisher who handles all the writing, publishing, and promotion himself, Dan is in the best position to advise a first time self-publishing author who is on a limited budget.

Dan was prompted to write this book because so many of his friends, noting his success, approached him to publish their manuscripts. Now he is revealing to you the secrets of writing, printing and selling your book. . . the good life of self-publishing.

ACKNOWLEDGMENT
Those Who Contributed to the Third Edition

I have not attempted to cite in the text all the authorities and sources consulted in the preparation of this manual. To do so would require more space than is available. The list would include departments of the Federal Government, libraries, industrial institutions and individuals.

Scores of people contributed to the earlier editions of this manual. Information and illustrations have been contributed to the this third edition by Judy Appelbaum, Ken Asher, Mindy Bingham, Jamie E. Bolane, Jerry Buchanan, Gordon Burgett, Klaus Burmeister, Patricia Burns, William Burns, E.N.G. Cleary, Mary Crest, Robbie Fanning, Ellen Ferber, Len Fulton, Alan Gadney, Peggy Glenn, Arthur Hallam, Hannelore Hahn, Rick Hartbrodt, Eileen Heilesen, Fiona Hill, Bob Holt, John Huenefeld, Lachlan MacDonald, Jim Maynard, John McHugh, Brian Pope, Carolyn Porter, Marilyn & Tom Ross, Deborah Michelle Sanders, Robert Sheldon, R.L. Shep, Maggy Simony, Aletha Solter, Virginia Wiley, Kathy Thompson, Jan Venolia, Beth Warwick, David Warren and Wilbur Zook. Special thanks to Shari Mueller for help with the graphics.

I sincerely thank all these fine people and I know they are proud of the part they have played in the development of the self-publishing movement as well as their contribution to this work.

Cover by Robert Howard

TABLE OF CONTENTS

WARNING — DISCLAIMER

This book is designed to provide information in regard to the subject matter covered. It is sold with the understanding that the publisher and author are not engaged in rendering legal, accounting or other professional services. If legal or other expert assistance is required, the services of a competent professional should be sought.

It is not the purpose of this manual to reprint all the information that is otherwise available to the author and/or publisher but to compliment, amplify and supplement other texts. For more information, see the many references in the Appendix.

Self-publishing is not a get rich scheme. Anyone who decides to write and publish a book must expect to invest a lot of time and effort. For many people, self-publishing is more lucrative than selling manuscripts to another publisher and many have built solid, growing, rewarding businesses.

Every effort has been made to make this manual as complete and as accurate as possible. However, there **may be mistakes** both typographical and in content. Therefore, this text should be used only as a general guide and not as the ultimate source of writing/publishing information. Furthermore, this manual contains information on writing/publishing only up to the printing date.

The purpose of this manual is to educate and entertain. The author and Para Publishing shall have neither liability nor responsibility to any person or entity with respect to any loss or damage caused or alleged to be caused directly or indirectly by the information contained in this book.

WARNING — DISCLAIMER

Chapter One

YOUR PUBLISHING OPTIONS—
WHY YOU MUST SELF-PUBLISH

Everyone wants to "write a book." Most people have the ability, some have the drive but few have the organization. Therefore, the greatest need is for a simple system, a "road map." The basic organizational plan in this book will not only provide direction, it will promote drive and expose ability no one thought existed.

Magazines devoted to men, business and sales are littered with full page advertisements featuring people with fabulous opportunity offers. Usually these people discovered a successful system of business in sales, real estate or mail order, and, for a price, they are willing to let the reader in on their secret. To distribute this information, they have written a book. Upon close inspection, one often finds that the author is making more money from the book than he or she did at the revealed original enterprise. The irony is that the purchaser gets

---

"The No. 1 reason any professional writes is to pay the bills. This isn't the Lawn Tennis Association, where you play just for the thrill of it" — Jimmy Breslin.

the wrong information; what the reader needs is a book on how to write a book.

Writing a book is easy! If you can voice an opinion and think logically, you can write a book. If you can <u>say</u> it, you can <u>write</u> it. The trick is to break a mammoth project down into little, bite-sized chunks. Most people have to work for a living and, therefore, can spend only a few minutes of each day on their book. Consequently, they can't keep the whole manuscript in their head. Being overwhelmed and confused, it is easy to quit the project. The solution is to break up the manuscript into many small easy-to-attack sections (and never start at page one where the hill looks steepest.) Then concentrate on one section at a time and do a good job on it.

Since poetry and fiction are very difficult to sell and, even when sold, have a short sales life, we will concern ourselves with nonfiction. Nonfiction doesn't require any great literary style, it is simply the sale of well researched, reorganized, up-dated and, most important, repackaged information. Some of the recommendations here may be applied to fiction just as the chapters on publishing, promotion and the mail order business may be taken separately and used elsewhere. However, all the recommendations are written toward and for the reader who wishes to become an author or an author/publisher of useful information.

People want to know "how-to" and "where-to" and they will pay well to find it. The information industry, the production and distribution of ideas and information as opposed to goods and services, now amounts to over one-half of the gross national product. There is money in information. To see how this market is being tapped by books, check the best seller lists in the back of <u>Publishers Weekly</u> noting especially the "Trade Paperback" section.

Your best sources for this saleable information are from your own experience plus research. Write what you know. Whether you already have a completed manuscript, have a great idea for one or need help in locating a suitable subject, this book will point the way.

"People can be divided into three groups: those who make things happen, those who watch things happen and those who wonder what happened" — John W. Newbern

---

The prestige enjoyed by the published author is unparalleled in our society. A book can bring recognition, wealth and an acceleration in one's career. People have always held books in high regard, possibly because in past centuries they were very expensive and were, therefore, purchased only by the rich. Even a hundred years ago, many people could not read or write. To be an author then was to be an "educated" person.

Many enterprising people are using books to establish themselves in "the ultimate business." Usually starting with a series of non-paying magazine articles, they develop a name and make themselves visible. Then they expand the series of articles into a book. Now with their credibility established, they operate seminars in their field of expertise, command high speaking fees and issue a high-priced business advice newsletter. From there, they teach a course in the local junior college and become a consultant advising large corporations and commenting on legal briefs for lawyers. They find they are in great demand. People want their information or simply want them around. Clubs and corporations fly them in to consult because it is cheaper than sending all their people to the expert.

This "dream product" is the packaging and marketing of information. Starting with a field you know, then researching it further and reducing it to paper will establish you as an expert. Then your expert standing can be pyramided with interviews, articles, TV appearances, talks at local clubs, etc. and most of this activity is to promote your book sales. In turn, all this publicity not only sells books but opens more doors and produces more invitations leading to more opportunities to prove your expert status and make you more money. People seek experts whose opinions, advice and ideas are quoted in the media. Becoming an expert does not require a great education or a college degree. You can become one on a small particular area if you are willing to go to the library, read up on it and write down the important elements.

> *"You cannot avoid making decisions. Every time you fail to act on a question, you have, in effect, made a decision to do nothing."*

A book is like a new product design, similar to an invention but usually much, much better. A patent on a device or process runs only 17 years whereas, since the 1978 change in the law, a copyright runs for the author's life plus 50 years. Patents cost hundreds, usually thousands of dollars to secure and normally require a lot of legal help. By contrast, a copyright may be filed by the author with a simple form and $10; there is no waiting period. Once you write a book, it is yours, you have a monopoly and there is no direct competition.

The next secret is to cut out the middlemen by by-passing the commercial publishers to produce and sell the book yourself. You can take the author's royalty, the publisher's profit, the distributor's markup, the retailer's piece of the action, all of the reward because you are all of them. Now, in addition to achieving the wealth and prestige of a published author, you have propelled yourself into your own lucrative business: a publishing house. This shortcut not only makes more money (why share it?) it saves you the time and trouble required to sell your manuscript to a publisher. You know the subject and market better than some distant corporation anyway.

Publishing doesn't mean purchasing a printing press to actually put the ink on the paper yourself. Some people feel this is the best part and enjoy the actual printing process but most would prefer to write and publish leaving the production to a printer.

In addition to the writing and publishing of your book, you will want to investigate its distribution. Today, more books are sold through the mail than through book stores. In fact, books are the leading mail order product. One-third of all these books are in the "how-to" category. Mail order is considered one of the best ways for the beginner with no previous business experience to start a venture of his or her own. Selling books by mail is a good, solid day-to-day business opportunity.

Mail order is not only the simplest way to distribute books, it is an ideal way to build a second income or a new life. You don't have to give up your job, there is little overhead, there are tax breaks, you work for yourself and it can be operated anywhere: you need only be near a Post Office. No one knows about your age, education, race or sex; your opportunities are indeed equal.

Mail order marketing is like fishing. You throw out a line by promoting your products and you find out almost immediately if you have made a sale. Everyday is like Christmas; opening envelopes and finding checks is great fun.

Initially, you will warehouse your books in a closet and will slip them into padded bags for mailing. It is really quite easy and starting out is not expensive or time consuming.

Your writing/publishing/mail order company is actually combining three profitable fields and concentrating on only the best parts of each. A business of your own is the great American dream and it is still an attainable possibility. In your own business, you make the decisions to meet only those challenges you find interesting. This is not "goofing off," it is making more effective use of your time; "working smarter, not harder." After all, there are only 24 hours in a day and only one day at a time to each person. You have to concentrate on the good areas if you are to prosper.

Running your own enterprise will provide you with many satisfying advantages. You should earn more money because you are working for yourself rather than splitting your efforts with someone else. You have job security and never have to worry about a surprise pink slip. If you keep your regular job and "moonlight" your own enterprise as recreation, it will always be there as a fall back position should you need it. You start at the top, not the bottom, in your own company and you work at your own pace and schedule. You will meet interesting people because as an author and publishing executive, they will seek you out.

In your own small business, you may work when and where you wish; you do not have to go to where the job is. You can work 'til dawn, sleep 'til noon, rush off to Hawaii without asking permission: this is flexibility not available to the clock punchers.

> *"By nature of the business, every writer is an entrepreneur. Take one more risk and self-publish. The dividends are well worth it."* — Mindy Bingham, Self-Published co-author of Choices/Challenges.

Being an author-publisher sounds like a good life and it can be. Working for yourself requires organization and discipline but work doesn't seem so hard when you are counting your own money. To help you understand what is ahead, here are some definitions and some background on the book publishing industry.

"PUBLISH" means to prepare and issue material for public distribution or sale or "to place before the public." The book doesn't have to be beautiful, it doesn't even have to sell, it needs only to be issued. Saleability will depend upon the content and the packaging.

A "PUBLISHER" is the one who puts up the money, the one who takes the risk. He or she has the book printed and then distributes it hoping to make back more money than has gambled. The publisher may be a big New York firm or a first-time author but he or she is always the investor.

A "BOOK" by international standards is a publication with at least 49 pages not counting the covers. The U.S. Post Office will accept publications with 24 or more pages for "book rate" postage. Books should not be confused with pamphlets which have less than 49 pages, or periodicals. Magazines and newspapers are examples of periodicals. They are published regularly and usually carry advertising.

THE BOOK PUBLISHING INDUSTRY in the U.S. consists of nearly 13,000 firms by R. R. Bowker's count but there are many thousands more publishers who do not bother to apply for a listing. For example, over 140 book publishers are located in Santa Barbara, California, but Bowker lists just 10% of them. About 100 publishers are considered to be the big firms and most of them are located in New York City. Altogether, more than 60,000 people are employed in book publishing in the U.S. Sales amount to nearly $9-billion per year for the over 600,000 active titles listed in Books in Print. Even though most of the titles are reprints of older books, the volume of brand new titles still amounts to about 100 each day for every day the bookstores are open.

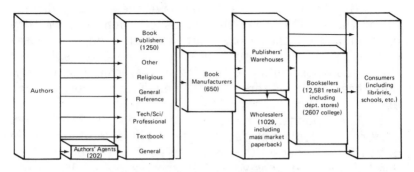

How books get from writer to reader

YOUR CHOICE. An author who wishes to get into print has many choices. You may approach a large New York general publisher or a smaller specialized "alternative" publisher. You may work with an agent or deal with a "vanity" press. If you decide to self-publish, you may go to a book printer, a regular printer who can manufacture books or get your own press. If you choose to go your own route, you will be one of the many small presses. As you expand your list of titles, you may graduate to the ranks of the alternative or small publisher. With drive and desire, you could, one day, even become a major conventional publisher. Now let's take a look at the choices.

THE BIG PUBLISHING FIRMS concentrate on books which anticipate audiences in the millions. Many houses were absorbed by much larger soap and oil companies in the 1970's but were sold off in the early 1980's when they found book publishing was not as predictably profitable as other media. A look at the economics of big publishing will help us to better understand their problems. It has been estimated that some 350,000 book length manuscripts are written each year but that only 32,000 go into print. Many of the larger publishers receive 15,000 to 20,000 unsolicited manuscripts each year. Reading manuscripts takes an enormous amount of editorial time and a very high percentage of the submissions are poorly written or do not fit the publisher's line; they are a waste of editorial time.

> *"I hope you get as much pleasure reading my book as I got spending the money you paid me for it."*

15

The 9,000 bookstores don't have the space to display all of the 40,000 new titles published each year so they concentrate on the books that move the best. Consequently, most publishers figure than even after selecting the best manuscripts and pouring in the promotion money, only three books of ten will sell well, four will break even and three will be losers.

Ever wonder why all the books in the store have very recent copyright dates? They are seldom more than a year old because the store turns them over so fast. Shelf space is expensive and in short supply. The books either sell or they go back. If one title doesn't move, it is replaced by another.

Most initial print runs are for 5,000 books. Then the title remains "in print" (available for sale) for maybe a year. If the book sells out quickly, it is reprinted and the publisher dumps in more promotion money. If the book does not catch on, it is pulled off the market and "remaindered" (sold off very cheap) to make room for new titles. The publisher has a business to run; there is overhead to consider and bills must be paid.

The financial demands cause him or her to be terribly objective about the line. To many publishers, in fact, a book is a book. If they already cover a subject, they won't be interested in a new manuscript on the same topic. They already serve that interest and do not care that yours might be better. Many big publishers are not interested in whether it is a good book, all they want to know is whether it will sell. Therefore, they concentrate on authors with good track records or Hollywood and political personalities who can move a book with their name. Only occasionally will they accept a well-written manuscript by an unknown and then it must be on a topic with a ready and massive audience. A published writer has a much better chance of selling than an unpublished one, regardless of the quality of the work. Large publishers usually must sell close to 10,000 copies in hardcover to break even. They hope to make their money on

> *"A little publishing house may surface with one or two books — How-to, self-help, pop psychology — and start a trend"* — Patricia Holt, western correspondent for *Publishers Weekly.*

subsidiary rights for the paperback edition, book clubs, movie rights, etc. They spend several thousand dollars on promoting most titles and often more than $50,000 on a blockbuster. This makes it tough on the small publisher with less volume who must compete on the basis of sales and can't afford large scale promotion.

Publishers, like most businesspeople, seem to follow the "80-20" principle. That is, they spend 80% of their effort on the top 20% of their books. The remaining 20% of their time goes to the bottom 80% of their line. Most books have to sell themselves to induce the publisher to allocate more promotion money.

> There is a story about one author who sent her relatives around to bookstores to buy up every copy of her new book. The sudden spurt in sales excited the publisher who increased the ad budget. The increase in promotion produced greater sales and her book became a success.

The author will get a royalty of 5% to 15% usually on a sliding scale and the economics here are not encouraging. For example, a print run of 5,000 copies of a book selling for $8 will earn $40,000 and 10% royalty on this is $4,000. That isn't enough money to pay for all the time spent at the typewriter. The chances of selling more than 5,000 copies is highly remote because after a year or two, the publisher takes the book out of print. In fact, the publisher will probably sell less because some books will be returned by the bookstores unsold.

If your manuscript is a blockbuster with potential sales in the millions, you may need a big publisher and they certainly want you. They will take care of all the printing and distributing and you can have your royalty checks sent to you in Bimini. If your's is a nonfiction book, they will ask you to furnish sales leads and, in any case, you will be expected to go on tour. You will wind up doing most of the promotion yourself while losing control over the program. When sales drop off, you will probably

---

"One person in the sales department has to love your book, or it's gone." — Charles, Oviatt, McGraw-Hill.

ask to buy the book and the remaining stock back from the publisher so you can pursue the marketing yourself. At this time you may also discover to your dismay that your contract provides that you must submit your next two manuscripts to this same publisher.

The big publishing houses provide a needed service but for many first-time authors they are unapproachable. Once in, the author doesn't get the best deal and getting out may be very difficult. To begin with, the publisher may sit on the manuscript for many months prior to rejecting it. Then if he or she does accept it, they will chop it up editorially and change the title; you lose artistic control of your book. The publisher's experts will change everything in the name of enhancing commercial appeal.

All these changes might be acceptable if the big commercial publishers were great financial successes. They aren't, or at least, they haven't been so far. One publishing house even admits it would have made more money last year if it had vacated its New York office and rented out the floor space.

The publishing industry attracts lovely creative people who find their rewards in its nonmaterial aspects. They come from tax-supported academic or library communities; they have never been marketing oriented. In fact, the editorial function in most publishing houses jealously guards its independence so it won't be "corrupted" by the marketing department. This leads editors into the greatest trap in publishing: producing titles which "should be published" but do not sell. When a book fails to earn back its investment, the publishing house calls it a "prestige" book and justifies its production as a public service.

Many of the people working in the big firms know the editing-marketing approach is wrong (or that losing money is not what business is all about) and they are frustrated by it. But no matter how many seminars they attend or books they read, they can't move their companies out of their rut.

> *"If you would be thrilled by watching the galloping advance of a major glacier, you'd be estatic watching changes in publishing."* — John D. MacDonald in *InfoWorld*

In the big firms, salaries are too low to attract highly motivated marketing people. Without better marketing, the companies can't afford to pay more. It is a vicious circle and there been little effort to reverse it. The answer is for the marketing department to select the manuscripts they feel they can sell and to confine the editors' work to editing.

"I'll be damned if I'll do my publishers' job for them. If I had wanted to become a hustler, I would have hit the streets long ago. I am a creative artist—I know it sounds pretentious, but that's what I am. I am no businessman or salesman." (From an article by Rebekah Jordan in Publisher's Weekly.)

But there is a brighter side for the small publisher who understands what the public wants to read. Since the old line big publishers do not pursue marketing and the new big ones concentrate on the top selling books only, there is a lot of room left for the smaller publishing house and self-publisher.

Be careful if you hang around with people from the book industry. Learn but don't let their ways rub off. Study the big New York publishing firms but don't copy them. You can do a lot better.

THE SMALL PRESSES or "alternative publishers" are the smaller firms which specialize to serve certain minority interests such as specialized technical fields, particular geographic regions or their own personal interests. One definition of a small press is a publisher with no more than 12 full-time staff members, issuing fewer than 25 titles per year for receipts under $400,000. Many small presses emerged from the anti-establishment movement of the sixties and their entry into publishing was made possible by the coincidental introduction of newer, simpler, cheaper (offset) printing methods. Some of these publishers are very small while others are fairly large but

---

"Small publishing is exhibiting robust health, while the traditional industry is ailing." — Paul D. Doebler in *Book Industry Trends*

most are specialized. Many people in the industry are attracted to the flexibility offered by small publishing. When their firm grows too large, they break off to form a new small firm. There are thousands of small presses and because of their relatively low overhead, they can produce their books much cheaper than the big publishers.

Two of the more successful new presses are Bruce Lansky's Meadowbrook Press in Minnesota and HP Books in Tucson. Both combine their instincts about the marketplace with the best research they can buy to direct quality products at the right buyer. The key to their success is that these publishers came from the world of marketing, not from the academic or library communities.

However, while the smaller publishers may be closer to their market, their royalty rates are the same and some do not promote a title any harder than a big publisher. Most will agree that small publishers are usually nice to deal with and provide good personal attention but they are faced with many of the same economic problems as the rest of the industry and don't always have the resources to combat them. To find a small press, consult Dustbook's International Directory of Little Magazines and Small Presses and Literary Market Place. Look for a publisher who specializes in your type of book. Do not take an aviation book to a cook book publisher. They will not take it and would not know where to sell it if they did. You want a publisher who knows the market, one who can plug your book into their promotion/distribution system.

THE "TINY PRESS" has been defined as those publishers who normally make press runs of 500 books or less. Often these firms concentrate on fiction, poetry or very specialized material. Many do their own printing and some do quite beautiful work.

> "I can't understand why a person will take a year or two to write a novel when he can easily buy one for a few dollars."
> — Fred Allen.

CO-OP PUBLISHING HOUSES have been formed in many areas. Usually three to ten people join together to share the work of editing, design, layout, typesetting, compilation and financing. Often these people contribute more labor than money to the publishing venture. A good article on this subject appeared in the August, 1978 edition of Writer's Digest magazine.

VANITY OR SUBSIDY PUBLISHERS produce around 6,000 titles each year; some twenty firms produce about 70 percent of all the subsidized books. Many of these businesses advertise in the Yellow Pages under "Publishers." Subsidy publishers offer regular publishing services, but the author invests the money. Under this arrangement, the author pays the full publishing (more than just printing bill) costs, receives 40% of the retail price of the books sold and 80% of the subsidiary rights, if sold. According to The Wall Street Journal, the cost is between $2,000 and $15,000 to get into print. Others say you can figure roughly on $25 per page.

The vanity publisher claims he will furnish all the regular publishing services including promotion and distribution. All this might not be so bad if they had a good track record for delivery. But according to Writer's Digest, vanity publishers usually do not deliver the promotion they promise and the books rarely return one-quarter of the author's investment.

The ads reading "To the author. . ." or "Manuscripts wanted by. . ." easily catch the eye of the writer with a book length manuscript. Vanity presses almost always accept a manuscript for publication and usually with a glowing review letter. They don't make any promises regarding sales and usually the book sells fewer than 100 copies. The vanity publisher doesn't have to sell any books because the author has already paid him for his work. Therefore, subsidy publishers are interested in manufacturing the book, not in editing, promotion, sales or distribution.

> *"Subsidy publishing is closer to trade publishing than it is to self-publishing"* — Freda Morris.

Since binding is expensive, the subsidy publisher often binds a few hundred copies; the rest of the sheets remain unbound unless needed. The "advertising" promised in the contract normally turns out to be only a "tombstone" ad listing many titles in the New York Times. Results from this feeble promotion are very rare.

The review copies sent to columnists usually go straight into the circular file. The reviewer's time is valuable and they do not like vanity presses because they know that so little attention was paid to the editing of the book. Further, they realize there will be little promotional effort and that the book will not be available to readers in the stores.

Only a local bookstore might be persuaded to carry an author's vanity press book. The rest know there won't be any public demand for it.

The vanity publisher can get your book into print if this is all you want and they will not cut the manuscript all to pieces but, even then, they are not the least expensive way to go. It would make more sense to contact a book printer or even a regular local printer who has the equipment to print books. Publishing yourself should save 25% to 35% over vanity publishing.

Before considering a subsidy or vanity publisher, send for Does it Pay to Pay to Have it Published (Writer's Digest, 9933 Alliance Road, Cincinnati, OH 45242.) From everything you read, it appears that no one likes vanity publishers. Some have been in trouble with the Federal Trade Commission (FTC) and at least one has been sued by a client author. But then, many tyro authors don't like any publishers at all. Reasoning that they must do most of the work anyway, they opt for self-publishing.

OTHER PUBLISHING CHOICES. Textbook publishers offer the author a royalty based on the net amount received by the publisher. University presses don't pay well because they accept manuscripts on the basis of merit, not sales potential. Contract books are those written for a company on a subject of their choice. For

---

"Legitimate publishers don't have to look for business."
— L.M. Hasselstrom

example, a mail order house might need a book on a particular subject to round out its line. Sponsored books are commissioned by a company. They are usually about the company and, in addition to their regular sale, may be used as a promotional tool.

LITERARY AGENTS provide publishers with a valuable service by screening out the bad manuscripts and most new material comes to big publishers through them. The agent has to serve the publisher well for if he or she submits a poor manuscript, the publisher will never give him or her another appointment. Therefore, agents like sure bets too, and are reluctant to even consider an unpublished writer. When they do, their fee is often higher than their normal commission of 10%.

For the author, the agent will make manuscript suggestions, negotiate the contract and try to sell the book to one of their many contacts; the agent will exploit all possible avenues. If your manuscript is a winner, it is wise to have professional management. If you deal with an agent, it is best to contract with one in New York; he or she will have closer contacts and can deal in person.

According to Literary Agents '83-'84 Marketplace about 40% of the book agents will not read manuscripts by unpublished authors and a good 15% will not even answer query letters from them. Of those agents who will read the manuscript of an unpublished author, 80% will charge for the service. 80% of the agents will not represent professional books; 93% will not touch reference works; 99% will not handle technical books; 98% will not represent regional books, satire, musicals and other specialized manuscripts. While most agents will handle novel-length fiction, only 20% are willing to take on either novelettes or short stories, and only 2% have a special interest in literature or quality fiction.

On the fringe, there are a number of "agents" who charge a "reading fee" and then pay students to read and critique the manuscript. They make their money on these fees, not from placing the manuscripts. For a list of

---

"Vanity publishing is to legitimate publishing as loansharking is to banking" — Martin J. Baron

literary agents, see <u>Fiction</u> <u>Writer's</u> <u>Market</u> and <u>Literary</u> <u>Market</u> <u>Place</u>.

SELF-PUBLISHING is where the author bypasses all the middlemen, deals directly with the printer and then handles the marketing and distribution. You maintain complete control over your product. You have to invest your time as well as your money but the rewards are greater; you get it all.

Self-publishing is not new. In fact, it has solid early American roots; it is almost a tradition. Many authors have elected to go their own way after being turned down by regular publishers and many others have decided to go their own way from the beginning. Well-known self-publishers include Mark Twain, Zane Grey, Upton Sinclair, Carl Sandburg, James Joyce, D.H. Lawrence, Ezra Pound, Edgar Rice Burroughs, Stephen Crane, Mary Baker Eddy, George Bernard Shaw, Edgar Allen Poe, Rudyard Kipling, Henry David Thoreau, Walt Whitman, Robert Ringer, Richard Nixon and many, many more. These people were self-publishers though today the vanity presses claim they were "subsidy" published. Today's success stories are usually in the nonfiction how-to books.

There are thousands of these very small author/publisher firms, many of them in California. Some are growing and some are withering, but practically all are hanging on. They are proving that a self-published book is not inferior to one marketed by a big New York firm. Some self-publishers are very successful and some are making a lot of money.

Self-publishing is not difficult. In fact, it may even be easier than dealing with a publisher. The job of the publishing manager is not to perform every task, but to see that everything gets done. The self-publisher deals directly with the printer and handles as many of the editing, proofing, promotion, and distribution tasks as he or she can. What they can't do, they farm out. There-

---

"I was thrilled at the cooperation of agents, but was a little alarmed when I found, more than once, a rejection letter from the last recipient in the manuscript." — Ruth Notkins Nathan in *Publishers Weekly*

fore, self-publishing may take on many forms depending on the author's interests, assets and abilities. It allows you to concentrate on those areas you find most challenging.

Properly planned, there is little monetary risk in self-publishing. If you follow the plan, the only variable is the subject of the book. Poetry and fiction are difficult to sell but most nonfiction topics sell easily. In fact, many authors publish themselves because this method provides the best return on their labor in the long run. Because the big publisher only tries a book for a year or two and then lets sales dictate its fate: reprint or remainder, the first year is most important. The self-publisher, on the other hand, uses the first year to build a solid market for a future of sustained sales. While a big publisher may sell only 5,000 copies total, the self-publisher can often count on 5,000 or more each year, year after year.

Here are eight good reasons to self-publish:

1. To make more money. Why accept 6% to 10% in royalties when you can have 40%? You know your subject and you know the people in the field. Certainly you know better than some distant publisher who might buy your book. While the trade publisher may have some good contacts, he doesn't know the market as well as you, and he isn't going to expend as much promotional effort. Ask yourself this question: will the trade publisher be able to sell four times as many books as I can?

2. Speed. Most publishers work on a $1\frac{1}{2}$ year production cycle. Can you wait that long to get into print? Will you miss your market? The $1\frac{1}{2}$ years begins after the sale of the manuscript and all the contract negotiations. Publication could be three years away! Why waste valuable time shipping your manuscript around to see if there is a publisher out there who likes it. Richard Nixon self-published "Real Peace" in 1983 because he felt his message was urgent; he couldn't wait for a publisher's machinery to grind out the book.

Typically, bookstores buy the first book on a popular subject. Later books may be better but the buyer will pass on them since the store already has the subject "covered."

3. To keep control of your book. According to <u>Writer's Digest</u>, 60% of the big publishers do not give the author final approval on copy editing. 23% never give the author the right to select the title, 20% do not consult the author on the jacket design and 36% rarely involve the author in the book's promotion.

    The big New York trade publishers may have more promotional connections than you but with a stable of books to push, your effort may get lost in the shuffle. Give the book to someone who has a personal interest in it--the author.

4. Save your energy. Unless you are a movie star, noted politician or have a recognizable name, it is nearly impossible to attract a publisher.

5. Self-publishing is good business. There are far more tax advantages for an author/publisher than there are for just authors.

6. Self-publishing will help you to think like a publisher. You will learn the industry and will have a better understanding of the big picture.

7. You will gain self-confidence. You will be proud to be the author of a book. Compare this with pleading with people to read your manuscript.

8. Finally--you may have no other choice. There are more manuscripts than can be read. Most publishers won't even look at your manuscript.

A book is a product of one's self. An analogy may be drawn with giving birth. The author naturally feels that his book is terrific and that it would sell better if only his publisher would dump in more promotion money. He is very protective about his book (ever try to tell a mother her child is ugly?). The publisher answers that he is not anxious to dump more money into a book that isn't selling. So, if the author self-publishes, he gains a better understanding for the arguments on both sides. It is his money and his choice.

SHOULD YOU SELF-PUBLISH? Would-be author/publishers should be cautioned that self-publishing is not for everyone. Writing is an art while publishing is a business and many people are unable to do both well. If you are a lovely creative flower who is repelled by the "crass commercialism" of selling one's own product, you should stick to the creative side and let someone else handle the business end. On the other hand, some people are terribly independent. They will not be happy with the performance of any publisher no matter how much time and effort are spent creating and promoting the book. These people should save the publisher from all this grief by making their own decisions. What is important is that writers understand all the alternatives so that they may make an intelligent, educated choice.

SELLING OUT. Many self-publishers find that once they have proven their books with good sales, they are approached by the big publishing houses with offers to print a new edition. Some use self-publishing to break into the big time. Others keep on self-publishing, keeping the work and the money to themselves.

BOOK PRINTERS are those print shops which specialize in the manufacture of books. They are not regular publishers or vanity presses, they are simply specialty printers with book machinery. The major book printers are listed in the Appendix. Many of them advertise in magazines like Small Press and Writer's Digest, and every self-publisher should compare their quote with that of the local printers. Incidentally, some of them have an interesting sales tool: a book on how to self-publish. Of course, they strongly recommend their own press. Some of the other book printers are running seminars for the same purpose: to make contact with potential clients.

> *"Self-Publishing: Your short-cut to fame and fortune"*

THE FUTURE. Packaged information is becoming increasingly specialized. More and more books are being printed in smaller quantities. The information in books is going out of date faster. Books are being produced more rapidly. Computerized equipment is being used to write, edit, layout and print books. The customer wants more condensed information fast.

The chapters which follow describe in detail an alternative route to traditional publishing. They will enable you to get your book into print at minimum cost. There is no reason why you shouldn't gain great fame and considerable financial reward.

This book could be your "second chance." It will show you the way to the wealth and prestige you never thought possible. Even if you just want the satisfaction of being published and are not interested in, or do not require, the extra income, this book will lead the way.

Obviously your success cannot be guaranteed but many people are doing very well in the writing/publishing business. This isn't a pipe dream, there is work involved. While you are working for yourself, at your own pace, it is still work. You won't get rich overnight. Building a sound business venture takes several years.

The secret is to invest your labor. Your time is more precious than gold. There is a finite quantity; you have only 24 hours of it each day. You may use your time in several ways: you may throw it away, sell it or invest it. You can waste your valuable time in front of the television set; time is easy to "lose." Most people punch in at the clock, go to work and get a check. They trade their labor for money on a one-for-one basis. If you don't punch in, you don't get paid. How much better it is to spend your time on a book which will sell and generate income while you are away doing something else. Your labor becomes an investment which pays dividends for years while you are playing or working on another investment.

Before going on to Chapter Two, turn to "Your Book's Calendar" at the beginning of the Appendix. You might also like to skim Chapter Twelve. Before you start, it is nice to know where you are going.

Chapter Two

WRITING YOUR BOOK
HOW TO GENERATE
SALEABLE MATERIAL

Where are your talents and what do you want to do? Do you enjoy writing or do you want to be a published author without the "pain" of writing? Analyze yourself. Do you want to write, publish or sell books, any combination or even all three? Here we will cover all three to help you make an educated choice. We will discuss both sides of publishing: as seen by the author and as seen by the publisher.

PICKING A SUBJECT is the first step. Sitting there waiting for inspiration is called "writer's block." You cannot write about a subject until you select it. So, do not waste time thinking about what to write, think about what to write about. Consider the four elements necessary for producing good nonfiction.

"There are three rules to writing: 1. Have something to say, 2. Know how to say it, and 3. Be able to sell it." — David Hellyer.

---

1. The subject is interesting to you.
2. You have the necessary expertise and the information is available.
3. The subject is of interest to others and is, therefore, saleable.
4. The subject matter is tightly focused.

The book should be on a subject in which you are interested and where you are an expert or would like to become an expert. You have spent years working at, specializing in and learning something and there are thousands of people out there willing to pay good money to get the inside information on it. Write what you know! If you select your hobby, there are a number of advantages: you know what has been written in the past, you have the contacts for gathering more information and your further participation in that hobby will become tax deductible.

Poetry does not sell well and few people will purchase your autobiography. Protest subjects usually have a short life and built-in audience limitations. As entertainment, fiction must compete with other media such as television and films which require less conscious work.

FICTION. It is possible to sell fiction or, at least, some people are doing it but it isn't easy. Dorothy Bryant, a novelist in Berkeley, California, publishes and promotes what she writes. She calls her publishing company Ata Books. You might be able to sell your fiction if you consider the market first. Stories tailored to a specific area might sell well locally.

In Santa Barbara, John Martin's Black Sparrow Press is well-known for successfully publishing quality fiction and poetry. Martin has a publishing formula and an established following. He knows just how many books to publish in softcover, hardcover, signed editions, etc. and many buyers take everything he produces, sight-unseen. He is so sought after by writers that he operates Black Sparrow from a Post Office box and maintains an unlisted telephone.

Fiction writers who are ready for the test may send their manuscript to the West Coast Review of Books for review. A good review here will get the attention of several publishers. A bad review cuts deep. Send for a sample copy or subscribe to the magazine to see what they do (address in the Appendix.)

For more information on selling unpublished novels, see the January 1983 edition of Writer's Digest. For a list of fiction publishers, see Fiction Writer's Market and Alan Gadney's How-to Enter & Win Fiction Writing Contests.

Very generally speaking, a large New York publisher will do a better job on fiction while you will do a better job yourself with nonfiction. In 1984, genre fiction such as romances were selling well. You must decide whether you wish to write, publish and/or make money.

NONFICTION. The subject of a book, not the name of the publisher or the comments of a reviewer, is what really sells it. Every new national craze requires how-to-books. According to Newsweek there are over 1,300 books on fitness and health currently in print. Do not be discouraged if your subject has already been covered. That just proves someone else thought it to be important. Using your own experience and the latest information, you can do it better. The subjects with the best sales potential are how-to's, money, health, self-improvement, hobbies, sex and psychological well being. Find a need and fill it.

Women provide a growing market for nonfiction books which is taking on new importance. Many have entered the world of business with a lack of necessary education or experience. Once out of the kitchen and into the office, they are also faced with a shortage of time. They need information and their employment provides them with the money to pay for it. Books aimed at women have great sales potential.

One specialized book that has been selling for years is Kershner's The Student Pilot's Flight Manual which has gone through the press 26 times for 485,000 copies.

"The writer does the most who gives his reader the most knowledge and takes from him the least time" — Sydney Smith.

Anticipate reader interest and pick a subject which will sell on its own even if the buyer has never heard of the book.

Local guide books are relatively easy to write and market. The information and the distribution is all local. Tourists guides, restaurant guides and historical books are a good way to get started in publishing.

You do not have to be an expert--yet. If you are new to a subject, you could produce a better book than an old hand because you are better able to understand and relate to the reader-novice. You know what his reactions and needs are as well as what he is thinking. Once you are finished researching and writing, you too will be an expert.

There may be more money publishing your information in short monographs than in longer books. Timely monographs usually command a higher price, can be published in shorter runs and they take less time to produce.

Now, to obtain a manuscript you have the choice of buying it from others or writing it yourself (are you an author or a writer?) In this chapter, we will discuss the many possibilities. Only one has to be right for you. If one possibility "clicks," you are on your way. This discussion of both sides of publishing will provide you with the whole picture. First we will cover how to write material yourself and then we will show you how to obtain some or all of the material from others.

WRITE IT YOURSELF. Creating your own material is easy if you have a system; all it takes is organization and discipline. Following the system outlined below, creating copy becomes challenging fun and it allows you to easily see the progress you are making which is encouraging. While this method may be of some help in writing fiction, it has been developed specifically for nonfiction.

While writing a book is not difficult, it is not for the lazy. Like AA or a diet, you will have to change your life-style. This means waking up one morning and making

> *"To avoid writer's block, do not sit waiting for inspiration, get out and search for a subject."*

a decision: to do it now. To get into the system and develop good habits will provide you with a sense of purpose and a feeling of accomplishment. Once you have selected a topic, only the decision to go stands between you and the finished book.

TIME or lack of it is the most frequently heard excuse. But somehow we always find the time for those things most important to us. We just put them first. Often we can fit in an hour of writing time each day by completing our other chores faster. One way is to get up one hour earlier each day. This is perfect scheduling as the house is quiet, the telephone does not ring and most writers find the early morning to be their most creative and productive time. Once you gather momentum in your project, you will find arising early will be easy; you won't even miss that hour of sleep. You must put this hour first and not let anything interfere with it.

Set up a writing area in a spare room or a corner of the living room. Keep all your writing materials and research tools there. Your creative writing time is precious, do not waste it trying to get started.

WRITE YOUR AD BEFORE YOU WRITE YOUR BOOK in order to set your sights on your objective. Layout a full page advertisement with a bold headline, a sub-head and wall-to-wall body copy. End with a coupon asking for the order. Tell the readers what the book is about and how it will change their lives. Make the headline an attention grabber, write and rewrite the copy. Only when you have a polished ad should you begin to write the book. The ad will help you to focus on who your audience is and what they want so you will be able to slant the book to their needs. Now all you have to do is to deliver on all your promises.

Most non-fiction books are written without a specific market in mind and since the book does not provide what the potential buyers want, it does not sell. Do not

> *"Faulty research is like a faulty septic tank. Sooner or later the evidence will surface and become embarrassing."* — Rex Alan Smith.

ignore other markets though. If you have an instruction book aimed at students of flying schools and the bookstores pick it up, so much the better. But the bookstore sales are the frosting, not the cake. The more areas the book may be fitted into, the better its chances of success.

RESEARCH is simply reading, making notes and rearranging the gathered pertinent information. The importance of the use of the library cannot be over-emphasized. All research must begin there and most of the required information will be found within its walls. The first library visit will be to determine whether the subject has already been beaten to death. If not, then on to the book.

Ask the reference librarian for Bowker's Books in Print which lists all books currently available by subject, title and author. Make a list of those you would like to review. Research the library's card file to see which books may be obtained there. The others you may purchase at your local bookstore or by writing direct to the publisher; addresses are listed in the back of Books in Print. You will find that some of the book listed in BIP never went to press. And remember that this is probably not the only library in town, try the local college, too; it will have different types of books. Research the Reader's Guide to Periodical Literature which lists magazine articles on every subject. There are thousands of associations and many have their own special interest magazine. Be a detective. When you run out of leads, ask the librarian. Libraries carry hundreds of indexes, listings and source books. Gather everything ever written on your subject. Load yourself up with so much material you will have to decide on what to leave out. Overdo it and you will be proud of the result, secure in the knowledge that you have covered the subject completely.

Check out those books and magazines you can. On those restricted to the reference room, make notes of small bits of information and use the photocopy machine to record longer pieces. Where you wish to use photos and drawings of material with expired copyrights, use a plain

---

"Researching is fun because when you are researching, you aren't writing." — Rex Alan Smith.

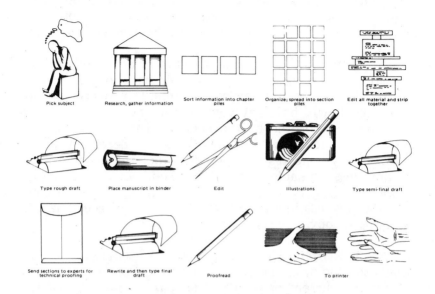

The flow of your manuscript

paper photocopier for the drawings and use a camera to reshoot the photos (more on this later). But even where the copyright has not expired, make a photocopy of valuable illustrations to guide you in your research. Photocopy checked-out books and magazines at the local copy center. They will have a a plain paper copier which is cheaper, cleaner and easier to read than the wet process models used in many libraries.

After exhausting the library of its information, there are many other sources. Write for Selected U.S. Government Publications to the Superintendent of Documents, USGPO, P.O. Box 1821, Washington, DC 20402. This is a monthly catalog of government publications. Many of these pamphlets are also available at U.S. Government bookstores in the larger cities. Check the white pages. For more information on your field of study, there are interviews with the experts you uncover in your research. You may write or call them. Now that you are researching, you are a member of the print media and will be able to attend a lot of related events free. Use your new business card to get a press pass, media packet and preferential treatment.

COPYRIGHT is the subject which most interests potential authors. They want to know how to protect their precious material from others and to know how much they may steal.

A copyright covers exact printed words, not ideas or thoughts so you are safe if you just do not copy word-for-word. The copyright law was completely overhauled in 1978 and it will be many years before every aspect of it has been interpreted by the courts. The courts seem to deal with each case individually when determining infringement. One test has been whether the original work is any less saleable once it has competition from an alleged infringer. Make it a personal rule never to copy any three words in a row. If your book is not recognizable as being a copy, you should be safe.

MANY DOCUMENTS ARE NOT COPYRIGHTED. If you want to find whether some material is protected under either the current or pre-1978 law, the Copyright Office will conduct a search for you. Send them as much information as possible, such as the author, title, publisher and publication date. The cost is $10 per hour and they should be able to make two searches per hour. Government and military publications are in the public domain. Even if they weren't, they would probably be covered by the Freedom of Information Act. If you really need a piece of material, military or civilian, ask for permission. It is safer and cheaper than hiring a lawyer to prove you have a right to it.

YOUR COPYRIGHTED MATERIAL is valuable property, or it may be so one day. File copyright forms on all those magazine articles you don't get paid for. You may need an article for inclusion in a book someday and the expenditure on fees will justify to the IRS that you really are in the word business.

If you are asked for permission to reprint some of your work, you might consider a limit of a section or two and stipulate that an editor's note indicate that it was used with your permission and came from your book. This

---

"Other people copy, we adapt."

will further indicate you as an expert and is good publicity for the original work. A copyright on your book is not only for protection, it is prestigious; it shows you are a professional. Copyright is discussed in several places in this book. See the Index. For more information on copyrights, see the discussion in Writer's Market and read John McHugh's Permissions, Copyright and Fair Use: A Guide for Book Publishing Managers and the other copyright references listed in the Appendix.

ORGANIZE YOUR MATERIAL WITH THE "PILOT SYSTEM." Start by drawing up a preliminary table of contents. Then sort all your research material and "pile it" as required. Decide on your chapter titles and, using scissors, tape and staples, sort all this copied material into the applicable chapter piles. During your library research, you must have written down a number of interesting observations, many of your own experiences. Add your own notes to the piles.

Now spread out the individual chapters. They will probably completely fill the living room. Pick an interesting pile, any one, not necessarily the first, and go through it, underlining important points and writing in your additional comments. Write out longer thoughts on a tablet and file them in order in the pile.

This floor spread will enable you to see the whole interrelated project, lending excitement and encouragement—a great incentive. Move the piles around to insure a good, logical flow of thought and to avoid duplication of copy. Discard bad and duplicate material.

This use of other information from other sources is not plagiarizing, it is research. Your notes insure that you will not leave out any important points. However, you will be entertained as you compare what other authors say about the same item. The similarities are often remarkably coincidental, sometimes to the point of including the same words and phraseology.

> *"Every conceivable piece of information imaginable is available somewhere in your local library. There are indexes and references on everything. Ask the reference librarian for help."*

As you read what others say on a particular point, your memory will be jogged. You will have additional points, a clearer explanation or an illustrative story. Where you disagree with another author, you can always say "some people believe. . ." and then tell it your way. You have the advantage of the most recent information since you came last.

Carry paper and pen with you at all times, especially when driving, running or engaging in any solo activity. This is the time to think, create, compose; this is when there is no one around to break your train of thought. Some authors keep a pad in their car and compose while commuting. When you are confined, captive, isolated, you have nothing else to do but create. Make use of any available time. A lot of good material develops while attending dull meetings.

Some people like to work with a small pocket tape recorder, but remember that someone must transcribe this noise onto paper. It all depends on what you are used to, how you perform best. If you often dictate letters and have a secretary to transcribe your tapes, this may be the most comfortable and most efficient method for you.

When a particularly original thought or creative approach hits you, write it down or you will lose it. Keep on thinking and keep on note-taking. Add your thoughts and major pieces to the piles. As you go along, draw up a list of questions as they come to mind so that you will remember to follow them up for an answer.

STRIP your notes by cutting, sorting and taping. Paste the strips together with Magic Transparent Tape. If your photocopies were made on a plain paper copier, you will be able to write on the tape and the paper when adding notes.

Type on 3-hole punched mimeo paper; it is substantial and inexpensive. The holes even help you to see when the bottom of the page is coming up in the typewriter; it comes quickly when you are double spacing. Do not use erasable paper, the ink comes off on the hands. Type, do

---

"I love being a writer. What I can't stand is the paperwork."
— Peter De Vries

not handwrite. You will need a typed copy of your draft to better visualize it so typing will save you one complete step.

WRITING from the pasted strips may be done, as above, with a tape recorder, typewriter or word processor. With practice you will learn to think, create and compose at the machine. Many law schools allow their students to take their exams by typewriter and the students type in spite of the racket in the typing room. Type out or dictate the manuscript rough the first time. Write as you speak; relax and be clear. Make notes where you are considering illustrations. Type the manuscript double spaced as you would the final copy. Initiate good habits.

Do not start with chapter one—to do so makes book writing look like an impossible mountain climb. Select the chapter pile that looks the easiest. It may be the smallest or the most interesting but it is sure to go the fastest. Once you have written it, take the next most interesting chapter and so on. Soon you will be passed the half-way mark and the going will be down-hill. You will be encouraged and will gather momentum. Using this approach, you will probably find you are writing the first chapter last. This is as it should be as the first chapter is usually introductory in nature and you cannot know what the first chapter should say until the rest of the work is drafted. Many authors wind up rewriting and reslanting the first chapter because they wrote it first.

Do not be concerned with what goes down on paper the first time around. The important thing is to get it down. Often these first impressions are the best; they are complete, natural and believable. Later you will go through the draft, making corrections, additions and deletions. Major changes will require rewriting while minor corrections only need some proofing marks. Sentences and paragraphs will be added through cutting and pasting-in the new material. Set up the material in a loose leaf-form; it will be easy to add to the manuscript with a little cutting, pasting and page additions.

> *"There's nothing to writing. All you do is sit down at the typewriter and open a vein."* — Red Smith

Read the whole pasted-up section to grasp the overall theme. Then boil it down and use your own words. Think about the section and how you might explain the basic message better. Can't you say it better with fewer words?

Do not just write from the strips sentence-by-sentence, that approaches plagiarism. For organization, list the main points and rearrange the pieces. If you are having trouble with a section, arrange it as best you can and then sleep on it. If you still cannot bring it all together with a few well-chosen sentences, you may have to call another expert for his or her explanation of the subject matter.

As you type up the rough first draft and later as you review it, you will decide whole paragraphs are misplaced and belong elsewhere. Using three-hole punched paper and a binder, it is an easy matter to cut, move and paste material.

If you lack a certain piece of information, a number or fact, leave a blank space, put a note in the margin and go on. Do not lose momentum. Similarly, if you find yourself repeating material, make a note in the margin so you may compare it with the other material later.

Remember, this is not plagiarism but solid, thorough research and an efficient system made possible by Xerox. There is nothing new in the universe. Practically every non-fiction book is simply a repackaging of existing material.

Type one complete section at a time if possible. One chapter at a time is better and the whole book straight through is the best way to go. Most beginning authors must work and are able to devote only a short period each day to their writing. But, the more time you can put into each piece of the book, the better, as there will be greater continuity, less duplication and clearer organization. If you can only do a small section at a time, try arranging the pieces in the evening, reviewing them in the early morning, thinking about them while commuting, etc. and then come home to type it all up.

"The ideal best-seller would be about a quiche-eating cat with thin thighs."

On the other hand, if you can, take two weeks off from work, shut out all distractions and become totally involved in the manuscript. Do not pick up the mail or answer the telephone. Eat when hungry, sleep when tired and forget the clock except as a gauge of your pace. Keep up the pressure and keep on typing. Pace yourself at, say, one chapter per day. You should not have to force yourself to write but it will take organization and discipline.

After a couple of books, you will find yourself making very few changes in your original draft. In fact, using an IBM Correcting Selectric typewriter, you will even change the type balls to indicate to the typesetter which type faces you want for body type, bold face, italics and captions. Incidentally, many writers say the hum of an electric typewriter or word processor--knowing the electricity is on--prompts them to work.

Do not throw out your materials once your draft is typed. Put them in a cardboard carton. Someone may ask where you found a particular piece of information and you may wish to find it. This is especially important with photographs and artwork.

WRITING STYLE. Before writing a magazine article, always read one or more editions of the magazine thoroughly to absorb the style. It helps one to subconsciously adapt to that magazine's way of writing. The same technique may be used in writing a book by reading a couple of chapters of a book by a writer you admire.

Writing is a communication art. You should not try to impress. Write as you speak, avoiding big words where small ones will do. Most people regularly use only 800-1,000 of the some 26,000 English words available to them. Use simple sentences and be precise in your selection of words. Vary sentence and paragraph length and favor the shorter ones. Try to leave yourself out of the copy: avoid the word "I."

Use action nouns and verbs. Help the reader draw a mental picture by introducing sight, sound, smell, touch and taste to your copy. Be precise by avoiding superla-

---

Don't use "I", the perpendicular pronoun.

41

tives and overuse of adverbs and adjectives. Study newspaper writing and place the words you wish to emphasize at the beginning of the sentence. The important sentence should start the paragraph and the main paragraph should head up the chapter.

Relax, talk on paper, be yourself. Explain each section in your own words as you would trying to help a friend who is new to the subject. Do not use contractions in your writing as you do in your speech as they're (there is one now) more difficult to read. "Which" and "that" can usually be left out to the benefit of the sentence. Keep your writing short. You are paying for the words so edit out the junk.

Writing is hard work; it is an intellectual and emotional workout. Some authors enjoy the discipline it requires but more have a greater appreciation for the reward of the results.

Like a speech, every paragraph should have a beginning, a middle and an end. The paragraph should tie together with both the preceding and following paragraphs (good transitions.) The first sentence of the paragraph is called the "topic sentence"--stay with one subject per paragraph.

As a published author you have the responsibility of being a recognized expert. Be accurate; you will be quoted. Use proper terms; don't start a new language. Steer away from highly technical language; you will only turn off your reader.

A few years ago, hang gliding was a hot new subject. It was the rebirth of aviation using a wing made in the sail industry and whose participants were kids off the streets. The terms for flying and parts of the glider could have come from the aviation community, the sail industry or popular (new) jargon could have been used. Obviously aviation terms were in order. This was impressed upon the early book and magazine writers; aviation terms were used almost exclusively and this usage aided the introduction of hang gliding into the community of sport aviation.

One technique for educating your readers to the correct terms is to use the proper term and then follow it with the more popular word in parentheses. Educating the reader as you progress through the book is preferable to making them wade through a glossary.

Be a professional and give the readers their moneys' worth. Your material will be used by others in coming years and you will be quoted. If you are accurate and correct now you won't be embarrassed later by the written legend you have created.

Anticipate trends to keep your work up to date. Use metric and non-sexist terms wherever possible. Cookbooks may not be ready to switch to metric and books on printing will deal with 17 x 22 presses and 6 x 9 books for a long time, but many measurements may be avoided by using comparisons. For example, instead of telling a parachutist to prepare for landing at "30 feet," say "at tree top height." The comparison is clearer anyway.

HELP is available to those who still cannot write even after learning the tricks mentioned above. If you can talk, you can write, so get a tape recorder. Do the transcriptions yourself or hire it out. Type the manuscript as you said it. Then either correct the language or leave it as it is. Sometimes a basic speaking style adds to the book.

If you still cannot get your thoughts to paper, try the team approach. There are a lot of writers out there without an original idea—people who love to put good thoughts into words. Look for a moon-lighting newspaper reporter. They are trained to listen and put your thoughts down accurately. Once they have your material written out, you may edit the work for rewriting. The reporter may even wind up doing a feature story on you and their media contacts are invaluable.

Perhaps you can get your thoughts down on paper but all that good information does not read very well. What you need is an editor, someone who can take your information and put energy into it.

"If you do not write for publication, there is little point in writing at all." — George Bernard Shaw

---

Doctor Hartbrodt wrote a medical book about a common disease. The manuscript contained a lot of solid, helpful information but was hard to read. He contacted writers' groups, editorial services and secretarial services through the Yellow Pages and located four people who were willing to help. He gave each a copy of the first chapter and asked them to edit a couple of sample pages and to quote their fee. Some editors only want to dot "i"s and cross "t"s while other want to do complete rewrites. Using this method, he was able to compare their work and select the one he liked at the best per-page price.

Many big name authors cannot type or spell so they hire people who can. To contact people in the "word game," go to libraries, PR firms, advertising agencies, college English departments and see the Writer's Digest Yearbook. For a list of freelancers and ghostwriters, write Research Associates International, 340 East 52nd Street, New York, NY 10022. There are a lot of people out there who will be happy to work for you at a reasonable rate. You have the knowledge of the subject and a writer knows how to put your thoughts on paper. The big winner is the reader/bookbuyer who receives good information expressed well.

Whenever one is using the team approach to book writing, they must have a contract stating clearly whose name will be on the book and who is working for hire. Many people who are not professional writers get into print. If they cannot pick up the skills, they ask for help. You can too.

COMMISSIONED WRITING. Many of the more successful book houses approach publishing from a hard-nosed marketing position. They know what they have been able to sell in the past and they stay in their field of expertise often by assigning writers to produce more of these

> *"I just sat down and started all by myself. It never occurred to me that I couldn't do it as well as anyone"*—Barbara Tuchman.

"commissioned books." Once you have decided on an area of concentration, you too may approach others to write for you by paying cash outright or using modest royalty advances as an inducement. The accounting is easier and the arrangement is often more cost effective to pay outright for material rather than paying royalties. Flat fees are often around $2,500, half on assignment and half on acceptance. These books may be wrapped up in less than sixty days by moonlighting advertising copywriters.

AUTHOR SUBMISSIONS. Another source of material is the traditional one of unsolicited author submissions. If you are concentrating on a certain interest area and are selling books to a select market, you are also in contact with those people best qualified to generate new material for you. And once you publish something they like, they will come to you. Many people have always wanted to be an author and they will seek you out once they recognize your success.

Of course, you can always wait for manuscripts in your interest area to come to you but you will save time and a lot of useless copy reading by issuing one-paragraph outlines of books you need to round out your list. Next, contact Writer's Digest and fill out a form for a listing in Writer's Market. Most publishers will not waste their time reading an unsolicited manuscript; they are interested only in outlines of the proposed book and biography of the author. They want to be sure they can use the material and that the author knows what he or she is writing about before investing their valuable time in manuscript reading.

CO-AUTHORSHIP. If you have a book you want to do yourself but recognize that you lack the required technical expertise, consider co-authorship. Find an expert in the field to write part of it while you write the other part and then each of you can edit the other's material. This

---

"The How-to article is to writing as McDonald's is to restaurants; it enjoys no epicurian status. Nevertheless, McDonalds advertises "28 billion sold," a point the writer might keep in mind." — Leonard S. Bernstein

has many advantages including the endorsement of an expert, credibility and you have someone else to send on the promotional tour. The disadvantages are smaller royalties, extra accounting and author hand-holding.

This author shared the responsibilities for the <u>Frisbee Players' Handbook</u> with disc expert Mark Danna. Danna wrote the throwing and catching chapters while Poynter wrote on history, record attempts, competition and assembled the appendix. Poynter came up with the unique package and marketing idea but did not have enough expertise or credibility as a Frisbee player. Mark Danna rounded out the team well.

Spouses without experience outside the home may choose to co-author a book with their partner on their area of expertise. A project like this gets both of them published, provides them with a common project (which may do great things for the marriage) and elevates their job stature.

REPUBLISHING ARTICLES. Many author-publishers have gone the easy route by simply editing the material of others. Deeply interested in an area, they have thoroughly researched a subject only to find that many fine experts have already written good material on several aspects of it. The collection of these articles, one per chapter, formed a book. To pursue this course, contact each author for permission to use his material and ask him to go over a photocopy to update it with any new information or changed views. This makes your chapter better than the original article. If the chapter must be shortened, ask the author to do it. This is faster and easier than doing it yourself and then negotiating your changes with him.

If, for example, you are deeply involved in the sport of parachuting, you might contact the national association and their magazine about gathering like articles which

> *"Publishing is an active life while writing is a quiet life."* —
> Linda Meyer

have appeared over the years and republishing them in a series of booklets. Booklet Number One might consist of all the best articles on student training. Your primary market would be the members of the association: you would sell them through the organization's "store" and via mail order by advertising in their magazine. Thus, the association is providing both the material and the customers. As an editor, you simply repackage the information.

Bill Kaysing discovered an out-of-copyright book called Thermal Springs of the World. He abstracted just the data on hot springs in the western U.S., added some original comments and reprinted it as Great Hot Springs of the West. Review copies sent to several major magazines resulted in an entire column of flattering coverage in Sunset. $3. orders poured in for a book that cost him 50¢ to print and some 3,000 copies were sold in a little over a year.

NEGOTIATING AND CONTRACTING WITH AUTHORS. The object of an author-publisher contract is to clarify thinking and positions by laying out all the details on the table and arriving at a mutually beneficial agreement. There will never be a second book if one side takes unfair advantage of the other; it pays to keep the future in mind. Small publishers should not offer less than the industry norm unless they will be satisfied with just one book per author, and there is no need to offer more. Most likely, if the author had a chance with a big publishing concern, he would not even be talking to you. Then again, he may be working on one of your ideas. Each contract will be a little different but you can start with a standard one. For a sample and some published references on book contracts, write The Authors Guild, 234 West 44th Street, New York, NY 10036, Society of Authors' Representatives, Box 650, Old Chelsea Station, New York, NY 10113 and the American Society of Journalists and Authors, 1501 Broadway #1907, New York, NY 10036.

"Today, as always, if a talented author remains unpublished and unnoticed, the fault is the author's" — **Bill Henderson**

First-time authors will be eager to become published and may not be terribly concerned about the contract initially. Many creative people are not business or commercially oriented. It is imperative that contract negotiation and signing be taken care of first. Rough draft the contract and ask the author whether it is generally acceptable. If he or she has made any other commitments, such as for some subsidiary rights, this information must be added into the contract. Include a schedule and a clause allowing you to cancel if he or she fails to meet deadlines; always keep the pressure on writers to perform.

Unless you have a narrow field of interest or the writer has very strong feelings about a particular area, you will want a contract which includes all possible rights. Once you have published the basic book, you will want to entertain the possibilities of translations to other languages or co-publishing in other English-speaking markets (however, unless the market is quite large, it will be more economical to ship your own print run in "direct sacks of prints"). Then there are book club adoptions, film rights, magazine excerpts, newspaper serializations and the mass market paperback rights. Your promotion will rub off on all areas so take advantage of it by taking complete control of the manuscript. Remember that people who write contracts slant them their way. The author will want to check the publisher's track record; how long do his books normally stay in print?

ADVANCES AGAINST ROYALTIES depend on the proposed selling price, projected print run and the sales potential of the book. The advance seals the deal which is an important legal consideration while it puts pressure on the author and the publisher to perform. The advance makes the author feel accepted and has great psychological value; it does not have to be large to work as an incentive.

Advances generally range from $100 to $5,000 and small publishers often keep them low. A good rule of thumb is to offer an advance equal to the projected first year royalties. One way to create an incentive, or at least make the author feel morally obligated, is to make progress payments. One-third may be paid on signing the contract, one-third when the writer submits the first draft and one-third when he or she completes the proof reading. Advances are paid against royalties, they are not in addition to this percentage. Ordinarily, advances are non-refundable; the author keeps them even if he or she fails to deliver. This is another good reason to protect your money with progress payments.

Advances work both ways. Authors demand high advances from publishers in order to commit the publisher to the book. The publisher with a lot invested in a book, has to bring it to market quickly and market it well. The advance is the publisher's gamble. The author keeps it even if the book fails to sell and generate enough royalties to cover the advance. Some authors with little faith in their manuscript or the publisher will, therefore, request larger advances.

FLAT FEES OR ROYALTIES. Should contributors get a percentage of the book or be paid a flat fee? Obviously flat fees are simpler and occasionally cheaper. An illustrator creating a major portion of the book should get royalties while someone doing basic research, typing or contributing a drawing should be paid a set fee. Everyone must understand clearly what is in it for him. If you require a few drawings, go to a graphic artist and have them drawn to order. Then pay the bill and be done with it. The artist deserves a piece of the action no more than the person who painted your car prior to your selling it. One exception is a book for children where the illustrations are usually as important as the text.

Normally, the author supplies, and is responsible for, all illustrations (but this is negotiable). Royalty reports are a time-consuming chore which may be avoided if you pay a flat rate for material received.

THE ROYALTY FORMULA, traditionally, has been to pay the author 10% of the list (cover) price for each hardcover book sold through regular channels such as book

---

"The publisher is financing the author on the one end and the bookstore's inventory at the other." — **Sol Stein, President of Stein and Day.**

wholesalers, book stores and libraries. Remember that after discounting the book to dealers, this amounts to 15-20% of the publisher's budget. Or graduated royalties for the hardcover edition might be 10% of the list price on the first 5,000 books sold, $12\frac{1}{2}$% on the next 5,000 and 15% on sales over 10,000. Often softcover authors command 7% for the first 12,000 sold and 9% above that number.

Recently some small publishers have attempted to force their authors to assume some of the publishing risk by offering a flat 15% of the **net** on books marketed through normal trade channels and 10% of the net for mail orders. Percentages of the net rarely work out to the author's advantage as it is too easy for the publisher to pad the expenses. Even if the publisher is referring to "net sales" (both wholesale and retail), the author's royalties will be less. Further, the accounting required is a heavy burden and this is another expense to be considered. A percentage of the **list price** is preferable as it is easy to calculate and difficult to pad.

Royalties for college texts range between 10% and 18% while those for heavily illustrated elementary and secondary schools are between 4% and 10%. Royalties for juvenile books range between 10% and 15% to be split between the author and illustrator. Mass market paperback publishers usually pay 4% to $7\frac{1}{2}$% but print in much greater quantities.

Most contracts call for the author and publisher to split the subsidiary rights (films, book clubs, etc.) 50-50. Many of the big publishers barely break even on the book itself and hope to make their money on the subsidiary rights. Book clubs often want a lower price on their print run to make their deal look better; the author and publisher should not project their royalties based on the price of the original book.

TRANSLATIONS offer another source of material and are a royalty consideration. A good translator is a highly skilled artist who issues a product which does not read

---

"Professionals sell, then write, while amateurs write, then try to sell." — Gordon Burgett

like a word-for-word translation. He or she will spend hours searching for the single right word or phrase to convey the original meaning. Translators must not only be bilingual, they must be good writers, too. There may be some 1200 literary translators in the U.S. but few are very good. To find a translator, write the American Translators Association, 109 Croton Avenue, Ossining, NY 10562. The going rate is $30 or less per 1,000 words so few can make a living at translating. Citing their creative input, translators are now requesting royalties but few have been successful so far. The English language rights to foreign language books are rarely expensive so this is another interesting source of material.

COPYRIGHT CLEARANCES are the responsibility of the author and this should be spelled out in the contract. The author knows his sources better than the publisher and should be responsible for obtaining permission and paying the fees for extracted material, articles, photos or drawings. This includes the right to translate foreign material. See the discussion in Chapter Five.

PROMOTION is the responsibility of both the author and the publisher, though they play much different roles. Most contracts are very general on this point, recognizing that if the book sells, the publisher will be more agreeable to expanding the promotion budget. The author must agree to devote his or her time to these promotions in author tours, TV talk shows, autograph parties, etc.

TERM AND CONTINUITY OF THE CONTRACT. The agreement may be for a stated period or for the copyright life of the book. It should be made binding on those who succeed both sides: the heirs of the author and the new purchaser of the publishing firm. Most contracts give the rights back to the author if the publisher goes bankrupt or does not reprint the book.

NEXT WORK OPTIONS are often written into contracts with first book authors. They give the publisher the right to take the next couple of books from the author on the same terms as the original. The clause is written into the original contract when the new author is eager to sell. It is often doubtful the author would agree to such an arrangement at a later date, once he or she sees the editing done to the manuscript and the lack of promotion provided by the publisher.

As a result, many authors rebel at this roping technique that creates friction between them and the publisher. Sometimes, these authors send in obvious trash to fulfill their end of the hated contract.

FURTHER CLAUSES include arbitration agreements in case of dispute, a paragraph saying the contract is being entered into on the basis of "good faith" and a statement that this is the only agreement, that neither party is bound by any other discussion during the negotiations.

The help of a lawyer is advised especially in drawing up the first contract. It may then be used as a general model for subsequent agreements. A well-written contract which is fully understood by both sides will avoid many later problems assuring a long and satisfying author-publisher relationship.

LAYOUT THE BINDER. Now that you are generating copy, you need a place to store it. Find a large 3", three-ring binder and add divider cards corresponding to the chapters you have selected. Insert the rough typed pages as you complete them. They should be numbered by chapter and page. For example, "6-14" would be page 14 in Chapter 6. As the piles come off the floor, cross the desk and flow through the typewriter into the binder, you will gain a great feeling of accomplishment.

Author and publisher (in this case you are both) should decide whether secondary matter is of value or just window dressing. An index, appendix, bibliography or directory may add to the usefulness of the book or it may just cost more than it is worth to include. It depends on the subject and your treatment of it. But all these items should be decided upon early, so a running list may be maintained as you do your research. Remember, some books are composed of nothing but lists.

> *"No man but a blockhead ever wrote except for money."* — Samuel Johnson

You will be further encouraged by setting up the front matter of the book. Soon you will have a partial manuscript, the book will be taking shape and you will have something tangible to carry around. This makes you feel proud and gives you the flexibility to proof and improve your manuscript away from home. Carry the binder around and work on it whenever you can. If the book is a short one, you may even use the binder to collect your material and this will allow you to avoid the piles of notes. Write your name and address in the front of the binder with a note that it is a valuable manuscript. You do not want to misplace and lose your future book.

It is wise to photocopy your manuscript periodically so that a copy may be stored in another location. You may lose a lot of important things in a fire but to have the fruit of your creativity destroyed would be a financial and emotional disaster.

PARTS OF A BOOK. Most books are divided into three main parts: preliminary pages or "front matter," the text and the back matter. We will discuss them in order so you can add a sheet for each to the binder with as much information as you have so far. It is not necessary to have all the pages mentioned or even to place them in any given order, but it is recommended that convention be followed unless you have a good, specific reason to stray. Set up these sections as best you can so the book will begin to take shape. You will make additions and revisions to the binder later.

There are two pages to each sheet or leaf of paper. The "verso" pages are on the left-hand side and are even numbered while the "recto" pages are opposite.

THE FRONT MATTER is that material placed at the beginning of the book. It includes everything up to the start of Chapter One.

END PAPERS may be plain or printed, usually of heavier paper, and are glued to the inside front and back covers of

---

"There are books of which the backs and covers are by far the best parts." — Charles Dickens

a hardbound (casebound) book. They hold the book together.

TESTIMONIALS and other sales copy are being seen more
and more on the first page of softcover books. This is
important sales material.

THE BASTARD TITLE or half title is usually the first
printed page of a book and is more often found in
hardbound books than in paperbacks. It contains only the
title and it is a right-hand page.

THE FRONTISPIECE is a photograph found on the reverse
of the bastard title page. Often this page is left blank
instead or it is used more economically to list other books
by the same author.

THE TITLE PAGE is on the right-hand side and lists the
full title of the book with its subtitle if it has one. This
page may also include the name of the author or editor,
the publisher, whether this is an original or revised edition
and the date.

CHOOSING A TITLE. Spend some time on your title.
Title testing has shown a good one will sell some 15%
more books. In some cases, the title made the book go.
    Start with a short, catchy and descriptive title, and
a lengthy explanatory subtitle. The first word of the title
should be the same as the subject to make the book easy
to find. The book will be listed in Bowker's Books In Print
by title, author and subject. If the title and subject are
the same, you have doubled your exposure. Most other
directories list only titles in alphabetic order; position
your book where it can be found.
    Book listings in BIP include only the title, not a
description of the contents so get more mileage with a
sub-title to tell what the book is about. For example,
COMPUTER SELECTION GUIDE, Choosing the Right
Hardware & Software: Business-Professional-Personal is
listed under the most common heading "computers" while

"It is easier to edit than it is to create."

the rest of the title and subtitle tell what the book is about.

Many self-published books are sold by mail order and to be marketed they must be advertised. Here the title must grab the attention of the reader and make him a promise such as: "buy this book and make a million." Test proposed titles out on your friends and acquaintances.

Good book titles are your best teaser copy whether they are selling the book from a magazine advertisement or the book shelf. Brainstorm the title and come up with a good "one-liner" which tells a complete and compelling story. The title is perhaps the single most important piece of promotional copy you will draft for the book.

THE COPYRIGHT PAGE or "title page verso" is on the reverse of the title page and is the most important. Proofread it a dozen times! Here you print the copyright notice, indicate the printing history (number of printings and revisions), list the Library of Congress Catalog number, the ISBN, the Library of Congress Cataloging in Publication Data, name and address of the publisher (you) and "printed in the United States of America" (to avoid export complications).

Those who know the trade will turn to the copyright page first when picking up a book. Next to the cover, this page is the most important in selling a book so make it look good. See Chapter Five regarding copyright, ISBN's, etc. and list all your numbers. You want to look like a big time publisher, not a basement word shop.

Each time you revise the book, it is worthwhile to restrip and reshoot the copyright page in order to add "Second Printing, revised, 1986," as this lets the potential purchaser know the book is up-to-date. The big publishers do not make any changes and print a string of numbers on the copyright page instead. You will note: "1 2 3 4 5 6 7 8 9 10" which indicates to the trained eye that this is the first edition. On reprinting it, they will opaque out the "1" on the photographic negative. Actually, the big publishers will print the full number of books they think

---

"Writing is one of mankind's most important endeavors, the primary vehicle by which man leaves his mark" — **James Warren** in *Writer's Yearbook.*

they can sell. They never really intend to go back to press.

THE DEDICATION PAGE usually contains a short statement, if one is made at all, but some authors like to praise their friend(s) in great detail. It is not likely that anyone else other than the person mentioned will care about the dedication. This right-hand page was used historically by writers to acknowledge their patrons: the person or institution that supported them during the writing.

THE EPIGRAPH PAGE contains a pertinent quotation which sets the tone of the book. Using a separate page for an epigraph is usually a waste of space.

THE TABLE OF CONTENTS should start on the right-hand side. This page will include the chapter numbers, chapter titles and beginning page numbers. You can leave these page numbers blank for now. They will be filled in by the typesetter when the book is laid out. Remember, when buying technical, professional or how-to books, most people turn immediately to the Table of Contents to check the coverage.

A LIST OF ILLUSTRATIONS is in order if the book is heavily illustrated or if it is a picture type book. Usually this page is a waste of space. The same goes for a list of tables, especially if they are tied directly to the text.

THE FOREWORD is positioned on the right-hand side and is a pitch for the book by someone other than the author. It is doubtful that many people read them; most turn directly to the action. The name of the contributor appears at the end. If you include a foreword, note the correct spelling, it is not "forward."

THE PREFACE is written by the author and tells why and how he or she wrote the book. It gets about as much attention from the reader as a foreword and appears on the right-hand side. If you have an important message and want to be sure the reader receives it, put it in Chapter One, not in the preface or introduction.

ACKNOWLEDGEMENTS are a great sales tool. List everyone who helped you in preparation of your manuscript. People love to see their name in print and each one will become a disciple spreading the word on your great contribution to literature. They may even purchase a copy. On this blank sheet in your binder, add names of contributors as you encounter them so that you do not forget anyone.

THE INTRODUCTION was covered above in the discussion of the preface.

THE LIST OF ABBREVIATIONS is only required in some very technical books.

THE REPEATED BASTARD TITLE is next, is optional and is a waste of space.

DISCLAIMERS are showing up in more and more books today. Chapter Three lists some of the reasons.

Obviously, if all the front matter pages listed above were included in your book, you would have a number of pages already. You do not need all these pages and it is recommended that you do away with most except the title page, copyright page, acknowledgements and table of contents. Check over several other books for layout, especially old hardbound books which followed convention.

THE TEXT of the book is the meaty part on which the front matter and back matter hang. This is the second or main section.

Start your book off with an "action" chapter. Like the introductory part of a speech, it should arouse the reader and whet his appetite. Too many authors want to start from the "beginning" and put a history chapter first. The reader wants to know where-to and how-to. Do not lose him in the first chapter.

> *"The best and most businesslike way to write for money— and consistent publication—is to find out what editors want and try to produce it. — Kay Haugaard in The Writer.*

DIVISIONS are sometimes made in long books with distinct but related sections. Their title pages contain the name and number of the section and their reverse sides are usually blank.

CHAPTER TITLES should reveal the subject of the chapter to aid the reader in finding what he or she wants. The reader may be skimming the book in a store pending possible purchase or may be referring back to something he or she read. In either case, you want the description to be as clear as possible.

THE SUBHEAD is a secondary heading or title, usually set in less prominent type than the main heading, to divide the entries under a subject. Subheads can contribute a logical progression, aid in finding needed material and help to break up long chapters.

FOOTNOTES are not needed except in technical publications. If your book will be used as a research tool, the readers may want the footnotes so they can follow up on the material. Where footnotes must be used, some people recommend they be placed at the end of the chapter or in the appendix as it is more time consuming and therefore costly to place them at the bottom of each page.

THE BACK MATTER is all that reference material such as the glossary and index placed at the back of the book. It is less expensive to revise lists at the end of the book when reprinting; do not print lists subject to change in the text.

THE APPENDIX contains important charts, graphs, lists, etc. and it may be composed of several sections. It is permissible to set this reference material in smaller type.

THE ADDENDUM has brief, late additional data. It is printed as part of the book or on a loose sheet.

"The last thing one discovers in writing a book is what to put first." — Blair Pascal

ERRATA are errors discovered after printing. The list is printed on a separate sheet and may be pasted in or loose.

AUTHOR'S NOTES come next and include additional information in chapter order.

THE GLOSSARY is an alphabetically arranged dictionary of terms peculiar to the subject of the book. Some authors like to save space by combining the glossary and the index.

THE BIBLIOGRAPHY lists the books you used in writing your book.

THE INDEX aids the reader in locating specific information in the pages and is particularly important in reference works. Many librarians will not purchase books without indexes. Assembling the index is very time consuming unless you have a word processor and the index must be revised every time the book is updated because the page numbers change.

THE AFTERWORD is sometimes seen in manuals. Often it is a personal message from the author to the reader wishing the best of luck and/or requesting suggestions for improvement.

"COLOPHON" is Greek for "finishing touch" and details the production facts by listing the type style, designer, typesetter, printer, kind of paper, plate maker, binder, etc. It is not as common as it once was but is used more and more today in special "labor of love" type publications.

COUPON. The last page of the book should contain an offer for more books and a coupon; place it on a left-hand page—facing out. Some readers will want to purchase a

---

"I quess every normal writer has a desire to give birth to a book someday—to become, in fact, an author. Books are...a chance at immortality" — **Margaret Bennett** in *Publishers Weekly.*

copy for a friend while others may want a copy for themselves after seeing your book at a friend's home or in the library. Make ordering easy for them. This coupon system works. Several orders on the coupon are received for The Self-Publishing Manual each week.

Make a page for each of the sections listed above that you wish to include and fill in as much information as you now have. Keep adding with a pencil as you progress. The collected information does not have to be neat or in order, the important thing is that now you have a place to store your material. As you add pages, as the book fills up, you will have more work to carry as you venture away from home. When you find a few idle moments, open the book, draft and revise it, bit by bit. Tighten your writing, change words, cut out those which fail to add to your message. Revise and improve.

EDITING your manuscript is where you cut, rearrange and add material. You will probably make fewer changes than you predict. Go through the manuscript section by section and clean it up. Ask a couple of friends to read over the material and to pencil in their suggestions.

THE FINISHED MANUSCRIPT must be typed, never hand-written. It should be neatly double spaced on one side of $8\frac{1}{2}$ x 11 white paper and contain a minimum number of changes. Check all spelling, punctuation and grammar. Using a binder to hold the manuscript, it is easy to change, add or subtract material. To delete, line it out. To change, type out new copy and paste it over the old. To add, just insert an additional page and give it the same number as the previous page with the suffix "a", as in 16a. The result will be several strips of paper pasted onto each page. Fill an empty Elmer's Glue-All bottle with rubber cement to simplify the job.

PHOTOS AND DRAWINGS are easily indicated in the manuscript with page and position numbers. The second photo on page 40 of Chapter Three would be marked "3-40-B", for example. Mark the location both in the manuscript and on the back of the photo or drawing. Mark the photo near its edge and do not press too hard, you may push through to damage the photo. Incidentally, it is sometimes necessary to indicate which side of the photo goes up if it is not obvious to someone not familiar with the subject. Type the captions into the manuscript under the photo position number. Make a photocopy of the photos or contact prints and paste them into the manuscript (set the machine on "light"). This will make the draft clearer to both you and the typesetter or printer. Never paste in the photos themselves, they are hard to get off and make a mess.

TYPING THE MANUSCRIPT. If you lack either the ability or desire to type the final draft of the manuscript, there are many typists who specialize in this work. Check with your printer, call other printers, business schools and look for secretarial services in the Yellow Pages. Typists' rates are moderate.

START EACH CHAPTER about one-third of the way from the top of the page and make it appear just as you want it in the book by listing the chapter number and title. At the top of each page, type your name and the chapter/page number. Leave about a one inch margin all around the page so you and the typesetter will have room for penciling in notes. If you maintain consistency in line length and in lines per page, it will be easier to project the length of the finished book. If you type the final draft yourself, you will have an opportunity to clean it up and make the text flow even better.

TYPESETTING NOTES should be made on a page in the front of the manuscript. List your name, address and telephone number; the typesetter may wish to call you to clarify something in the manuscript. Include the hours you expect to be by the telephone if you are not always there. List the typestyles you want for each type face used in the manuscript. Some subjects use words that are

---

"An awful lot of junk is released today, and such books are quickly read and discarded. The author's name floats off. Your best work on every page is your gift to yourself and to publishing." — Aron Mathieu *in The Book Market.*

similar and easy to interchange. For example, one set in aviation is "altitude" and "attitude." Tell them to watch for these. And you may have some other special notes to include.

TYPE STYLES may be indicated in the manuscript in a couple of ways. The usual system is to code each one with a number and then to mark the manuscript with them only when there is a change. The typesetter does not want the text all cluttered up with notes such as "10/11 Bodoni Bold." Another very neat way is to use different IBM type balls in a Selectric typewriter. Whatever your system, place an explanation in front of the manuscript for the typesetter. For an explanation of type, see Chapter Four.

PROOFREADING has to be done again and again. You will proof your manuscript for content and style, and then you will proof the book as it makes its way through the various stages of production.

Ask friends to proofread your manuscript for grammar, punctuation and content. Do they find it easy to read? Do they understand what you are saying? If no one has time to read the whole book, ask them to go over an interesting chapter. For technical proofing, send chapters off to various experts. Just make a photocopy of your draft and ask them to make notes right on the copy. Enclose a self-addressed, stamped envelope and remember to give them credit in the acknowledgments. You will not only produce the very best book, you will gain their support for it and this is very important to its marketing. Incidentally, it is customary to pay an honorarium of $50–150 to experts reviewing a book-length manuscript and it is worth much more to you.

There will be a lot of proofing. The manuscript must be proofed and marked prior to final typing, the final draft has to be proofed for the typesetter, the set type or "boards" have to be proofed and the blueline prints of the book signatures have to be proofed. You will have some errors anyway but without careful proofreading, you will have more. Being familiar with your own writing style, you will find it difficult to catch all of your own errors. Try reading syllable by syllable, slowly. Find a friend to proof for you.

There is an interesting story about a professor who wanted to publish the error-free book. He brought it out in mimeographed form and offered his students 10¢ for each error they could find in the course of the term. They found quite a few. Then he corrected the stencils and ran off another set. This time he offered the new class 25¢ per error. They searched harder and found fewer. By the fourth time around at $1 per error, only a very few errors turned up and the professor was satisfied. Incidentally, this proved to be an effective way to encourage the class to read the required text thoroughly.

Proof well. Get it right the first time. "What you (don't) see is what you get." There is no practical way to take ink off paper.

Some typesetters will want you to proof the "galleys," the composition before it is pasted down on the boards. This is a holdover from letterpress when it was less expensive to make changes at this point. (Actually in letterpress, this is the last chance to proofread before the plates go on the press.) The only good reason to proof galleys today is if the author turned in a messy manuscript. The typesetter should proof his own galleys for typographical errors and proceed with the pasteup.

Proofing the "boards" is what you will do if the book is being printed offset. These are the pasted-up pages and the typesetter will provide you with a photocopy to mark up. Usually the typesetter will proof the boards before sending them to you. They will catch the obvious punctuation and spelling errors but not the technical or look-alike words (altitude and attitude). Many of the errors will be from the typesetter, not from your manuscript. Proof carefully; a page is not error-free just because it looks clean. You will not be charged for errors made by the typesetter, so correct them no matter how small. On the other hand, you will be charged for any deviations from your submitted manuscript. But if the changes are important, this is the cheapest place to make them. Do it now.

Proofing the blueline prints comes next. These are large folded blueprints of the actual stripped-in negatives which were photographed from the pasted-up boards. Bluelines are assembled into signatures just like the proposed book. They enable the printer to make sure the pages are in order and that everything is in place. This is your last chance to proofread. Check especially the page numbering, sentence continuation from one page to the next, the chapter page numbers in the table of contents, chapters beginning on a right-hand page, proper insertion of the illustrations (right-side-up?) and captions, the numbers on the copyright page, the ISBN on the cover, etc. Most important, hold the pages up to the light to check registration. The blocks of text and page numbers should be superimposed.

To change even a punctuation at this point, it is necessary to reset the entire line, paste it on the board, reshoot the negative, strip it into the flat and reshoot the blueline. Expensive! If you delete or add words, entire pages may have to be reset and this may affect more than one page. It may be necessary to reset the rest of the chapter or even the rest of the book. So count the characters and make the new line the same length as the one it replaces. Ask for a tour of the plant and you will better understand the situation.

Compare the set type with your manuscript. Use "PE" (printer's error) next to your correction in the

---

"There are no problems in publishing, only challenges."

PROOFREADER'S MARKS

ℓ	delete; take out	S.C. or Sm.cap	set in small capitals (SMALL CAPITALS)
◯	close up; print as one word	lc	set in lowercase (lowercase)
◯	delete and close up	ital	set in italic (*italic*)
∧ or ˃ or ⋏	caret; insert here *something*	rom	set in roman (roman)
#	insert a space	bf	set in boldface (**boldface**)
eq #	space evenly where indicated	= or -/ or ⌵ or /N/	hyphen
stet	let marked text stand as set	⊬ or en or /N/	en dash (1965-72)
tr	transpose change/order the	⫫ or em or /M/	em – or long – dash
/	used to separate two or more marks and often as a concluding stroke at the end of an insertion	∨	superscript or superior (∨ as in r2)
		∧	subscript or inferior (∧ as in H_2O)
⌐	set farther to the left	◌̂ or ⋋	centered (◌̂ for a centered dot in p · q)
⌐set⌐	set farther to the right	∧	comma
⌢	set ae or fl as ligatures æ or fl	∨	apostrophe
=	straighten alignment	⊙	period
‖	‖ straighten or allign	; or ;/	semicolon
✗	imperfect or broken character	: or ⊙	colon
⧠	indent or insert em quad space	∨ ∨ or ∨ ∨	quotation marks
¶	begin a new paragraph	(/)	parentheses
(sp)	spell out (set 5 lbs. as five pounds)	[/]	brackets
cap	set in capitals (CAPITALS)	ok/?	query to author: has this been set as intended?

manuscript where the typesetter made the mistake so you will not be charged for the change. If the change is your fault, it is called an "author's alteration" and they cost. Use a red pen to mark the proofs so your notes cannot be missed. Do not proof blueprints outdoors; the sun will turn them solid blue fast. Write in small corrections but type out and paste in large ones. Proof with a dictionary. Double check all numbers, dates and facts. Recheck the spelling of names, places and unusual words.

"Press proofs" are where the printer runs off a few sheets and then lets you do a final proofing. Press proofs should not be necessary, you had your chance with the blueline prints. It is very expensive to leave a press idle so people rarely request press proofs.

No matter how carefully you proofread, some errors will always show up in the final printed book. Do not be too concerned; resign yourself to it and make the corrections in the next printing.

Many publishers like to make a small press run the first time to help them catch the errors. Keep a "correction copy" of the book near your desk and pencil in changes as they come to your attention. Then when you are ready to reprint, you will be ready to go. Major errors may require the insertion of an "erratum" slip. They are slipped into the front of each printed book.

PROOFREADER'S MARKS are standardized to enable you to communicate clearly with your typesetter and printer. A complete set of marks can be found in your dictionary under "proofreader's marks." Stick to the standard marks. If you make up your own, you will only confuse those who must understand them. Use these marks throughout the editing/proofreading process.

ARTWORK consists of line work and halftones. Line work is a clean black on white drawing without any shading. Line drawings may be pasted directly on the boards unless their size must be enlarged or reduced. Camera work costs extra. Halftones are made from photographs, or drawings with shading, by taking a photograph of them through a screen. You will notice the result using a magnifying glass to look closely at a printed photograph. A screened photograph is composed of many tiny dots of various sizes (shading). This takes camera work and you will be charged for each one. Camera charges are a start-up cost; the cost of an individual photo when spread over the entire print run is very small. It is foolish to be cheap at this point.

　　If you need line work and cannot draw, you can hire a commercial artist. Most typesetters have illustrators on their staff or know some and they usually work inexpensively. Your typesetter or printer may also have a large file of "clip art" and you may find something there you can use. These are commercially provided drawings on a large variety of subjects that may be used without permission. Many people lift art from reprints of old Sears catalogs and other publications where the copyright has expired. Depending on your subject, you may be able to clip drawings from certain military and government publications which are in the public domain or are supposed to be yours under the Freedom of Information act.

PHOTOGRAPHS, rarely seen in fiction, are almost a requirement in nonfiction, especially how-to books. The most successful how-to books are those that manage to integrate words and pictures into an attractive teaching tool. Unless you are writing an art-type book, you will use black and white rather than the more expensive color. Color requires four trips through the press plus pre-press "color separations." The best photos are large, (they become sharper when reduced) glossy, black and whites with a lot of contrast. Color photos and slides may be reproduced in black and white but will not be as clear. Photographs which have already been printed once may be pasted-in direct or reduced and rescreened but the results are not as good as with an original glossy photo. When in doubt about the suitability of a photo, ask your printer. Occasionally the screening actually improves the photo.

CAMERAS. Unless you are an accomplished photographer with a good set of equipment, you will want to get a good camera with attachments and buy a book on how to use it. There are many types of camera but the most popular and versatile is the single lens reflex. Many used models and accessories are available at your discount photo shop and they have good resale value. If all your subjects are still, you can get by with a cheaper match-needle model. If you are shooting fast-moving people or objects, you may need a camera with automatic features and/or motor drive. (Aircraft mounts may dictate motor drives and a remote firing device too.) And do not overlook the new zoom lenses which make framing faster and easier. Olympus has the fastest motor drive, (five shots per second) and that still is not fast enough to get a series of photos to show the windup and throw of a Frisbee disc. But it is fast enough for most subjects and allows you to keep your eye on the subject rather than pulling away to advance the film. Some good automatic cameras are the Olympus OM-2, Nikon FE, Minolta XD-11, Canon A-1 and the Konica C35-AF.

USING THE CAMERA. As you compile your manuscript, make a photo list so you will know what you need. Then set out with your gear to take them. Try to frame your shots on the object, person or activity you are trying to show; avoid distracting clutter. For good black and white

---

"Life is too short for reading inferior books" — James Bryce.

contrast, avoid tonal shades. Put people in your photos. If you are showing a number of pieces of equipment which are better modeled, such as parachutes, invite as many different people as possible to wear them. You can bet that each model will buy a copy of the book. When taking still shots of people, make them smile. Get their teeth in the picture. Most people do not know how to pose for a photo and complain that they do not photograph well. Catch them smiling and they will love you for it. Try to capture action in your photos, make them move. Seek the unusual, tell a story, look for human interest, shoot from a different angle. Then have your film processed by a custom photo lab. Do not send it out through your supermarket. Slides don't matter as much but in b/w processing the negative must be focused.

Handle negatives and photos carefully, you have a lot invested in them. Keep them clean and mail them flat between cardboard sheets. When you wish the typesetter or printer to crop a print, do not take out the scissors, make crop marks on the edges. If a photo needs retouching, such as to remove an extraneous object like your camera bag, let the graphic artist do it. Do not use paper clips. When writing on the back, use a fine point felt tip pen, concentrate on the edge and do not push down too hard. Make sure the ink is dry before restacking the photos and to be safe, ship photos back to back and face to face. For more information on cameras and photography, see the discussion in Writer's Market.

Photo release forms are advisable, particularly for pictures of minors. Permission might cost $20-500 but normally your subjects are just tickled to be in the book. A news photo does not require a release unless it is used in an advertisement. Permission fees are paid by the author on publication.

Often you will overlook getting permission and occasionally a subject will inquire about his rights. The best way to handle this is to tell him or her that you are about to go back to press with a revised printing and while it will cost you to replace the photo, you can take him or her out. I have yet to hear of a subject who wanted to be deleted from a book.

OTHER PHOTO SOURCES. Freelancers with a stock of photos will sell them for a couple of dollars each. Or you can have them custom shot for $5-$20 per photo. Photo syndicates are in the business of selling stock photos. The chamber of commerce, private firms, trade associations and some governmental departments have public relations departments who provide photos as part of their function. Libraries and museums sometimes have photo files. Photos from old books with expired copyrights are easily copied with your camera. Just carry the book over to the light, lay it out flat and snap a photo. These photos of photos come out very nicely. When covering an event, make contact with the other photographers and get their cards. They may have just what you need. Picture sources are listed in World Photography Sources, Writer's Market and Literary Market Place.

WHEN TO FINISH. If the book is 100% accurate and 99% complete, go to press. That one last photo and that one extra item can wait for the reprint. If you delay the printing, you are tying up your money longer and you may miss the market.

MAILING THE MANUSCRIPT. If you are not dealing with a nearby typesetter and printer, you will have to ship the manuscript. Stack the photos and drawings and enclose them in cardboard to avoid folding. Send the manuscript in a binder. Enclose both in plastic bags and pack them in a sturdy cardboard carton. The Post Office does offer a special manuscript rate (same as book rate) but most authors prefer United Parcel Service because the service is good and the parcel must be signed for on the receiving end. Another alternative if you are not near a UPS office is certified, priority (air) mail through the Post Office. A couple of extra dollars now is well worth the expense. Be sure the carton contains your complete return address.

Always keep a copy of the manuscript. This is to protect you in case the original is lost in the mail or by the printer and it is your ready reference when the printer calls with questions. Take the manuscript to a copy center which has a plain paper dry type copier. They usually give reduced rates for overnight service and are reasonably inexpensive. After the book is printed, turn the copies over; the paper makes a fine scratch pad and people love to get notes on it.

Writing a book can be easy if you have a system. With the organization outlined here, a decision to go and some discipline, you will start a whole new rewarding life.

See the list of books on how to write on specialized subjects listed in the Appendix.

Dan's first book took eight years to produce. He worked on this labor of love without guidance or direction. The huge, steady selling manual on parachutes became the base for his publishing company. His second book was a study guide for an obscure rating; it sold better than expected.

In 1973, he became interested in the new sport of hang gliding. Unable to find any information at the library, he wrote the first book on the subject. He foresaw a trend and cashed in on it; the book has sold 125,000 copies and is still going strong. Total writing time: two months.

By this time, he had developed a writing formula. His fourth book took less than 30 days from conception and decision until he delivered the manuscript to the printer. And most of this time was used in waiting for answers to his many letters requesting information. The first draft took only five days.

From there he concentrated on several high-priced, low-cost course pamphlets, turning out most within a week. His ninth book took all of two weeks to first-draft and it was typed "clean." Very few editing changes had to be made to the original copy and he even used different type styles in his IBM Selectric typewriter to indicate those he wanted in the book.

Using a word processor, Dan spent 31 days to write, edit and typeset a book on computers. The actual time spent was just 18 3/4 days.

Writing a book is easy if you know the formula. Now Dan will reveal his system to you.

Chapter Three

STARTING YOUR OWN PUBLISHING COMPANY

Forming your own publishing company is not difficult and many of the requirements may be postponed until you are ready to send your manuscript off to the printer. You do need a system and must get into the habit of using it. This is, after all, a business.

HAVING A BUSINESS IS JUST GOOD BUSINESS. Tax laws favor business. Businesses get to deduct goods and services the wage earner must pay for with after-tax dollars. If you don't have a business, you do not get to deduct very much.

Gross ⟶ Taxes ⟶ Net
Job

Gross ⟶ Expenditures ⟶ Net ⟶ Taxes
Business

If you own a business, a lot of what you are already spending becomes deductible (car, dues, subscriptions,

71

travel, etc.) A wage earner would pay for these items with what is left after taxes.

THERE ARE THREE FORMS OF BUSINESSES: sole proprietorship, partnership and corporation and each choice has advantages and disadvantages which you will have to weigh. You do not have to make the choice right now. If you do not file for corporation status, you will be operating as a sole proprietorship anyway. Here are a very few things to keep in mind while you are concentrating on the most important project: your manuscript.

In a sole proprietorship you have the choice of keeping your financial records on a cash basis or an accrual basis. The cash system is easier to understand, allows you to defer more income and requires less bookkeeping which makes more sense for a small business. You may always switch to accrual when you grow larger. Once you use the accrual system, however, you cannot switch back to cash and you must get IRS permission to make any switch.

Many business consultants discourage the formation of partnerships as they are not much more successful than marriages—for a lot of the same reasons. It is a rare pair who compliment each other well enough to divide the work so that both are happy. If two or more people want to form a company, they should consider a corporation.

In a corporation, you are an employee, not the company itself. This means more accounting, payroll taxes, paperwork, annual meetings with published minutes, more taxes and annual registration fees. In California the fee is $200 per year.

Corporations are separate legal "beings" and can be sued but their stockholders cannot be touched. A sole proprietor does not have the protection of this "limited liability" and could lose his home and other possessions if he lost in a legal action. There is more to consider in publishing than just the debts of the business. Someday, a reader may sue, claiming a book mislead him to his great damage. In fact, this has already happened with a cook

---

"Many of us are small because we want to be" — Charles Nurnberg in *Publishers Weekly*.

book and a diet book. The plaintiff will, of course, join both the author and publisher as defendants trying to collect from both you and your incorporated company. Since you are the author, incorporation will not protect you from suits. Today, many books contain disclaimers warning readers not to rely on the text.

Libel might be another reason to sue, but again, the plaintiff would seek damages from both author and publisher. Keeping some of these problems in mind and considering your book's subject, talk to other people around you in small businesses and to your accountant and attorney.

PUBLICATIONS. When your manuscript is near completion and you have a "product," you will want to concentrate on the business end of publishing to get it printed and off to market. The Small Business Administration has many free publications and some at a slight charge which should help you. Write SBA, Washington, DC 10416 and request publication order forms #115-A and 115-B as well as Booklet #71, a checklist for going into business.

The Bank of America publishes several helpful reports in its Small Business Reporter series. Send to B of A Marketing Publications #3120, P.O. Box 37000, San Francisco, CA 94137 and request both a publication index and a copy of Steps to Starting a Small Business.

It is strongly recommended that you subscribe to Publisher's Weekly and Writer's Digest magazines. You will learn about the writing/publishing trade, obtain many ideas and gain enthusiasm. Purchase a copy of Literary Market Place, it is the resource of the book industry. I used to recommend referring to it in the library whenever it was needed but it has become too important for just occasional use. Check the Appendix of this book for accounting and business books such as Kamoroff's Small Time Operator. Your writing references such as dictionaries, thesauri and style manuals can be purchased inexpensively in used book stores.

SCORE is the Small Business Administration's volunteer network, the letters of which stand for "Service Corps of Retired Executives." These are retired executives who will call on you to assist in your problems. There is no charge for this service except for occasional out-of-pocket traveling expenses. There are several hundred SCORE chapters around the country. Call the SBA office nearest you to see if there is a nearby SCORE chapter. Look in the White Pages under U.S. Small Business Administration. Tell them what you need and they will find someone tailored to you and your business. Naturally, it is always best to get this advice before you get into trouble; do it sooner, not later.

YOUR COMPANY NAME will have to be decided before you go to press so keep thinking about it. You could name it after yourself, say Mindy Bingham Enterprises or Alan Gadney Publishing Co., but these choices do not make you look as big as a separate name. The use of "enterprises" is the sign of a rank beginner; as though you don't know yet what your company is going to do. If the business succeeds and one day you decide to sell out, the name will be sold with it. A good name will have more value. After all, what is the value of Scott Hamilton Publishing without Scott Hamilton? Looking big may be important when applying for credit from your vendors or asking a paper mill for samples. A company name will create the impression that you have a going business.

Starting the name with an "A" will place your company high in alphabetic listings. Peggy Glenn change her PiGi Publishing to Aames-Allen to assure top billing in directories.

Foreign names can pose cataloging problems. Would you list "La Cumbre Publishing" under "L" or "C"? If people do not know where to catalog you or where to look for you, you may not be found and this could amount to a loss of business.

Geographical names can be limiting. Which sounds larger, East Weedpatch Press or North American Publishing? Which would you rather run and what happens if you move to West Weedpatch?

> *"An entrepreneur spends 16 hours a day to avoid having to work someone else for eight hours."* — James Healey.

To find a new name, one that isn't being used in the publishing industry, go to the library and look through Writer's Market, International Directory of Little Magazines and Small Presses, Books in Print, Literary Market Place and your local telephone directory. This search is fun and you will note that the newer companies have some pretty interesting names. As a new, little outfit, it does not hurt to have a handle that attracts attention. Pick a name that isn't being used by anyone else.

After you select a name for your new publishing company, you will probably be required to file it as a "fictitious business name" and run a notice in a local newspaper. This notice is your way of letting the public know that you and the publishing company are the same person.

YOUR LOGO is a graphic image, an easily recognizable symbol; it may consist of a drawing or just the company name in a distinctive style of type. If you can dream up something clever and easily recognizable, start putting it on all of your letterheads, labels, business cards, etc.

YOUR PLACE OF BUSINESS will be your residence for awhile. You will not need a lot of space to write or even to store and ship books initially. When you have several titles and need more space and employees, you will have to move out, but for now home has many advantages. Working out of your home (house, mobile home, camper, wherever you live) will save additional rent, utilities, the headaches of a second property, etc. And, as we will discuss later in this chapter, you can write off part of the household expenses on your tax return. Working at home takes some organization and discipline but for many it is very comfortable working in this no-stress atmosphere.

Before you actually begin sorting, shipping and selling books in your front room, quietly check the zoning ordinances. Local regulations may allow one or two firms in one house. Your business will be small at first and as long as you don't have employees and large trucks aren't

---

"No-one takes better care of your money than you do." — Cliff Leonard in *License to Steal*

pulling into the drive every few minutes, no one is likely to complain. Avoid walk-in traffic and refer to yourself as an "author" rather than a "publisher" and you shouldn't encounter any difficulty. Sometimes when local regulations prohibit operating a business in a residential neighborhood, author/publishers post their business licenses at a friend's store and continue to quietly work out of their home.

Working from your home should not be confused with "office in the home." The IRS has cracked down on the offices which are in addition to one's place of business. If you use one-half of your home for your business activities and do not have another office, you may deduct 50% of most of the house expenses. Some of those deductions are for mortgage or rent, electricity, heat, insurance and water.

If you are worried that a vendor or client might not be favorably impressed with your setup, make a lunch date in a restaurant. Actually, he or she will probably envy you. In the U.S., two percent of the work force enjoys the "short commute." Working out of your home is more comfortable, more efficient and cheaper.

P.O. BOX OR STREET ADDRESS. There are many good arguments for each one. Some people feel quite strongly that a street address is more effective in a mail order ad because the business reflects more substance and stability. But today, even the big firms are using boxes. This is probably the result of the high incidence of urban crime. There was a time when the mail was sacred and no crook would dare to touch it, but not anymore. Depending on your address ("1234 Northwest Whispering Valley Parkway, Suite 1701" or "Box 3") a long street address could cost you more in classified ads where they charge by the word.

You will have to go to the Post Office regularly to ship books so you might as well pick up your mail there and with a box, you will be able to pick up your mail a few hours earlier. Another advantage of a box is that you can

---

"You're a living, breathing, embodiment of the American Dream — free enterprise division."

76

maintain the same address even though you move (the Post Office forwards mail for one year). Perhaps the most important reason to maintain a box is to keep your excited, loyal readers from dropping in at all hours to meet their author who must be interested in them and their project.

Apply for a box now and consider a big one. In some areas boxes are in short supply and there is quite a waiting list. It may take you months to get one. Write your name, your company name and the title of your book on the box registration card so you will get your mail no matter how it is addressed. Remember, all your stationery and business references need an address so get a box now.

YOUR STATIONERY is you. It should look nice but you do not want to tie up a lot of money here. One attractive, inexpensive, simple system is available from The Drawing Board (see the appendix and write for a catalog.) All you will need are #10 window envelopes, # ML5-N72 memo sized letterhead (without reply) and some invoice forms to fit. Windowed envelopes save time as you only type the name and address once. Also order business cards and a rubber stamp with your company name and address.

YOUR TELEPHONE may be listed under your name or the company name and if you request a commercial listing or a Yellow Page ad, you will get hit with the higher commercial rate. Keep costs down when doing your research by dialing direct during the early morning, evenings and on weekends. For exact hours, consult the initial pages of your telephone directory. The power company may also wish to charge you commercial rates if they find out you are running a business from your home.

YOUR TYPEWRITER or word processor (see Chapter Eleven) is your most important piece of machinery; spend the money and get a good one. You are a "wordsmith" now and require the best word processing machine you can

---

"My take home pay won't take me home anymore."

afford. If you choose a typewriter, the new electronic machines are less tiring to operate and they will make your work look better. These machines can be used to create brochures, forms, etc. because of their clear, sharp type. There are a few electronic typewriters on the used machine market and there will be more now that offices are switching to computerized, video display text editing equipment. See an office supply store. Even if you have to go new, consider paying for it over several months or years. After all, you will be using it over a long period. If you are already in a high tax bracket, you should consider leasing all your office equipment. The costs are tax deductible and you tie up less money. Ask your accountant.

Better yet, are the new computerized systems. It is hard to beat the combination of the IBM Personal Computer with Spellbinder word processing software and a Diablo 630 printer. Not only will this system speed up your writing, it may be used for correspondence, mailing list maintenance and bookkeeping. Set up with a carbon single-strike ribbon, a metal printwheel, and clay-coated repro paper, it may be used to set strike-on type for your book. When you figure in the money saved in typesetting, investment tax credits and the mechanization computers provide your business, they are really quite inexpensive. For specific details see the Computer Selection Guide by the author.

THE BETTER BUSINESS BUREAU may offer some credibility to a mail order business operating out of a Post Office box with a name like "Joe Smith Enterprises" and many people recommend joining. Look up the BBB in your telephone directory and call to request literature on what they have to offer. Membership fees vary from one locality to the next and often run $100 per year for the small business.

THE LEGAL REQUIREMENTS of operating a business are covered in many parts of this book just as you will encounter them in every facet of your daily publishing life. The following is what you need to run your business, but remember that most of this may be postponed until you are ready to go to press, move out of the house or

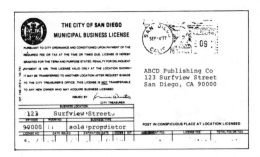

DISPLAY CONSPICUOUSLY AT THE PLACE OF BUSINESS FOR WHICH ISSUED

hire employees. These tips, of course, are food for thought, not a substitute for legal counsel.

Interview a friend or acquaintance who has recently set up a small business in your community. They will be happy to tell you what happened to them, where to get various licenses, recommend an accountant, etc. In some areas you must register your business with local authorities, but not in all. Ask this same friend where to find the office. As a sole proprietorship, your business won't need a separate bank account and until you hire employees, you will avoid tax numbers and special accounts.

SALES TAXES. Most states have a sales tax. If your state does, you will be required to collect it ONLY on those sales shipped to destinations within the state which are NOT for resale by another dealer. The sales tax is collected only once at the retail level from the ultimate purchaser. In some states, shipping supplies are not subject to the sales tax. Other states exempt certain

---

"We don't charge sales tax here, we just collect it."

Example of a California resale number request card

non-profit or public institutions such as libraries and schools. As a commercial firm, you must either collect the sales tax, show by the shipping address on the invoice that the goods are going out of state or claim to be selling the books "for resale." Many states will require you to maintain a file of customer resale numbers. Some dealers will list their resale number on purchase orders but usually you have to send a standard resale number request card, available from your stationer, with the invoice. Type "for resale" on the invoice and record the resale number there if you have it.

Before you go to press, obtain your resale permit so you won't have to pay sales taxes on your books when you pick them up from the printer. Find the office in the telephone directory. In California it is called the Department of Equalization, in Massachusetts it is the Sales and Use Tax Bureau of the Department of Corporations and Taxation. Check the posted resale permit at a nearby store, the name of the controlling agency will be on it.

When you apply for your resale license or seller's permit, say you are just starting out as an author and hope

> *"More trouble than you ever dreamed may be as close as your nearest tax office."*

to sell a few of your books. Tell them that most sales will be wholesale to bookstores or shipped out of state. This way you may be able to avoid giving them a deposit and you will be allowed to report annually instead of quarterly, thus saving both money and paperwork. For example, in California, if you say your taxable sales (retail and within the state) might amount to more than $300 per month, you must place at least $100 on deposit with the Board of Equalization before you start. If you say you might be collecting over $12.50 per month in sales taxes, they will want you to fill out the forms and remit the taxes quarterly instead of annually. When you apply, the tax office will supply you with an explanatory sheet detailing your responsibilities toward the sales tax in your state.

When drafting ads, don't say: "California residents, please add 6% sales tax." This is a sure way to lose sales. Your potential buyer is not a mathematician and he may be embarrassed if he doesn't know how to figure percentages. Just ask for so many cents for sales tax. For example: "Californians please add 54¢ sales tax."

THE LAW YOU MUST KNOW as an author/publisher concerns copyright, defamation (libel), right of privacy and illegal reproduction. Briefly, copyrights work both ways: they protect your work from others and their work from you. Take pride, do your own original work and make it better. For a detailed explanation of the copyright, see Chapters Two and Five.

DEFAMATION is libel in the printed word and slander when spoken. Black's Law Dictionary defines it as: "The offense of injuring a person's character, fame or reputation by false and malicious statements." Defamation may take the form of either words or pictures. The offense is in the "publication" of the matter so you are not "covered" if you read it somewhere else first. You are safe if the statement is true; this is the perfect defense, but check the source. The best advice is never to say anything nasty about anyone. You will need all the

"Profit is not a dirty word"

support you can get to sell your book. If you disagree with another authority, write "some people will argue. . ." or "many authorities believe. . ." and then tear up the position with your view. If you don't like someone, the worst thing you can do to them is to leave them out of your book altogether. Cover yourself and stay out of court; the legal game is expensive.

RIGHT OF PRIVACY is another area of law you may face. Unless part of a news event, a person has a right to keep his photo out of publications. Most people love to see their photo in a book and, in fact, they are prime customers for the finished product. But if you suspect there may be a problem, have them sign a written release.

ILLEGAL REPRODUCTION covers the promoting of lotteries, financial schemes, fraudulent activities, printing of securities, stamps, etc. In other words, don't print money. If you are writing about these subjects, you probably already know about the problems and the Postal and other laws relating to them. If not, seek legal advice.

TAXES are one place an author/publisher gets a big break. Not only are the costs of printing your book deductible, so are all the direct expenses incurred while writing and promoting it. If you are writing about your favorite hobby, you can deduct the expenses in pursuing it, too. For example, if you are writing on aviation, you can probably deduct flying lessons and trips to the national convention. There are sales and publicity tours and you can even write off a portion of your home, its rent or mortgage, utilities, etc. Assuming you are already employed and Uncle Sam is withholding 30% or more from your weekly check, that amounts to thousands of dollars a year. The game is to see how much you can get back. How much did you pay last year? Would you like to get a full refund? Getting money back is fun and rewarding. Of course, if your book is a great success, you will make more money and have to pay taxes on it. For complete

> *"You know you have arrived when you don't have to check the balance before writing a cheque."*

details, purchase a copy of the <u>Small</u> <u>Business</u> <u>Tax</u> <u>Guide</u> from your nearest IRS office. Under "record keeping", below, we will detail possible deductions.

RECORD KEEPING must be done from the beginning of your writing because you cannot deduct what you do not have written down. Many small business people get themselves into a jam by coming up with a great business idea and then charging off pursuing it. At the end of the year they suddenly realize that they have forgotten to fill out forms or record expenses. At that point their only choice is to hire an accountant to straighten out the mess. Accountants charge much more for this sort of work and they are never able to completely reconstruct the records or take all the deductions the business is entitled to take. The IRS is plugged into your bank and when they notice that $25,000 went through your bank account when you reported only $15,000, they will be by with questions. And you can't really avoid the bank as you have to cash all those checks which come in the mail for your book.

Dun & Bradstreet claims that 80% of all business failures are due to poor records. A University of Pittsburgh survey found that 40% of the retailers surveyed did not keep proper records. It is silly--no tragic--because recordkeeping is easy with a simple system. As the business grows, you will also need financial information on your past to properly project the future.

Start right now. Pick up a few sheets of ledger paper from your office supply store; get paper with at least 20 columns. Label the columns in the expense ledger as follows: meals & lodging, gas/lube/wash, office supplies, shipping & postage, advertising, entertainment, air, etc. fares, travel expenses, cost of supplies (books), dues & licenses, subscriptions, telephone, electricity, water, mortgage/rent, parking & tolls, car repairs, car tires & supplies, refunds and miscellaneous. The income ledger sheet will probably only reflect sales from your wholesale invoices and retail labels (see Chapter 10). For a detailed explanation of the items that fit into these

> "You can't deduct it if it isn't recorded. If you don't make a note now, you'll forget it."

columns, see the IRS publication Small Business Tax Guide mentioned above. The best way to get into the habit and to learn what is deductible is to list EVERY cent you spend the first year. Get receipts whenever possible, at the Post Office, for parking, tolls, meals, motels, etc. Your accountant will decide what is deductible when he or she does your taxes.

You have already decided to carry pen and paper at all times to record your thoughts for your manuscript so carry one more sheet for recording expenditures. Any money spent in the pursuit of income is deductible so write down every cent. As you learn what is deductible, you will find that you become generous where an expenditure can be written off and stingy where it can't. This is good discipline and good business. Keep an envelope in the car. Each day as you get in and start the car, let the engine warm up a moment as you record the date, mileage reading and places you intend to go. Use the envelope to hold the receipts you acquire during the day. Use a new envelope every month.

Every few months or even at the end of the year, sit down at the ledger and post the expenses for each month from your pocket notes, car envelope and check book. If you are not sure what column an expenditure might go in, place it in miscellaneous. In March, total up the columns and take the ledger and totaled figures to your accountant. The accountant will do the rest and the charge will be reasonable. You will be amazed at the size of your refund and the accountant will compliment you on your work. Record keeping is so easy and yet many people think there is some great mystery to accounting.

You don't even have to make money to claim deductions. You can claim a loss for at least three years in a row before the IRS deems you to be a hobbyist rather than an author/publisher. Some companies such as Chrysler lose money for years and still take deductions. Keep good records and you will be able to easily prove you are in business. See the tax discussion in Writer's Market.

RAISING THE MONEY YOU NEED to pay for the production and promotion of your book will take you into the world of finance unless you have a lot of loose, ready cash lying about. Insufficient capitalization is one of the greatest problems facing most new businesses. Money won't come looking for you. You have to find it by selling yourself and your book. But the money is there, it is available.

According to the Wall Street Journal most entrepreneurs spend their own money to start their business. 48% rely on savings, 29% borrow from banks, 13% shake down their friends, 4% look for individual investors, less than 1% strike deals with venture capital firms or government agencies and 5% are successful with other sources.

In the beginning, you won't run up bills by hiring help or renting space and you will even save some leisuretime money by staying home to write. So you will not have any immediate needs for large sums of cash. Most people have more money than they really need for necessities; they throw away their disposable income on frivolous purchases. Going without booze, cigarettes and nights out is not only healthier, the time can be better spent writing your book.

Some people advise the use of "OPM" (other people's money) rather than your own. Then if your business goes bust and you lose all the borrowed funds, you still have your own money in reserve. But as you tuck your prized manuscript under your arm and venture off you are going to find that locating OPM takes some searching.

THE SMALL BUSINESS ADMINISTRATION has prohibited financial assistance to book publishers ever since it came into being in 1953. The SBA treats the whole opinion-molding media this way. This is to avoid financing radicals who might print seditious literature and then file for bankruptcy. This would leave the taxpayers with a social problem and the bill for starting it.

BANKS don't search for loan applicants in the publishing industry. They like "going" firms with upbeat balance sheets; like everyone else, they are in business to stay in business. Banks look on manuscripts/books as "speculative." Even armed with a detailed market research report

---

"High cash flow": Taking in lots of money but being unable to find any of it.

on your product, you may find that you can't even get an appointment with the loan officer. A stack of books is not considered good collateral to a bank; if you defaulted, they would not know how to turn the books back into money. If you ask for money to go into business, the bank won't be interested.

Basically, there are two ways to borrow money from a bank. The first is the "term" loan which is normally used to finance purchases such as a car. Term loans are paid back monthly and are usually limited to 36 months. The second is an ordinary signature loan with interest at the prime rate plus about 5%. A signature loan runs for a period of months and you pay it off at the due date. But while the loan is written for a stated period, it is common to pay just the interest and renew it. Many authors have been successful in acquiring money by leaving the manuscript at home and asking for a "vacation" loan.

You may need collateral, perhaps a second mortgage. If you have enough real and personal property, you will be able to get the money on your signature alone. Don't think small, large amounts are often easier to borrow.

All banks are not the same, shop around not only for loans but for the bank itself. Banks are not doing you any favors, you are doing them a favor by dealing with them. Stop in at several and pick up pamphlets on their checking account and loan policies. Take the brochures home and compare them. Do they charge for each check deposited? You will be receiving a lot of small checks and any check charge will add up fast. Do they pay interest on checking accounts and if so, what is the minimum required balance? Will they let you bank by mail and will they pay the postage? Don't just think of your present needs, think of the future.

Incidentally, you may be better off working your new publishing company part time initially. Then if it fails, at least you are not out of a job, too.

ALTERING YOUR W-4 FORM is advocated by some people as a way to have the IRS lend your withholding taxes back to you. If you have a regular job and a lot of money is being withheld from each paycheck, you may claim an exemption from withholding by making out a new

W-4 form for your employer. If you are in the 30% tax bracket, this is like getting a 50% raise. Of course, you must be serious about starting your business, keep good records and take deductions. Done correctly, you should be able to spend and deduct the formerly withheld money and "zero-out" at tax time. Once you are working for yourself full-time, you will file estimated tax forms rather than W-4's.

PRE-PUBLICATION SPECIALS are often used to raise money. As the book goes to press, send out a brochure to all who might be interested in the book and offer them a break on the price for a pre-publication order. Emphasize that the manuscript is complete and that the book is on the press. Tell them you won't cash their check until the book is shipped. Mention a shipping date but give yourself an extra month or two. Make another mailing to dealers. The offer is often 55% off for 500 or 1,000 copies on a non-returnable basis and it is made to wholesalers, organizations and anyone else who might be interested in a quantity. Pre-publication sales sometimes bring in enough to pay the printing bill.

SELLING STOCK in your business is another way to raise money but there are a lot of problems. You are not big enough to make it worth your while and you should give money-raising it a great deal of thought before sharing the rewards of your work. If you can find someone to risk an investment in your book, you can find one to give you a straight loan at a good rate of interest where his risk is lower.

GRANTS are available from numerous foundations for worthwhile publishing projects. The Glide Foundation tells you all about them in The Bread Game. Check into your state arts agency, the National Endowment for the Arts, 2401 E Street NW, Washington, DC 20506 (Government), Alicia Patterson Foundation (private) and see the listings in Grants and Awards Available to Writers. Ad-

---

"A person who does not read good books has no advantage over the person who can't read them." — Mark Twain

ditional listings may be found in <u>Literary</u> <u>Market</u> <u>Place</u>, UNESCO'S handbook <u>Study Abroad</u> as well as in magazines such as <u>CODA: Poets and Writers Newsletter</u> and <u>The Writer</u>. The Dramatists Guild and the Theatre Communications Group also publish useful periodicals. See listings in the Appendix. Most of the grants and fellowships are for fiction and poetry. If your book qualifies, it can mean a large amount of money but there is a lot of paperwork to go along with it.

WRITERS' COLONIES often supply free room and board to support budding authors. Some have rigid rules limiting the length and number of stays. For a list, see <u>Writer's Market</u>.

YOUR PRINTER may be interested in helping you in exchange for an interest in the book. Typically, the printing company would absorb the printing costs and would receive 10-15% of the sales in return.

PARENTS will often lend on a book. They have faith in their offspring and want to see your name on a book as much as you do. But if you do borrow from friends or relatives, make the same presentation to them that you would to a bank. Talk figures and do not get emotional. Then write a loan contract and pay them the 10-15% interest that you would pay the bank. Put the loan on a business basis and keep the friendship. The interest is all deductible and you will get more of your withholding taxes back anyway.

OTHER POSSIBILITIES include credit unions, retirement plans, the Veterans Administration (if appropriate) and the Farm Home Loan Association which is said to be very liberal in its definition of a "farm community." Shop around. All these suggestions for borrowing money assume you have a good saleable product to begin with.

> *"In this work, when it shall be found that much is ommitted, let it not be forgotten that much likewise is performed."* —Dr. Samuel Johnson upon completion of his dictionary, 1755.

HOW MUCH you will need is an important question and this will take some research. Money will not be coming in right away. There is a lot of lead time for writing, printing and promotion and the book industry is notorious for being slow to pay.

At 1984 prices, it might cost you $12,000 to launch a nice book. This would be 5,000 copies of a 5½ x 8½ softcover with 200 pages, lots of photographs and a four color cover. Initially you might spend $2,000 for research trips, photographic work and office supplies. The typesetting and printing might cost $8,000 and then the shipping supplies and early promotion may run another $2,000. A book with fewer photos, fewer pages and a one color cover could run much less but without a good looking book and some promotion money, the book will not sell. For details, see the chapters on pricing and promotion. Get a quote from your printer to firm up the middle number. Try to be more exact with amounts and dates.

On the first venture, the printer will probably want his money in installments: 1/3 to start, 1/3 when the plates are made and 1/3 on the completion of the printing. After a book or two, he will no doubt give you normal 30 day terms and want his money a month after he delivers the books to you. If he wants installments, agree to them and then request a "2% discount for cash." (2% of $8,000 is $160.) In fact, you should always take cash discounts when paying bills even if you have to borrow to do so. Invoices with terms marked "2% ten" mean you can knock off 2% if you pay on the 10th instead of the 30th day. This is the equivalent of 36% interest per year. If you pay money before it is due, you are financing someone else's business without receiving interest; unless they offer ten day terms, pay on the 30th day.

Realistically, not wishfully, project your other expenses. Then work up a projected income chart. How much money do you expect to come in, from where and how fast? Now you know what you will need.

"...writing. It was a private thing that I could do. I could just send it out and see what it did. If someone laughed, I could stand up and say, 'I did that'" — Erma Bombeck in *The Writer*.

If you wait until you need the money to approach the source, you have waited too long. If you can find the money at all at this point, it is likely to be more expensive. Line up your sources of credit now but don't borrow the money until you need it. Borrow the funds for one, two or three years, whatever you project the needs to be, and make sure you will not be penalized for paying the loan back early.

Run a streamlined, efficient operation. Do everything yourself and buy only those services you cannot perform. Avoid employees, they cost you time (management), money and paperwork. Print in small quantities to keep the inventory low. Once you have learned the business by doing every part of it yourself, farm out the repetitive and least enjoyable tasks. When contracting for services, remember that everyone is in business for himself first, you come second. The graphic artist, accountant and all the rest will try to sell you more than you need. They don't care about your business as much as you do because they have less to lose. Never take advice from someone who is trying to sell you something.

Keep on top of costs. If you can save $1,000 per year by streamlining procedures and your net profit is normally 3%, the effect is the same as if you increased sales by $30,000.

Don't waste anything. Save the stamps from the incoming mail. Stamp collecting is big business and you may be able to sell them to the big stamp companies.

MACHINERY. As your publishing company grows, look for labor-saving machinery to multiply your efforts. Personal computers, photocopy machines, cordless telephones and postage meters will save you time. They are much better buys than an employee and you will find that with investment tax credits and depreciation, machines are not very expensive. As machinery accumulates, you will begin to understand the advantages of owning your own business.

"Most people work at only 10% of there mental potential. There is much capacity for improvement."

The author has operated, and worked for, large firms but since 1969 has opted to go it alone. In terms of both dollar volume and books sold, he is probably the world's largest one-person publishing company. And this is by design.

Because he has committed himself to the luxury of a one-person enterprise, he must operate efficiently. He must concentrate on those areas which will provide a maximum return on his investment of time and money: the highest profit and best results for the time and energy expended (invested).

He knows small business and small publishing inside-out because he plays both roles: he sets policy as management and implements it as labor. Consequently, he has developed simple systems to handle every task.

Most publishers with his amount of business have 5-7 employees. Dan works more efficiently and keeps all the pay checks.

Dan is a small businessman. His background is in marketing and mail order. He did not come from the publishing industry and, consequently, he doesn't make their mistakes.

"We think that small presses and self-publishing individuals frequently preceed the market because they can more easily become involved in a new trend at the conceptual level and can bypass a lot of the red tape that slows things down in larger houses." — Bob Speer of Southwest Book Services.

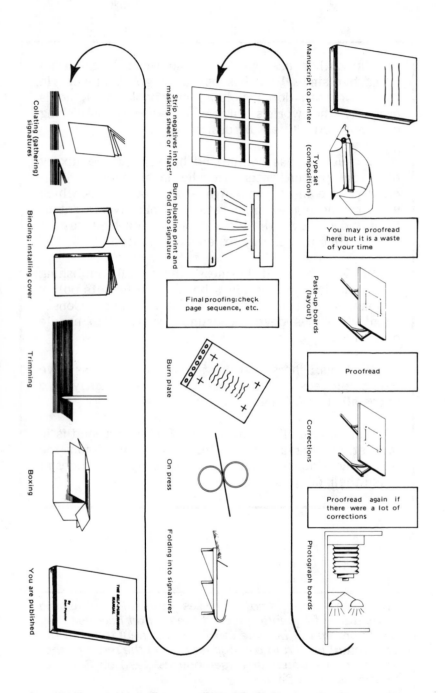

Manuscript to printer

Type set (composition)

You may proofread here but it is a waste of your time

Paste-up boards (layout)

Proofread

Corrections

Proofread again if there were a lot of corrections

Photograph boards

Strip negatives into masking sheet or "flats"

Burn blueline print and fold into signature

Final proofing: check page sequence, etc.

Burn plate

On press

Folding into signatures

Collating (gathering) signatures

Binding; installing cover

Trimming

Boxing

You are published

THE SELF-PUBLISHING MANUAL
By Dan Poynter

Chapter Four

PRINTING YOUR BOOK
MATERIALS — DESIGN
— PRINTING

Here is what you can expect when your book enters the production stage. This explanation of the printing process is meant to be brief and yet provide you with enough information to deal effectively with your printer. There are many excellent books on the printing trade. See your library. One good one is <u>Printing It</u> by Clifford Burke. See the Appendix.

INFORMATION PACKAGING. OK, you have the information and have written the manuscript. Now the project is to decide how to package the information to make it saleable. Some packages will bring in more money than others. You might print your information in a series of magazine articles, put it on cassette tapes, present it at a seminar or print it in a book. Or you might concentrate on one of them, such as the book, and spin off part to the rest. People are paying good money for well packaged information today. Some manuals cost $75 and some seminars run $200 per day. Obviously, the "package" must appear to be worth the asking price. It must be a professionally run seminar, a nicely printed book or an attractive article in a prestigious magazine. Here is what you should know about printing. This chapter will help you to select an appropriate design for your book.

PRINTING PROCESSES. There are two methods which may be used to print your book. Letterpress is the older one. It uses a linotype machine to set "hot type" or cast metal which is placed set into the press. Linotype (line of type) is more costly as it requires highly skilled trades-people, usually unionized and it is less flexible than your other choice.

Photo offset is a newer process where the original work ("cold type") is set by typewriter, composer (like a typewriter but much more versatile with variable type size, proportional spacing and a justified right-hand margin) or a computerized photo composition machine with a video screen. The pasted copy of type, line drawings and screened photos are transferred to a thin printing plate photographically. The "plates" are lighter, type is set faster, illustrations (and you may have a lot of photos) are easier to handle, the quality is better, accuracy is improved and it is more versatile than linotype. Most printers have switched to offset today, so unless you go to a specialized firm or a very small press which concentrates on letterpress work, all you will find is offset. You will hear of other methods of producing books such as gravure and belt press but these are used for large print runs or special work. What you want is offset at a good price; you aren't concerned whether the printer uses sheet fed or web presses.

Conversely, there are also some less expensive, short run methods. Wire stitched (stapled) booklets with up to about 60-5½ x 8½ pages can be reproduced very nicely on photocopy machines from typewritten material. Machines such as the Xerox 8200 and 9500 will print both sides of the paper and collate them. They will even handle heavy cover stock. Short run booklets may also be inexpensively produced by your local "instant print" shop.

"If you want your book to sell like a book, make it look like a book."

94

Ask them for a brochure. To learn more about producing small runs of booklets with your instant printer, read Publishing Short-Run Books by the author.

This book will concern itself with squarebound softcover and hardcover books, those you normally see in a bookstore. If you have a book-length manuscript, one which will fill a book of 100 pages or more, you will want a clean, sharp, professional-appearing product, one that will sell. You will be proud of it and it will be more acceptable to the stores.

You can figure on four to five weeks to print, bind and deliver your books to you but the work may take longer if your printer can't do all the work in-house and has to farm some of it out. Hardbound books will take a couple of weeks more because they must be sent out, in most cases, to install the cover. They take longer to bind. What will take a lot of time, perhaps months, will be the composition and layout. The variables here are the number of photos, number of pages, amount of corrections and whether you can keep up with the proofreading.

BOOK DESIGN serves two purposes. It aids communication by organizing the material for the reader and it promotes efficient book production by organizing the material for the typesetter. Most publishers have book designers who rough out the book layout and make up dummies. They show the position of the type on the pages, especially in the front and back matter. You may wish to give your typesetter specific instructions on some of your pages but there is no need to make up a dummy of the whole book. Your binder layout shows were illustrations are to be inserted.

Type may be set to run-around illustrations but it is simpler and cheaper to make a break in the text and insert the photo or drawing full-width, from margin to margin.

With a colored pen, so it won't be confused with copy, write your notes on the pages. Use the same color ink throughout for consistency; so the typesetter won't confuse changes in the copy with your typesetting notes. Only occasionally will you have special instructions for the layout of a page. Most of the copy and illustrations will simply be stripped in. There is no need to explain the

If all publishers thought alike, all books might look alike. Sometimes there is a good marketing reason to venture from the standard. This book is die-cut, nestled into a disc and shrink-wrapped.

obvious. Use other attractive books as a guide. You may vary from their format but strive for consistency through-out your book. Note that chapters start on a right-hand page. If this leaves you with a blank on the left, fill the space with a photograph. Never leave a blank page, fill it with something even if it is just a page number. Books with blank pages sometimes are returned by buyers who think there is a manufacturing defect. Just supply the typesetter with a few extra photos and provide instruc-tions to fill any blank pages with them.

"Running heads" are lines of type which appear across the top of the book page. Usually the title of the book appears on the left-hand page while the chapter title is on the right. Running heads are a good sales device and are educationally useful as they reinforce your message, but they take up space. The "folio" is the page number. Folios may be placed in the top outside corner, bottom middle or even on the side. In a die-cut circular book, the side might look best. Traditionally, pages received Ro-man numerals in the front matter and Arabic numbers in the text. This was because the text was set separately and then the front matter was expanded or contracted to use up most of the pages in the signatures. But today, many publishers take a tip from the magazine companies and start the count, though not the numbering, from the title page. This makes the final page count higher and makes the purchaser feel he is getting more for his money. The argument goes: "I paid for those pages so I'm going to count them."

STANDARDIZE AND SAVE MONEY. If you vary from the norm, the creativity will cost you. Occasionally variations can be justified, as in a die-cut circular book on Frisbee play, but make sure the special work will contribute to the sales of the book. Remember, too, that libraries and bookstores have standardized shelving. You want your book to fit. Most short-run books are 5½ x 8½, perfect bound (glued) paperbacks with or without photos and drawings on a 50 or 60-pound stock. The cover is two or more colors on a 10 pt. C1S (coated one side) cover stock. Beyond this basic specification, a number of variations are possible. Each page will accept about 400 words, less with illustrations.

MEASUREMENTS. The conventional 5½ x 8½ size is suitable for both hardcover and soft, it is one of the most economical, fits a library shelf well and is by far the most popular. One hundred-twenty 5½ x 8½ pages make a much nicer book than 60-8½ x 11 pages. The only good reason to go oversize is if you have just too much material. If you have large illustrations such as charts, consider fold-out pages. The printer can insert them between signatures; specify where you want the foldouts. If you have a lot of material, over say 400 pages in the 5½ x 8½ measurement, select the 8½ x 11 size. Whatever size you select, make all your books in these measurements so as to standardize your shipping bags and cartons. If some books are 5½ x 8½ while others are 8½ x 11, they will still stack well together.

NUMBER OF PAGES. You need 24 to qualify for the Post Office's "book rate," 50 to get a Library of Congress Catalog Card Number and 100 pages to qualify for a listing in H.W. Wilson's Cumulative Book Index. Over 100

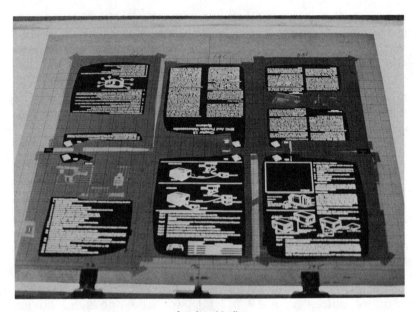

A stripped-in flat.
The photographic negatives of the pasted-up boards are "stripped-in" (positioned) to the masking sheet or "flat" prior to being "burned-in" to the thin metal printing plate.

is psychologically good and will help to justify your price so if you have just 99 pages, set the book in larger type, put more leading (space) between the lines, add some copy or an illustration.

Your book will be printed on several very large sheets of paper which will be folded down into "signatures" (originally, the person who sewed the pages together signed his work.) The number of book pages which will be in each signature will depend on the size of your printer's press, but 16 is common. This means that eight of the pages will be printed on one side of the sheet ("eight up") and eight will be printed on the other. Therefore, you will figure the pages in your book in multiples of 16.

Ask your printer how many pages his press can fit onto a sheet and you will be able to figure how many signatures will be required. Now, depending upon the size of the signatures, probably multiples of 16, try to come out close to even. 113 pages will cost much more than

112 (16 x 7) because of the extra press run which will be required for just one page. You might like to cut some material or choose a slightly smaller type style.

Often we want to have a page count before the boards are pasted up so that we can quote the number in our advertising. Simply look through books of the same size ($5\frac{1}{2}$ x $8\frac{1}{2}$, etc.) and find a type size and spacing you like. Count the words on the full page. Then compare the word count on a typical full page of your manuscript and add in more pages for photos depending on their to-be-reproduced size and number. Don't forget to count the front matter and back matter separately. While your printer can come up with an exact count through a long, involved computation, this method will be close enough. In your brochures, refer to the page count as: "More than 150 pages"; you don't have to be exact but people do like to know what they are paying for.

Poetry gets different treatment. Unless very short, each poem should have its own page.

TYPE FACES are many and varied; no typesetter could stock all the styles and sizes. With the help of your typesetter, you will select the type size and style, the width of the columns (4¼" in a 5½ x 8½ book) and whether you want the right-hand side justified (even or ragged right margin). Books set with a ragged right don't look professional and find it difficult to gain acceptance in bookstores and libraries. Four type factors affect legibility: type style (sans serif, italics, etc. are harder to read), type **size, leading (rhymes with "heading" and is the space between the lines) and the column width (the eye was trained on narrow newspaper columns). To give your book some variation, you may use italics, boldface, small caps and larger sizes for chapter heads, captions, subheads and for lending emphasis.**

8/9
Helvetica
Light

10/11
Helvetica Bold
Condensed

Here are some more type terms to make you sound as though you know what you are talking about. "Point size" is the height of a capital letter (and its mount) as in "10 pt. type." There are 72 points to the inch. "Pica" is the printer's standard measurement for the length of a line and the depth of a page. There are 12 points to a pica and six picas to the inch. Therefore, "24 picas" means a four inch wide column. "Leading" or slug is the space between the lines. Printers used to use a strip of lead, hence the name. So, if you have nine points of type plus two points of leading, it would be written out as "9/11".

10/12
Bookman Light
Italic

9/10
Garamond
Book

Nine on eleven is about as small as you should go for a legible book. Ten on twelve is very common though children and older people with failing eyesight prefer a 12/14. What you will decide to use will depend to a great degree on the length of the finished book. Look through books you like and ask your typesetter for type samples.

10/11
Times Roman

Some composing machines put more type on a page than others using identical type face, size and leading. "11/13 Century x 24 picas" is not always the same; it all depends on how the machine was originally programmed. You will want a sample of your typesetter's work in order to estimate pages.

11/12
Chelmsford

Do not venture too far from the common typestyles such as Times Roman, Palatino, Baskerville, Caledonia, Bookman and Granjon.

8/10
Souvenir

6 Helvetica
7 Helvetica
8 Helvetica
8½ Helvetica
9 Helvetica
10 Helvetica
11 Helvetica
12 Helvetica
13 Helvetica
14 Helvetica
15 Helvetica
16 Helvetica
17 Helvetica
18 Helvetica
19 Helvetica
20 Helvetica
21 Helvetica
22 Helvetica
23 Helvetica
24 Helvetica

Compare the various type faces

**Character height is measured in "points."
There are 72 points to the inch.**

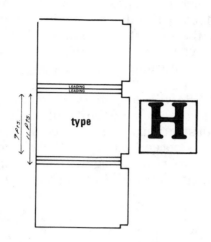

Type over 12 point is usually set with a headliner

Americana
Americana Italic
Americana Bold
Americana Extra Bold

Aquarian Script

Avant Garde Extra Light
Avant Garde Book
Avant Garde Medium
Avant Garde Demi Bold

Baskerville
Baskerville Italic
Bauhaus Light
Bauhaus Medium
Bauhaus Demi Bold
Bauhaus Bold

Bembo
Bembo Italic
Bembo Bold
Bembo Bold Italic
Brush
Caslon Antique
Caslon Open
Cheltenham Bold
Cheltenham Bold Condensed
Cheltenham Bold Outline

Commercial Script

Cooper Black
Cooper Black Italic
Deepdene
Deepdene Italic

The relationship between type and leading in point size. This is "9/11." Note that the character is not the full height of the type body. Leading is used to further separate the lines of type to facilitate reading.

HEADLINES, such as chapter titles, which are larger than 12 pt. are set on a headliner machine. Your typesetter will show you the type styles he or she has to offer. You may also set your own headlines using transfer type available at most stationery stores.

ILLUSTRATIONS will augment the text, enhance the appearance and aid the saleability of the book. Don't be cheap with illustrations. Each one is very inexpensive when the cost is spread out over the entire print run of books. If a photo or drawing will make the book more attractive, readable or useful to the buyer, include it.

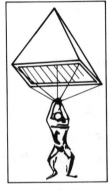

Line drawing

Extra lines were crowded into this line drawing to give it the appearance of shading.

Photo printed unscreened

Same photo screened.
Study with a magnifying glass or loupe.

LINE ART may consist of type, charts, sketches, etc. If you draw your own artwork or have it done, use a fine-point felt tip pen with black ink.

"Clip Art" is sold by the book or sheet and consists of line drawings on almost every possible subject. Clip art often lacks originality but it is less expensive than hiring an artist. Your printer or typesetter can tell you where to get clip art and they may have a lot of it themselves. See the list of clip art supplies in the Appendix under "Graphic Arts Suppliers."

Art may be taken from old magazines and books, too. If the copyright has expired, the art is in the public domain. Prior to January 1, 1978, copyright protection was for 28 years. The new law makes the copyright renewable for an additional 47 years. Therefore, anything printed prior to 1909 is safe and anything in print prior to 1956 is probably safe.

HALFTONES must be made of artwork which is not solid black-white, such as photographs. The original copy is re-photographed through a screen and the resulting print is composed of dots of various sizes. The eye blends the dots together into a continuous tone. Making a halftone of a photo, pencil drawing, water color, etc., costs $5 to $10 each. This is a one-time charge if you save the negatives; you won't have to pay again to screen photos for the next press run.

Screens come in several values and are measured in dots per linear inch. The more dots, the crisper the printed halftone. Newspapers commonly use a 65-or 85-line screen (85 dots per inch) while books are commonly done in 120, 133 or even 150 line. Black and white photographs screen best. Color prints reproduced in black and white tend to get muddy.

Photos taken from other magazines and books have already been screened and may be pasted right onto the boards. However, if they are to be enlarged or reduced, they must be re-screened and this usually reduces the quality.

With both photos and drawings, reductions are preferable to enlargements. Reductions become sharper while enlargements only magnify flaws, losing clarity.

A DUOTONE is a two color process which makes a halftoned photograph look significantly different from a plain black and white. Using a black and white original photograph, the paper goes through the press twice to be inked with black and one other color such as brown or blue. The second color is slightly offset from the first one.

FOUR COLOR PRINTING should be used on covers but it is normally too expensive for inside pages. To reproduce a color photo or slide, it is re-photographed four times, each time with a different colored filter over the lens. This produces four negatives consisting of the three primary colors (red, blue and yellow) plus black. the result is called a "four color separation." Then the paper is run through the press four times, each time with one of the colors and the color photo is re-created. Naturally, four color is more expensive because of the additional camera work and press time. Always ask for a "color key" before your color pages are run through the press. When checking these four plastic color overlays, remember simply that the sky is blue, the grass is green, clouds are white, wood is brown, etc. What you see is what you get.

Drawings may be pasted right down on the board. If illustrations are to be reduced, it is done photographically and there is a camera charge. You will be able to check the illustrations for position in your first proofreading. If there are just a few halftones (photographs), the board will only have empty spaces for them, you won't check them until the page negatives have been stripped into the flats. If, however, your text has several hundred halftones, your printer may wish to make screened prints of the photos and paste them onto the boards. This allows you to catch the errors sooner which could be cheaper. It is frustrating to proof copy without the accompanying photographs; you just cannot visualize the completed page or comprehend the entire message.

PAPER is even more confusing than type faces, and while you should know what to look for, you will need the guidance of your printer to make a final choice. In times of tight supply, not all types of paper in any quantity are always available. Some printers stock a very few grades in a narrow range of colors while others order paper for each job they do. If the printer has the storage space, he can save a lot of money buying in carload lots. Basically, you have four general paper choices:

1. Newsprint: inexpensive but it looks cheap, it yellows quickly and the photo reproduction is poor.
2. Uncoated book stock: looks good, photos OK. Most common.
3. Coated book stock (matte, coated or gloss): looks great, photos great, more expensive.
4. Fancy textured papers: may be hard to print, especially photos. Expensive.

Unless you are doing an art book, an uncoated book stock is what you need. Your printer will probably suggest a "50-pound or 60-pound offset."

Paper comes by the sheet or the roll (cut into sheets after printing). There are many variables which must be considered when selecting paper.

1. Weight is expressed in pounds per 500 sheets but the full size of the sheet varies according to the category to which the paper belongs. 60-pound cover stock and 60-pound book papers are not the same. For example: 16 lb. bond = 40 lb. book; 20 lb. bond = 50 lb. book; 24 lb. bond = 60 lb. book and 28 lb. bond = 70 lb. book. Cover stock is rated in point sizes with 10 point being very common.

Most books are printed on 50, 55 or 60 lb. stock. Generally, heavier paper is more expensive though some of the newer lightweight papers, developed for combating Postal rates, are even higher in price. If the paper is too thin, the book will look and feel "cheap", if it is too heavy, the book may not fold flat and, in either case, you have wasted your money.

> *"Never talk about what you are going to do until after you have written it."* — **Mario Puzo.**

In the metric system the weighing system is easier, all paper is simply weighed in grams per square meter of paper. There are no classifications.

2.   Texture. Some highly textured paper does not accept ink well, especially photos. Use a smooth paper such as "50 lb. offset book."

3.   Opacity. You don't want the type on the other side of the page to show through. Light-weight paper can be very opaque, especially when coated. Opacity may be tested by placing a printed sheet under the sample to see how much type shows through.

4.   Bulking factor is expressed in pages per inch (PPI). A 45 lb. paper may have a bulking factor of 640 pages per inch while a 55 lb. stock might be 370 ppi. Heavier weight does not always mean thicker paper. Bulking depends on the fiber content of the paper and the milling process used; A high bulk may also be produced by whipping air into the paper during manufacture. Whipping produces a thicker paper without increasing weight. However, this fluffed-up paper allows ink to diffuse more, so halftones are not as crisp. PPI is measured by the even inch.

5.   Grain in paper is similar to the grain in wood--it has a direction. Grain affects the way the text and cover lie. If the grain of the text is not parallel to the spine, the book will want to snap shut. Grain is also important if you plan to fold the paper since it may fold better in one direction than another. Grain is an important consideration in greeting card manufacture using heavy stock.

If the cover grain is not parallel, the cover will tend to curl or pop open. Sometimes the cover will even crack on the folds. The problem is that some automated book machinery trims the books cleaner when the grain is perpendicular to the spine than when it is parallel. When the grain is parallel, the trimmer makes small tears in the cover stock where it curls around the spine of the book. With such machinery, the choice is between cover curl and cover tear.

6. Grade refers to the type of paper, be it writing grade, book, cover stock, envelope, gummed, blotting, chipboard, etc.

7. Coating is done with a clay-like material and produces a smooth, shiny finish. Since the ink dries on the surface of coated stock, rather than down in the fibers of the paper, the printed pages looks crisper and cleaner. Coated stock, while more expensive, makes halftones look much better. It is a must for art books. Smooth finishes may also be produced by drawing the paper over a blade edge or through calendering (a heat and pressure roller process). The result may be a duller finish which is easier on the eyes.

8. Acid-free paper lasts longer and should be used for books of long term interest. Some printed products such as newspapers and magazines are made to be read and discarded, there is no need to save them. 67% of the university presses (which sell primarily to libraries) and 21% of other publishers produce their hardcover books on acid-free paper. Generally, some fiction, yearbooks and scholarly periodicals may be important fifty years from now while most nonfiction will not be.

Paper comes in a large variety of types and paper salesmen will be happy to deluge you with beautifully printed samples of all their wares. Don't buy paper any more expensive than you need. Ask your printer if he has any stock left over from another run. Perhaps you can shorten your press run and swing a sweet deal.

If you attend one of the many publishing seminars, you will probably be advised to purchase your own paper and "save about 15%." This makes about as much sense as taking your own oil to the gas station when you want it changed. The printer won't be happy about losing his markup and will probably charge you a "handling fee" or he may raise your price later claiming the job was "hard to print." If you buy your own paper, you will have to pay for it sooner, will be faced with storage and transportation problems and might lose it all if the printer botches a press run. It is far safer to simply get several quotes on the finished product and let the printer worry about the materials. After all, what you want is the least hassle and best price. Incidentally, printers and paper salespeople continually use the same pressure tactic claiming there will be a paper shortage soon. Expect it.

INK comes in a lot of colors and types, too, but both you and your printer will probably want black. If you are doing something special, ask to see his ink color sample books and run some tests. Remember that inks are transparent. If you print a drawing in blue and then overprint part in red, that part will become purple. Similarly, if you print blue ink on yellow paper, the print will be green. Unless you are doing a special art-type book, you will stick to the traditional black ink on white paper.

PAPERBACK AND/OR HARDCOVER. Traditionally, publishers printed in hardcover at a high price and would wait until sales dropped to come out with a cheaper softcover version. They might also publish a "library edition" with a supposedly reinforced hard cover, maybe an extra fancy "deluxe edition" on special paper, with gold stamped leather covers and even numbered and autographed. Then there might be "large type" editions for the elderly and, finally, an inexpensive "mass market paperback" edition. But what has emerged more recently is the very popular "oversize paperback," also known as the quality, trade, large format, large size, special or higher priced paperbacks. They fill the gap between the mass market pocket-sized book and the hardcover version. Today, more and more books are being published in a softcover edition only and the bookstores are stocking some 30% soft. This is not because paper cover books are cheaper to manufacture but because softcovers make

> *"Larger paperbacks...represent the greatest potential for growth in the book business today"* — *Publishers Weekly.*

more sense. Softcover books are printed on the same quality paper as the hardcover version. The differences are that the softcover edition is not normally sewn, has a thinner cover and (usually) does not have a jacket. So your field is narrowed to the hardcover and the quality paperback or simply "softcover."

Hardcover books are more expensive to produce and must carry a higher cover (list) price, but libraries like them and you don't want to miss out on this important market. However, libraries know how many times books can be loaned out (about 18 for paperback) before they fall apart. If the price difference between the two is too great, it becomes less expensive to purchase copies of the paperback and replace them more often. Often, libraries send paperbacks out to be "Permabound" with laminated hard covers. It costs about $2.50 to extend the book's life in this manner. Hardcover bindings are often used for reference works and it is estimated that about 20% are purchased gifts. They do make a nicer presentation than a paperback.

By far, most of your sales will be the softcover but you might produce some books in hard not only for the libraries but for those special presentation copies you will want for yourself. The problem is, however, with two editions, you want to make sure that they sell at the same rate so that you won't have a lot of one left over when you run out of the other and are printing a revision. On a 5000 book press run, you might consider doing 4000 in paper, 200 in hardcover and holding the texts of the remaining 800 to be covered later. But you must tell your printer to do this prior to the folding operation and you must print enough extra covers. Similarly, you must tell the printer you intend to use the same photo on both covers so he will make the color separation just slightly oversize. This allows for wrap-around on the hardcover while a small amount is trimmed off on the paperback.

Libraries are buying more and more softcover books. Many libraries do not have a policy on covers, they must only remain within their budget. In fact, many spend 20-25% of their funds on softcover editions.

The question is, just how long do you want a book to last? What good is a computer book that is five years old even if its condition is perfect? The package lasts but the contents is out of date. Better the library or retail purchaser pays a lower price for a softcover edition and replaces it in a year or two with a revised edition or another title. Some reference books, such as dictionaries, should be published with more durable hard covers but books that will be read once, such as fiction, annual references, such as the telephone directory, stand up very well in softcover. Another argument for the softcover book is that their covers last longer than the jacket on a hardcover book.

The major problem is that many reviewers do not take softcover books seriously; they do not consider a title to be a real book unless it is published in hardcover.

More and more softcover books are showing up as school texts today. Paper editions are lighter in weight and take up less space, making them easier to carry and cheaper to mail. Their lower manufacturing costs result in wider distribution, thus bringing the author greater recognition.

The cover of softcover books must be sealed. Traditionally, this was done with varnish. The cover made another pass through the press filled with varnish instead of ink. Today, ultraviolet set plastics and plastic laminates are more popular. The extra treatment to the cover protects it against scuffing during shipment and provides a shiny or wet look. The additional cost is easily justified as fewer books are returned damaged.

Workbooks and lab manuals must be durable enough to resist the flexing produced by constant use. Good results have been attained with Smyth sewing and perfect binding. The cover material may be 12 pt. C1S with a plastic laminate or a latex impregnated thick paper such as Lexotone or Kivar.

DUST JACKETS OR PRINTED CLOTH. You have a choice in the covering of your hardbound edition. The traditional method is to wrap the book in a colorful jacket. The problem is that the jackets are not durable and don't last long. In fact, many bookstores ask for extra jackets to keep the stock looking fresh. Another way is to print the cloth before it is installed on the book; this makes it far more attractive, especially on library shelves.

Dust jackets often contain a synopsis of the book on the inside front flap and a photo with a biography of the author on the inside back. If you use the printed cloth cover instead of a jacket, then like your paperback, you won't have any flaps. The alternative is to place the biographical information, lists of previous works, etc., in the front matter or back matter of the book.

THE COVER OF YOUR BOOK has two purposes: to protect the contents and to be a selling tool. According to The Wall Street Journal, the average book store browser who picks up a book spends 8 seconds reading the front cover and 15 seconds reading the back. And this assumes the book stood out enough to catch his attention enticing him to pick it up in the first place. In mass market (small size, high volume) paperbacks, this "hype" consists of about 12 words on the front cover and 75 on the back. The blurbs use words like "stunning," "dazzling," "moving" and "tumultuous."

Alan Gadney commissioned covers for three computer books he planned to write. He had the covers printed in four colors and made into dummy books for display at the ABA Book Fair in Dallas in 1983. His books were the talk of the show and he took a number of large orders. Covers must be important as he had not yet written one word on the subject.

The cover should include the title, subtitle (helps to identify the subject), the name of the author and a related photograph or drawing with impact. The print shouldn't be so fancy that it is hard to read at a glance. It is said that red attracts and sells best and many cover designers like to use it. Visit a bookstore and check the section where your book will rest. Consider what colors are there and pick something contrasting and bright that will stick out. Color definitely sells and the money should be spent to send the cover through the press four times. At the very minimum, two strongly-contrasting colors should be

> *"You can't tell — but you can sell — a book by its cover"* —
> *The Wall Street Journal.*

used. It depends upon your subject. For an action sport, an eye-catching color photo will sell more books than straight lines of types. The colors must contrast with each other. You will take black/white photographs of the cover for distribution with review copies. Darker colors may run together and look muddy.

Some of the things your cover should do are to make the author look like the ultimate expert on the subject. The copy should promise the buyer something such as health, wealth, entertainment or a better life. It must be bold, distinctive, intriguing so as to catch the eye and sell; it must stand out from the thousands of books around it. Depending upon the subject, you might include documentation and source material such as testing, surveys, case histories, etc. Stress the promise that the buyer is getting more than his or her money's worth. Important new information, such as a prestigious book review, may be printed on a sticker. Make the sticker a contrasting color and apply it at an angle so it doesn't look printed on.

THE SPINE usually has the title, the name of the author and an eye-catching symbol. If it is a dog book, include the outline of a dog. The symbol may attract the buyer more easily than the printed word. If there is room, you may include the subtitle, but make sure the title is big enough to be legible. Traditionally, the name of the publisher was included on the spine but in this case, you are the publisher and no one has heard of your company yet. Besides, people buy books by content or author, not by publisher. Some publishers also include the International Standard Book Number (ISBN) here. But beware of too much clutter. Your book will probably end up in the bookstore with only the spine showing from the shelf. Make the spine an eye-grabber.

THE BACK COVER usually has another attractive illustration or group of them, a blurb on the book, the price and the ISBN. Use whatever will sell the book. Many books have a photo and biographical sketch of the author. If you are an well-known celebrity put your photograph there but watch the ego trips. Many publishers print testimonials here. To get them, they send galley proofs out for review months before the book is completed. You will be anxious to get into print and onto the shelf so it is unlikely that you will have testimonials prior to your second printing. You can always print the reviews of your relevant previous titles.

Bookstores want a price on the cover. The Canadian booksellers don't want the price marked as they have to cover it with a sticker and they feel the customer dislikes seeing the apparently lower price underneath. The major problem is inflation. The price goes up with each revised edition and you reach a point where stores are returning an older edition for refund when you are shipping the latest edition. The older book cannot be recycled into stock and resold. Some people recommended that you use small stickers to allow flexibility. But this requires extra work and expense and even in these inflationary times, it makes little sense to raise the price once your printing bill is paid. Remember that changing prices, up or down, means new brochures, notifying <u>Books</u> <u>In</u> <u>Print</u>, etc. Sometimes the back cover is used to promote other books by the author but this valuable selling space shouldn't be wasted in this manner; mention your other titles inside.

Make every word on the front cover, spine and back cover count. There is no way to predict how the store will display your book.

DIFFERENT MARKETS are used to looking for different things on book covers. Target your primary audience and then try to cater to as many other markets as possible.

Mass market (smaller) paperbacks use a lot of color and "hype" because they have to compete with magazines for attention. It is assumed by some that these books are aimed at the less sophisticated people who don't frequent bookstores.

Mail-order books don't have to be flashy but their type must be large and clear so as to show up well in photographs in brochures and ads. The back covers don't show in the ads so they are often used to sell other books.

Trade books aimed at bookstores need a poster-like cover to aid in their sale. The back should also have a

---

"The Designer is expected to approach covers as though they were posters or ads" — John Huenefeld.

113

sales message as it is the next place a potential customer will look after the cover.

Textbook covers must be much more conservative or they will "turn off" the educators who make the purchasing decisions. Don't make wild claims.

Don't be confined by convention. The unorthodox cover may catch the eye better. Unless the cover is offensive, it will be the first step in selling the book. But look over other books you admire. Most follow the same pattern in layout. There must be a reason and you can bet it isn't lack of Madison Avenue imagination.

If the cover is not doing its job, consider changing it when you go back to press for a second printing. Once the book is in print the first time, you will come up with a number of ideas for changes.

Ask your printer to send you the overruns on the covers. You might even ask to have a few hundred extra printed. He will take these covers off the line before they are scored, folded and installed on the texts. These covers are beautiful and look very nice framed. You will be proud to hang one on your wall and you might like to send others to those who provided you with a lot of help, such as the photographer of the cover shot. Commissioned reps carry covers to the bookstores rather than heavy books. Many publishers use covers to make PR folders; they put all their sales information inside.

COVERING MATERIALS for your softcover edition will probably consist of a heavy, glossy, white coated paper. There is a great variety of cover stock to choose from. Your printer will tell you which is least expensive and easiest to print. You can also get special materials some of which look like leatherette such as Lexotone, Kivar, Graphitek, etc. Your printer will have samples. After printing, the cover usually gets another trip through the press to apply press wax or varnish to seal in the ink and protect the cover from fingerprints. More popular now are plastic coats or plastic laminates.

BINDING is your book packaging, the final touch. Consider your market (to whom will you sell it?) and the expected usage (will it be read once or used as a manual?). Because of the great expense of traditional hard

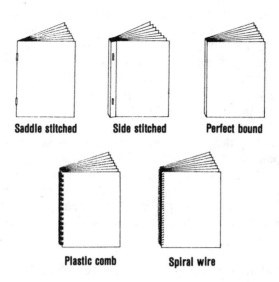

| Saddle stitched | Side stitched | Perfect bound |
| Plastic comb | Spiral wire | |

binding, there may well be a cross between the hardcover and the paperback one day. In Japan, it is common to place a dust jacket on soft cover books already. The choices are many and here are the most common types:

1. Perfect binding is the standard glued-on cover you see on most paperbacks. The pages are folded into signatures, often of 16 pages each, stacked, roughened and then the cover is wrapped around and glued on. The greatest advantage, besides lower cost, is that perfect binding presents a squared-off spine on which the title and name of the author may be printed. A text of more than fifty pages is required for a square spine and you might have to use a high bulk paper to achieve a sufficient thickness.

2. Cloth binding (case binding or hard binding) usually consists of Smyth sewing or side stitching the individual signatures together. Then they are installed (and glued) between two hard paper boards. Case bound books will accept a lot more flexing because they depend on thread, not glue, to retain the pages.

3. Wire stitches are staples and may be used in binding paperback books. This is the least expensive way

and many highly automated printing plants are set up for it. Wire stitches may be "saddle stitched" where the staple is on the fold or "side stitched" where the staple is driven through from the front to back cover. Saddle stitching will handle 80 pages (20 sheets) or less depending on the thickness of the stock because of the amount of paper "lost" in wrapping around the spine. On the other hand, side stitching may be used to bind even several hundred pages. Side stitched books won't open up to lay flat so this method shouldn't be used in manuals. Sometimes "Holland tape" is used to cover the staples making the book more attractive. The "stitches" come from a roll of wire and are adjustable in length.

4.   Spiral wire binding will allow books such as automotive manuals and cook books to open up and lay flat but it looks cheap. Spiral-bound books do not sell well in bookstores because the title doesn't show and libraries don't care for them. Consider your market.

5.   Plastic comb binding allows the book to open and lay flat and is often used for mail order books directed at professionals, short-run academic text and industry manuals. This system may be used on books to $1\frac{1}{2}$" thick. Comb binding is relatively expensive but looks cheap, the pages tear out and comb bound books don't stack well making shipping a chore.

6.   Velo-Bind is similar to side wire stitches but uses melted plastic rivets. This method is extremely strong and may be used to install either special Velo-Bind hardcovers or soft document covers.

7.   Xerox-Cheshire has an interesting hot melt hard and softcover binding machine which is good for short-run production.

8.   Binders are sometimes used in very expensive manuals directed toward professionals. They have the usual advantages of a binder but they are expensive, hard to ship and the pages tear out easily.

TO CALCULATE BOOK PRODUCTION COSTS, send a request for quotation (RFQ) to a number of typesetters and printers. Some printers set type and do pasteup but many of your more price-competitive book printers do not. This means you have to have your composition and layout done somewhere else, usually locally.

Request that all quotes for composition, layout, printing, halftones, reductions, etc. be made on a per item and per page basis. If your quotes are not figured this way, reduce them to these page/item figures yourself. Then when the book is finished and the exact number of pages, photos, etc. are known, both you and the typesetter or printer, individually and objectively, will come up with the same figure for the bill.

SELECTING YOUR TYPESETTER. Look under "Typesetting" in the Yellow Pages and send out several requests for quotation. Simply make up an RFQ like the one pictured, make enough photocopies and mail them to your list. Also send this typesetting RFQ to the printers mentioned later in this chapter. More typesetters can be found in the advertisements in Writer's Digest magazine and Literary Market Place but you may wish to have the work on your first book done locally.

You may wish to set your own type and do your own pasteup. While this is time-consuming and just one more large project on the way to publishing your book, it is a good way to justify the purchase of a word processing computer. See Chapter Eleven. To learn more about book pasteup, see Publishing Short-Run Books by the author. To learn about computer selection and the three ways to set type with a computer, see the Computer Selection Guide also by the author. Even if you do decide to do the work yourself, you should obtain typesetting quotes in order to compare figures.

> *"The horizon is larger in the West. And there's enough freedom for a small publisher to take a chance on a book that wouldn't get off the ground in New York"* — David Dreis in *West Coast Review of Books.*

(Your letterhead)

REQUEST FOR QUOTATION
Typesetting and Layout

To:

Please quote your best price and delivery for typesetting, pasteup and camerawork for the following:

SPECIFICATIONS
Name of book: (Skydiving For Fun & Profit)
Total number of pages including front matter: (152)
Trim Size: (5½ x 8½)
Ink
        Text: (Black throughout)
        Soft cover: (Four color plus plastic coat)
Binding
        Soft cover: (Perfect)
Typestyle
        (10/12 Press Roman)

QUOTE
Composition, per page:
Layout, per page:
(20) halftones requiring reduction and screening, each:
(40) line drawings requiring photo reduction, each:
Cover (Color separation from slide, typesetting):
Delivery charges to our address above:
Total price:

Delivery of negatives will be _____ working days from receipt of manuscript.

Terms: (To be arranged)

Remarks:

Signed:_____

Date:_____

Any item in this RFQ takes precedence over any industry convention. The boards, flats and all artwork shall be returned to customer on completion of job.

Example of a request for quotation.
Sample specifications are in parentheses.

REQUEST FOR QUOTATION
Book Printing & Binding

To:

Please quote your best price and delivery in producing the following book from our negatives:

SPECIFICATIONS

Name of book: (Sex and the Single Publisher)
Total number of pages including front matter: (152)
Trim Size: (5½ x 8½)
Copy: (Customer to provide negatives ready for stripping)
Cover: (Customer to supply color separations)
Paper: Inside: (60# white offset, book)
            Soft cover: (12 pt. C1S cover)
Ink: Text: (Black throughout)
            Cover: (Four color plus plastic coat)
Binding: (Perfect)
Packaging: (In plastic bags and tightly sealed cartons)

QUOTE

        First run of 3,000:   5,000:   10,000:
        Later run of 3,000:   5,000:   10,000:

Delivery charges to our address above:

Delivery will be: _____ working days from receipt of negatives:

Terms: (To be arranged)

Remarks:

Signed:_____

Date:_____

Any item in this RFQ takes precedence over any industry convention. The boards, flats and all artwork shall be returned to customer on completion of job.

Please send a sample of your recent work.

Example of a request for quotation.
Sample specifications are in parentheses.

SELECTING YOUR PRINTER. There are three types of printers: full-service, specialty and instant. You want a specialty printer who concentrates on books. There are over 40,000 independent commercial printing companies in the U.S., so there are plenty to choose from. This is the age of specialization. Some printers concentrate on books, while others do business cards, magazines or calendars. General (full-service) job printers cannot compete with the specialists who are set up for one type of work, may run three shifts on the same presses and buy just a few kinds of paper in larger lots. Many of the more competitive book printers are located in Michigan, close to the paper supply. Their prices are often very good because it is cheaper to truck finished books to you than it is raw paper. See the list of book printers in the Appendix. More are listed in Literary Market Place and 100 of them are evaluated in the Directory of Short-Run Book Printers by John Kremer ($4.95 ppd. from Ad-Lib Publications, P.O. Box 1102, Fairfield, IA 52556.)

Solicit several printing quotes. You will find some bids to be three times higher than others. These price differences are amazing and makes it obvious that it pays to shop around. Some printers are too big for you, some specialize in something other than books and some are too busy. You need a good one who is hungry and specializes in "short run" book printing.

If your state has an inventory tax, you might consider avoiding it by printing in another state and shipping books in small batches so as to avoid the tax date. Shipping is not too expensive as both the Post Office and trucking companies give special rates for "bound books." Your printer may even be willing to drop ship large quantities for you so you can ship direct to major customers. Some authors have found considerable savings on certain processes outside the U.S. They may have printing done in Taiwan, color separations made in Italy, or color printing done in Singapore, etc. See Printing in Asia by Bill Dalton (Moon Publications, P.O. Box 1696-P, Chico, CA 95927, $5.95 ppd.)

PRINTING BROKERS can often provide better service and prices. They know the industry and which manufacturers can do which part of the book most efficiently as well as who is busy and who is looking for work. They have buying power and often supply the paper, making their profit on the paper markup. Brokers can keep an eye on all the little typesetting, pasteup, printing and binding details for you. Get quotes from a couple of local brokers. If the quotes are competitive, you will get service with the price. Check under "printing brokers" in the Yellow Pages. The bottom line quote is the real difference so get quotes from brokers, distant book printers, local printers, everyone.

Request for quotations should be sent to the printers listed in the Appendix. Add to this list with two local print shops and two local printing brokers. Simply make up an RFQ like the one pictured, make enough photocopies and mail them to all on your list. Don't send your RFQ to just a few, the inquiry will not result in enough comparative data. The only way you will know you are paying the best price is if you get quotes from all. Don't worry about their reception of a photocopied RFQ, printers are used to making competitive quotes.

Adams, Delta, Dinner & Klein, Champion, McNaughton & Gunn, Maverick, Morgan, Multiprint, Prinit and some others provide "printing pricers" to help you estimate your costs.

When the RFQs arrive back, spread them out for comparison. Some printers will fill out your sheet while others will use their own form. Make sure the quotes are "FOB destination," that trucking to you is figured in. You will probably find that the distant printers quote much lower even with the trucking costs. If, however, the difference is small, you may wish to go with a local printer on your first book. A local job allows you to monitor the work at each step; a valuable learning experience. Next time, you will have more confidence to ship the job out of town.

Don't worry about hurting the feelings of your local printer. If his bid is not the lowest, show him the other bids. They are your excuse for not giving him the work. He will be interested in what the competition is quoting and will appreciate your openmindedness. He may even like to refigure his bid based on this new information.

EXCELLENT QUALITY costs more. Do you want your book to be an art form or an information storage system? Tell your printer what you expect and inspect samples of his work. He won't drop his standards to give you a lower price but he may use cheaper processes. You want clean, sharp work because your name is going on it. Communicate clearly with the printer initially and you won't be disappointed later. If you aren't in a great rush, the printer may be able to schedule your book into his "down time" and give you a better quote. In any case, don't rush the printer and you will get a better job. "Haste makes waste" and in printing waste can be expensive.

You might even decide to acquire a press and do the printing yourself. Be forewarned, however, that unless you have a simple job and are willing to sacrifice quality, the press run should be left to the professional. You have to decide whether you want to be a writer, printer or to concentrate on sales. Some people gain great satisfaction doing the whole job themselves. Unless you can use the printing press to capacity, your own printing won't be competitive in price.

GET IT IN WRITING, get everything in writing. You are new to publishing and what you assume may not be the same as what your printer assumes. Good faith and trust and friendship are fine until the bill arrives. Ask for samples and show him what you like, what you expect. Get a contract with the printer spelling out exactly what each part of the job will cost. Then if you have two more photos than your estimate, you and he will arrive at the same added figure. Count the books you pick up and get copies of the receiving slips. Monitor the production and make sure the book is coming out the way you want. If you see poor press work, tell the printer now. Don't wait to argue after binding. After the boards are pasted up and you have an exact page count, ask for a new quote on the press run. You should be able to calculate it using the original quote but it is best to avoid any possible misunderstanding.

> *"The universal object and idol to men of letters is reputation."* — John Adams.

You may be able to sell an unattractive book by direct mail where the purchaser can't inspect it first. But you may get the book back and you certainly won't sell this customer anything else, ever. In the mail order publishing business, you need repeat orders.

Make sure your contract includes a clause which states: "Any item in this contract takes precedence over any industry convention." You aren't familiar with the printing industry and aren't interested in how it is normally done. You want an attractive book and you want to know what it will cost.

Even if you keep up your end of the bargain on the schedule, others will not. Typesetters are usually late and printers are often late. Just plan on this.

KEEP YOUR ARTWORK. Maintain a file with a couple of clean copies of the book and all your reproduction materials. If you need them again, and you do hope for many happy reprintings, you don't want to have to regenerate lost material.

Put all the artwork, photos, drawings, etc. into a large envelope. You want to be able to find them easily if you contract for a translation or other foreign edition. Keep the boards and negatives of all promotional material such as brochures and order forms.

The art boards for the book are the publisher's property. Many printers will tell you the large and thin metal printing plates, stripped-in negatives (flats) and boards belong to them as they are the product of the printer's craftsmanship. A printer who argues this simply wants to make sure you return to him for reprints. The plates are difficult to store and printers often throw them out. Many also discard the boards, keeping only the flats. You may take possession of the plates and flats if you specify their ownership in the printing contract.

You should store the boards for future revisions. Find a cool, dry, clean place; they are subject to yellowing. If you think you might like to switch printers for the revision, you can always specify in the contract that you own everything. On the other hand, allowing the printer to store the flats while you keep the boards is good insurance. If one place burns to the ground, you won't lose everything. If you will want to make revisions when you go back to press, it is far more valuable to have the boards than the flats.

WHEN THE BOOKS ARRIVE from the printer, count the cartons. Compare the carton count with the amount on the bill of lading. Sometimes printers short-ship and sometimes books disappear in transit. Open random cartons and check for damage. If the books were loose in the carton, the top ones will be scuffed.

Para Publishing is a unique book business. It does not operate like a big traditional publisher and it doesn't lose money. Dan Poynter lays out the following reasons for the success of his company.

1. Publish your own material. Do not waste your time on, or split the money with, authors.
2. Perform every publishing and business function yourself. After your first book, farm out those tasks you do not wish to perform.
3. Operate as a sole proprietorship not a corporation and keep your books on a cash basis.
4. Do not mimic the big traditional New York publishers. Many are not making a sufficient return on their investment. Some of their procedures exist for a good reason while others are just convention (also known as a rut.) The trick is to know the difference.
5. If you cannot "find a need and fill it", then create a need and fill it. Decide on your market before you write the book and write to that market.
6. Market your books like breakfast food, not like a film. This is not one-shot entertainment, go after a market share and keep selling that book year after year.
7. You will have to spend more time on selling than you do on writing. Concentrate on marketing rather than editorial functions.
8. Produce valuable information, aimed at a small target audience and charge a fair price.

Chapter Five

ANNOUNCING YOUR NEW BOOK TELLING THE WORLD YOU ARE AN AUTHOR AND A PUBLISHER GETTING LISTED

Before you run off to promote your book, you must announce it to the industry, the government and the world. In fact, some of these announcements must be made before you go to press. For a clear understanding of when each of the following should be done, see the Calendar at the beginning of the Appendix.

As you use this chapter, remember, if the Library of Congress or any other office rejects your application, do not give up. Try to figure a way around their objection and file a new form. It is very doubtful they will remember your initial application rejection.

THE INTERNATIONAL STANDARD BOOK NUMBER (ISBN) is a world-wide identification system which has been in use since the late sixties. There is a different ISBN for each edition and each binding of every book so the number's use avoids errors in identifying the books ordered, shipped, received, etc. Publishers are finding that with the increased use of computers in the book industry, this system has become an essential element in the distribution of their books.

A typical ISBN might be 0-915516-21-7. Here, the initial "0" indicates a book originating in an English speaking country. The "915516" identifies the publisher. The suffix 21 identifies this particular title and edition of the book, hardcover or softcover. The last number, "7", is a check digit which is a mathematical function to make sure the rest of the numbers are correct, that they haven't been miscopied or transposed.

The ISBN is printed on the copyright page of the book and on the right foot of the back cover or jacket in 12 pt. OCR-A type. Jackets should also carry the number on the upper edge of the left-hand jacket flap. This special OCR-A typeface can be read by the automatic checkout equipment at the cash register. If your typesetter does not have the machine-readable OCR (optical character recognition) typeface, pick up a type ball for an electric typewriter and type it out yourself (IBM Element part number 1167229: USAS 1 OCR-2 or Royal part number CSA 49: OCR-A.) Print the ISBN in black on a light background so the OCR machine can see it.

Write to the International Standard Book Numbering Agency, 205 East 42nd Street, New York, NY 10017 and request a "Title Output Information Request Form," and a "User's Manual." There is no charge for this service. Since the ISBN people do not particularly like to list publishers with a single title (and who may never publish again), it is best to represent yourself as being larger. After all, this will not be your only book. Use different names for your company, publisher and author. "Deuel Publishing, Pam Deuel Publisher and book by Pam Deuel" is a sure tip off. Also keep this in mind when filling out the Title Output Form.

You may request a number and a log sheet for ten, 100 or 1000 titles. If you ask for ten, your publisher identifier number will be seven digits long and your suffix will be just one digit. If you ask for 1000, your publisher identifier will be five digits, leaving you with three in the suffix. Many starting publishers modestly ask for ten, run out of numbers in a few years and must apply for a new publisher identifier number--which is confusing. Ask for at least 100. The ISBN people will send you a card

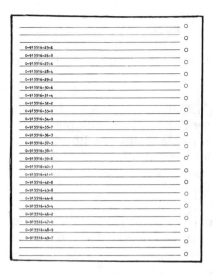

Example of an ISBN log book sheet.

bearing your ISBN publisher identifier and a log book sheet with enough room for listing 100 different editions.

Once started in the system, you will assign each of your new titles an ISBN suffix yourself. You do not have to start at the beginning of the log, the only requirement is that each title, revision and binding have a different number. If you use the first number on the log book sheet, the "0" will tip off those in the industry that this is a first book.

By now, you are probably finding there are a lot of agencies and offices catering to the book trade at 205 East 42nd Street. Bowker is a subsidiary of Xerox which publishes many references and performs many services for the publishing industry. Bowker administers the ISBN and SAN programs as well as publishing the magazines Publishers Weekly, Small Press, Library Journal and School Library Journal. Bowker publishes reference books such as Books in Print, American Book Publishing Record, Literary Market Place, Publishers Trade List Annual and many more. Treat each Bowker office separately, as though it was in a different building, so your mail won't get misdirected or lost.

UNIVERSAL PRODUCT CODE. The UPC bar codes are being seen more and more on books such as mass market paperback which are also sold through non-book outlets.

The machine-readable bar code includes the publisher, title, price and the ISBN. If your books are being sold in supermarkets or if your distributors start requesting the bar codes, it is time to consider the Universal Product Code.

STANDARD ADDRESS NUMBER. The SAN identifies each separate address of every firm in the book publishing industry from publishers, to wholesalers, to libraries, to bookstores. SAN's sort out the billing and shipping addresses and help to determine which "Book Nook" an order is going to.

A SAN may be requested when you apply for an ISBN. The seven-digit number should be printed on all stationery, purchase orders, invoices, etc.

The ABI form.

ADVANCED BOOK INFORMATION is another Bowker service. By filling out their ABI form, your book will be listed in <u>Books in Print</u> and several other specialized directories. <u>Books in Print</u> is published in November of each year and is the most important.

Everyone in the industry turns to <u>BIP</u> first when looking for a particular book. This multi-volumed reference lists all available books by subject, title and author. Ask for it at the library and become familiar with this important work.

Write to the ABI Department, R. R. Bowker Co., 205 East 42nd Street, New York, NY 10017 and request an ABI guide book and a half dozen ABI forms. There is no charge.

You should fill in an ABI form about six months before your book comes off the press but don't be too anxious. On your first book, wait until you have signed a contract with your printer to produce the book. Some new publishers act prematurely; they list the book and then never get into print. Your "publication date" will probably be six months away anyway, as discussed in Chapter Seven. Code your address on the ABI forms (see the discussion in Chapter Seven.)

Always use the ABI guide book when filling out the ABI form. Some of the questions may mislead a person not familiar with publishing terminology.

Bowker will send you a computer generated ABI checklist every other month to keep your listings up-to-date. This checklist must be returned every time even if all the information is correct. Failure to return the checklist may result in your books or company being delisted in Books in Print.

CATALOGING IN PUBLICATION is a program which enables publishers to print Library of Congress cataloging information on the copyright page of their books. Because the data block is already printed in the book, librarians are able to process new titles for library users rapidly and economically. First a publisher must be accepted into the program and then he or she must request cataloging data for each new book.

To participate in this program, write the CIP Office, Library of Congress, Washington, DC 20540 and request: "Cataloging in Publication - Information for Participating Publishers" and some "Publisher's Response" forms. The CIP people are eager to help and can be reached at (202) 287-6372. They even provide postage-

707-6372   Victoria Boucher

"If you don't know where you're going — you're there."

707-9813

paid mailing labels for the materials you are expected to send back.

The CIP people want to be sure each applicant is an established publisher. Accordingly, to be listed they require three past books and do not accept books which have been subsidy published. Sometimes they confuse self-publishing with subsidy publishing or privately published titles. Make your company look big when you apply for participation in the program. If you are turned down, make up your own data block and apply to the Library of Congress for just an LC number (see below.) Participation in the program has no affect on obtaining an LC number or a copyright.

Here is a line-by-line explanation of the CIP data block:

1. **Library of Congress Cataloging in Publication Data.**
2. Poynter, Daniel F.
3. Parachuting, The Skydivers' Handbook.
4. 1, Parachuting. 2, Skydiving. I Title
5. GV 770P69   797.56   77-83469
6. ISBN 0-915516-16-0 Softcover
7. ISBN 0-915516-17-9 Hardcover

Typical CIP data block.

1. The heading is made distinctive by setting in bold typeface.
2. The author's name
3. The title of the book.
4. The LC subject headings.
5. The "GV 770" is the LC classification number. The "P69" is keyed into the last name of the author. In this case "Poynter."

"From the time Gutenberg lifted the first sheet off the press, there has been a steady demand for books of instruction of all kinds" — Arnold F. Logan of Petersen Publishing Co.

AUTHOR NUMBER TABLE

Aa	-15	Ba-Bb	-3	Sa-Sc	-2
Ab-Ac	- 2	Be-Bh	-4	Sch-Sd	-3
Ad-Ak	- 3	Bi-Bn	-5	Se-Sg	-4
Al-Am	- 4	Bo-Bq	-6	Sh-Sl	-5
An-Ao	- 5	Br-Bt	-7	Sm-Ss	-6
Ar-As	- 7	Bu-	-8	St-	-7-8
Ast	- 8	Same for other		Su-	-9
Same for other		initial conso-		Q-Qt	-3
initial vowels.		nants except S		Qq-	-4

Letters not included are assigned next higher or lower numbers as required.

The second number group is the Dewey Decimal Classification Number (see The Dewey Decimal Classification and Relative Index) and the last is the LC Card Number.

6&7. The International Standard Book Numbers.

Once you are accepted into the CIP program, you will send in information on each book prior to printing. Send photocopies of the front matter of your pasted up boards and a filled out LCC Data sheet to the CIP Office. This enables them to select the proper classification numbers. They also like to have any other information you might have, such as a descriptive brochure on the book, a photocopy of your ABI form and a biographical sketch of the author. Within ten working days, the Office will send the CIP data and the catalog card number.

The CIP Office does not always catalog the book just as you might want it. Give them as much information on it as possible and read their "Information For Participating Publishers" carefully. You may even supply suggested data. Pay particular attention to the "subject tracings" (line 4 above). How a book gets cataloged can be just as important to small presses as how it gets reviewed or advertised.

LIBRARY OF CONGRESS CATALOG CARD. LC numbers appear on the copyright page of each book and are also included in the lists and reviews appearing in the leading journals of the book trade. The LC number differs from the ISBN in that one ISBN is assigned to each different edition of a work (hardcover, softcover, etc.); the LC number is assigned to the work itself, no matter how it is printed or bound. Use of the number enables subscribers to the Library of Congress' catalog card service to order cards by number and thus eliminate the searching fee. LC numbers are essential if you want to sell to libraries. About 20,000 libraries from all over the world subscribe to this service and some order almost every cataloged book. Additionally, most of the books are listed in The National Union Catalogue, issued several times a year in four editions. Most public and private libraries subscribe to it.

If you already participate in the CIP program, your LC number will be sent with your CIP data block. New Publishers, however, should write to the CIP Office, Library of Congress, Washington, DC 20540 and ask for "Procedures for Securing Preassigned Library of Congress Catalog Card Numbers" and their "Request for Preassignment of LCC Number" application (Form 607-7.)

The Library of Congress card number must be requested prior to the publication of the book so that the number may be printed on the copyright page. They do not preassign numbers to books that are already in print (it is too late to print the number in the book.)

Catalog card numbers are preassigned only to books which the Library of Congress assumes will be added to the collections or for which they anticipate substantial demand for LC printed cards. The types of material which the Library collects only in a very limited way and for which catalog card numbers are generally not available include: calendars, laboratory manuals, booklets of less than 50 pages, brochures, advertisements, bank publications designed for customers, blueprints, certain kinds of light fiction, privately printed books of poems, religious materials for students in Bible schools, catechisms, instructions in devotions, individual sermons and prayers, question and answer books, most elementary and secondary school textbooks, tests except for standard examinations, teachers' manuals, correspondence school lessons, translations from English into foreign languages, picture books, comic strip and coloring books, diaries, log and appointment books, prospectuses and preliminary editions, workbooks, and vanity press publications.

If the Library of Congress determines, on the basis of information submitted by a publisher that the book is to be cataloged, a catalog card number is preassigned and sent to the publisher on a typed 3 x 5 slip giving the author, title, imprint and publication date. The catalog card number appears in the upper right-hand corner of the slip.

The first two digits of the LC number do not indicate the year of publication, but the year in which the card number is preassigned. If you register after January first, your book will appear to be a year newer. Ever wonder why the dates on films are in Roman numerals?

The CIP Office must be advised of all subsequent changes in titles, authors, etc., and cancellations. This notification is important as it prevents duplication of numbers. A new number is not necessary when changes are made. Confirmations of changes will not be acknowledged unless requested by the publisher.

There is no charge for the preassignment of a card number. An advance complimentary copy of each publication must be sent to the CIP Office, Library of Congress, Washington, DC 20540. This copy is used for final cataloging so that cards may be printed before the book is released. The CIP Office provides postage-free mailing labels for use in sending these advance publications. The book is only for checking so send the less expensive soft cover edition.

The Copyright Office is operationally separate from the CIP Office. But the CIP and Catalog Card offices are the same. Catalog card numbers may be applied for per the above or when applying for Cataloging in Publication Data.

COPYRIGHT may be registered before your manuscript is published but, unless you are passing a lot of copies around for technical proofing and comment, you might just as well wait for books to come off the press. Your work is copyright protected, it just isn't copyright registered, yet.

Write to the Register of Copyrights, Library of Congress, Washington, DC 20559 and request three copies of Form TX (for registering books) and copies of Circular R1, Copyright Basics and Circular R2, Publications of the Copyright Office. Upon receipt, read over these publications and order any others you feel you need. They will also send you some business reply mailing labels so that you may send them the copyright form, your check and the books for registration.

To register your copyright, follow these three steps:

1. Print the copyright notice on the copyright page (title page verso). The notice takes the following form: " c 1985 by Robert Howard." You may use the word "copyright" but the " c " says the same thing and it is necessary for international protection. Also add "all rights reserved" and expand on this if you like. Check other books. The copyright notice must appear in all copies of the book to protect you, so double check it and all the numbers on the copyright page every time you proof copy, boards, bluelines, etc.

The copyright should be in the name of the owner. The owner may be the author, the publishing company or whomever created or paid for the work.

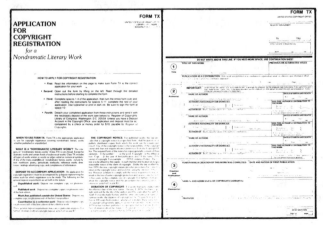

2.   Publish the book. Check for the copyright notice before any of the books are distributed.

3.   Register your claim with the Copyright Office within three months of the book coming off the press. To do this, send a completed Form TX, two copies of the "best edition" of the book and a fee of $10. The "best edition" would be the hard cover if both the hardbound and paperback came from the printer at the same time. However, since the hardbound edition often takes longer to produce, the softcover may be the "best edition at the time of publication." If you enclose softcover copies with the Form TX, be sure to note that they were produced first.

The Copyright Office will add a registration number and date to the form and will send you a photocopy containing a seal and the Registrar's signature.

The new copyright term is for the author's life plus fifty years. Your ownership of the book is now a valuable part of your estate, so be certain your copyrighted material is mentioned in your will.

Copyrights protect you like a patent but they are cheaper and much easier to secure. Like a patent, however, you must always be on the lookout for infringers. The copyright protects your text, photographs, drawings, maps, everything except the title.

THE CUMULATIVE BOOK INDEX is an international bibliography of new publications in the English language. All the bibliographical information necessary to identify a book is provided: full name of author, complete title, date of publication, edition, paging, price, publisher, International Standard Book Number, and Library of Congress card number.

In addition to bibliographical information, the Cumulative Book Index also provides subject headings to describe the contents of the book. These headings can usually be determined by an examination of the table of contents and a reading of the preface; sometimes, a careful examination of the text is necessary. Books must

Cumulative Book Index Information Slip

have at least 100 pages and a minimum press run of 500 copies to be eligible for inclusion in the Index.

A listing in the Cumulative Book Index gives your publication valuable publicity. Subscribers include most of the major libraries and booksellers around the world. No charge is made for a listing, but in order to record accurately the bibliographical description and subject content of each book, it is most helpful to base the listing on an examination of the book itself.

Although other units within the H. W. Wilson Company, such as the Vertical File Index, will make further use of the book, only one file copy is necessary. Send books to: Cumulative Book Index, H. W. Wilson Co., 950 University Avenue, Bronx, NY 10452.

BOOK PUBLISHERS OF THE UNITED STATES AND CANADA is a directory in which you may have a free listing. For an application form, write: Gale Research Company, Book Tower, Detroit, MI 48226.

INTERNATIONAL DIRECTORY OF LITTLE MAGAZINES AND SMALL PRESSES is another place you will want to list your new firm. Send to Dustbooks, P. O. Box 100-P, Paradise, CA 95969 for an application. Request information on their other directories, too.

PUBLISHER'S TRADE LIST ANNUAL is another Bowker publication. It is used by the publishing industry to announce books. Advertising rates for small ads are not high but many small presses find they get very little return on their investment. For information and an ad rate card, write: R. R. Bowker Co., P.O. Box 1807, Ann Arbor, MI 48106.

ANY BOOK is a lower cost alternative to Books in Print which is available on microfiche. To list your book, send for an application to The Library Corporation, P.O. Box 40035, Washington, DC 20016.

PUBLISHERS' INTERNATIONAL DIRECTORY is published by the K. G. Saur Publishing Co. Write to Saur, c/o Gale Research, 150 East 50th Street, New York, NY 10022 for information and a questionnaire.

1-800/637-0037   audray

ABA BOOK BUYER'S HANDBOOK is used by bookstores to find your shipping, discount, STOP and returns policies. A listing here will encourage STOP orders. Write to American Booksellers Association, 122 East 42nd Street, New York, NY 10168 for an application.

LITERARY MARKET PLACE is one of the most important reference books in the publishing industry. It lists every major publisher, publicity outlet, and supplier. An inclusion here will help your customers and suppliers to find you. Many firms use LMP to locate publishers as this reference is so much less expensive than Books In Print. To be listed in this annual reference, send for an application form to Literary Market Place, Attn: Janice Blaufox, Editor, 205 East 42nd Street, New York City, NY 10017.

WRITER'S MARKET. A listing here means you want manuscript submissions. For an application, write Writer's Market, 9933 Alliance Road, Cincinnati, OH 45242.

DIRECTORY OF DIRECTORIES will accept your book listing if it has an extensive appendix. Send for a form to: Contemporary Authors, Gale Research Company, Book Tower, Detroit, MI 48226. Visit the library and look for other directories which might list your book.

CONTEMPORARY AUTHORS is a large reference book containing over 54,000 biographical sketches. Authors of technical and vanity press books are not eligible. Send for a form to: Contemporary Authors, Gale Research Company, Book Tower, Detroit, MI 48226. Don't be modest, the more you write, the more space you get. After you fill out the application, make a few photocopies so you will be ready when someone else asks for extensive biographical information. The listing is free.

COSMEP is the international association of independent book and magazine publishers. The name Committee of Small Magazine Editors and Publishers is, however, misleading. They publish a very informative monthly newsletter, and membership will establish many valuable contacts. Write to COSMEP, P. O. Box 703, San Francisco, CA 94101 for a sample of the newsletter and a membership application.

PASCAL AND OTHERS. Many areas have local publishing groups like the Publishers' Association of Southern California (PASCAL.) These groups hold educational seminars, buy and share advertising space and operate booths at major book fairs. See the list of publishing associations in the Appendix.

FORMS. For a complete set of forms, including all of those mentioned in this chapter, see the coupon on the last page of this book.

With a listings in BIP, the Small Press Record and LMP; a membership in COSMEP and subscriptions to Publishers Weekly, Small Press, and Writer's Digest you will begin to receive a lot of writing and publishing mail. See the listings in the Appendix.

"Book buyers are less influenced by price differentials than almost any category of customers" — John Huenefeld.

Chapter Six

WHAT IS YOUR BOOK WORTH? PRICES, DISCOUNTS, TERMS, COLLECTIONS AND RETURNS

BOOK PRICING is a complicated affair which strikes a compromise between a price high enough for the publisher to stay in business and low enough to overcome customer price resistance. There are, perhaps, three reasons people write books: reward (fame and/or fortune, love of writing, and a desire to disseminate important material. While you may want to get the word out, your first book is usually for recognition, and once that is out of your system, the second is for money. Consequently, the author is likely to underprice the first book but work with a very sharp pencil on the price of the next.

THE LIST PRICE of your book will not be easy to set. Many first-time author/publishers ask themselves whether they want maximum financial return or maximum distribution, feeling they can't have both. Usually they wind up with a price on the cover which is too low. As a result, many small publishers have warehouses full of books which they cannot afford to market effectively. Without a sufficient price, there is not enough money for promotion and without promotion, a book will not sell. If the book fails to sell, there is no money for promotion or even to pay the printing bill.

One major reason small publishers stay small is their failure to think objectively about pricing their books. Low prices make you work harder for less and limit your growth.

You must also consider that the price printed on the cover is not what you will receive for it. Dealers require a percentage for their selling efforts. Your promotion costs, to let people know the book exists, are likely to be much higher than you originally anticipated. 10% of the books may be shipped out as review copies and 10% may come back from bookstores damaged. Discounts, advertising and returns take a big chunk out of the list price.

Books are becoming more and more expensive; visit a bookstore and compare prices. According to <u>Publishers Weekly</u>, the average prices for books in 1983, the latest year available, were as follows:

Hardcover (eliminating those priced over $81.): $23.38 and this compares with $17.32 in 1977 (Some areas more specifically were: Business $23.50, Science $34.76, Sports & Recreation $18.97, Travel $18.98, etc.)

Softcover: $11.64 and this compares with $5.93 in 1977. (Business $15.69, Science $17.60, Sports & Recreation $9.48, Travel $9.31, etc.)

Mass market paperback: $3.13 and this is up from $1.72 in 1977. (Business $5.02, Science $4.26, Sports & Recreation $3.47, Travel $9.92, etc.)

With the slowing of inflation in 1983, average prices of some categories of books actually dropped a little. Many economists consider these price drops to be a temporary condition.

"Retail price (of an commodity) should depend more upon the value the buyer places on the product than on the cost to the producer." — Leonard Shatzkin

Some publishers like to test prices before deciding on them. There are times when a higher price will make a product seem more valuable and will make the book sell better. These publishers run identical ads except for the price and then check the returns. Mail order book buyers are said to be the least price-conscious of all.

Your book is unique. Like you, it is one of a kind. While a customer will not pay more than what he figures to be a fair price, if your book is a good one and he wants it bad enough, he will pay what you ask. Underpricing a book to increase sales is often a very big mistake. In fact, it may even undermine the credibility of the book. And remember, price has a reverse impact when a book is purchased as a gift.

In a how-to book, you are selling unique information, not entertainment or stacks of paper; the selling price is not nearly so frightening to the buyer as it is to the author. According to Publishers Weekly, women are more resistant to book prices than men. Women buy most of the books on cooking, health, diet, and gardening as well as fiction.

Books you intend to sell through bookstores and mail order should be priced at eight times "unit production cost," textbooks at five times. Total production cost includes all composition, layout, printing, binding, etc. Pricing the book any lower than this is courting financial disaster. If the projected list price seems too high, consider reducing the print run, cutting out some of the copy or photographs or selecting a smaller type and narrower leading (space between the lines) to get more material on each page. Check with your printer for ways to reduce costs. Now, if the customer still won't pay that much, you picked the wrong subject to write about.

The 8X formula does not fit every case; there may be a few exceptions. Consider your audience and the cost of reaching them. If you write a pictorial history of your town and the Chamber of Commerce is buying all the books to give to tourists, your promotion and distribution costs will be much lower. For continuous-selling nonfiction aimed at a small target audience, you may be able to justify 8X the **reprint** costs (excluding the pre-press expenses.) If 8X seems like a lot, you should know that audio-visual materials are often marked up 11X.

141

It may seem old and silly, but $9.95 is still a lot cheaper to the subconscious mind than $10 and there is no good argument for a mid-price like $9.50.

Recheck your costs at reprint time; you may wish to raise the cover price. If you do raise the price, remember to change your ads, brochures, etc. and send off a press release on the reprint to <u>Publishers</u> <u>Weekly</u>. (Every little mention helps.) To ease the blow on your better dealers who have you listed in their catalog, consider offering them a one-time buy on the new edition at the old price in order to protect their catalog listing. This will also generate quick cash to help you pay your printing bill.

PRICE ON COVER. Bookstores in the U.S. like to have the price printed on the cover of the book to save them the stickering operation. Canadian bookdealers, dealing with an 80-cent dollar, do not like stickering-over prices. Booksellers feel they look bad to the customer who lifts the sticker to compare. Nobody buying a Honda in North America cares what it costs in Japan but books seem to be different. Customers feel ripped off.

Many publishers are leaving the prices off their books now because inflation causes frequent price changes. The problem surfaces when a store returns a third edition of a book when you are currently shipping the fifth at a higher price. Because of the price differences, the book cannot be returned to stock. On the other hand, perhaps you overpriced the book and it isn't selling well. You may wish to test it at a lower price. The only problem with non-priced books is that returns from bookstores have price stickers which must be removed—usually damaging the cover.

HOW MANY BOOKS? Once again, we must consider your purpose for writing the book and how many you can expect to sell. Do you want just a few for family and friends? Is it a high-priced mail order book with a small audience? Do you want to take a crack at the big chain

---

> *"Before you can sell a person anything you have to make him or her want it more than the money it cost."*

bookstores and hope you have a bestseller? How many will be review copies, gifts and other freebees?

INITIAL PRESS RUNS should normally be limited to the number of books one can reasonably estimate will be sold in the first year. Unless you have a substantial number of prepublication sales, it is a good idea to limit the first printing to no more than 5,000. No matter how diligently you proofread, some errors will not surface until they appear in ink. Also, once you see the book in its final state, you will wish you had done some things differently. By printing a smaller number, you can use the next few months to catch your errors and make some design changes. Then you will be much happier about the revised second edition.

Set the first press run conservatively. It is better to sell out and have to go back to press than to find yourself with a garage full of unsold books. You will be spending a lot of money on promotion so it is best to hedge your bets by tying up less money in the book even though you have to pay a slight premium in printing costs to do so.

But do not be too conservative. All the books will not be sold, many will be used for promotion. If you print 1,000 copies and send 400 out to newspapers and magazines for review, there will be only 600 copies left to sell. Reviews are your least expensive and most effective form of promotion and 400 is a realistic figure (see Chapter Seven.) Many publishers figure 10% of their print run will be used for review copies and promotion.

The economics of printing are as follows: the greater the quantity of books, the higher your bill but the less each book will cost you. The "start-up costs" make the first press run much more expensive than reprints. The major expenses, in fact, are the start-up costs of composition, layout, camerawork, stripping, etc. Once the type is set, you only pay for the paper, binding and press time. The more copies printed at one time, the lower the price per copy. Economy of scale is only true up to a point since the differences become smaller and

> *"The higher your markup, the better you can afford mistakes"*

143

smaller as the press runs increase. Again you must consider the number of books you may be able to sell in one year, because the price breaks fail to maintain significance after about 9,000 copies. Normally, between nine and ten thousand, you save so little that it isn't worth the storage space or the price of borrowing money at the bank. Therefore you do not want to print over 9,000 unless that number will move out within the year.

For example, you might receive printing/binding quotes such as:

No. of copies	500	1000	3000	5000	7000	9000	10000
Total cost	$1495	1784	4485	6778	8750	10530	11300
Unit cost	$2.99	1.78	1.49	1.36	1.25	1.17	1.13

So it is to your advantage to order as many books as possible in order to get the best unit price. And you want the best price as long as you are fairly sure you can sell the higher number.

Remember that a printer makes money on printing. Do not let him talk you into more books than you need. There is economy in scale but there are no savings in paying for books you can't turn into cash. Consider the total printing bill as well.

Print runs are never exact. Printers always run a few extra pages expecting some to be spoiled. When all the sheets are gathered, there are still some which must be thrown away. Accordingly, it is customary in the trade to have overruns and underruns and your bill may be adjusted higher or lower up to ten percent. A print run of 10,000 could wind up anywhere between 9,000 and 11,000.

ESTIMATING SALES for that first year will be difficult with your initial book because you don't have other books with which to compare it. You may get an idea from your own previous work experience and may be able to find out what similar books have done. But remember that bigger publishers have more clout in the trade and already have the connections for placing their titles; you will not do as well initially. Check with anyone you may know with other publishing companies for their educated estimate. With proper promotion, any reasonably good non-fiction book should sell 5,000 copies in its first year. If you cannot objectively project sales of 5,000 copies for the first year, you will have to raise the price substantially to justify printing the book.

REPRINTS have to be timed just right. If you order a reprint too early, you may tie up more money before the first run is paid for. And, many of those books could be sitting on the shelves in the stores—unsold. It is a good idea to make some telephone calls to find if the book is actually moving. On the other hand, if you wait too long to reprint, you run the risk of being out of stock and losing the all-important sales momentum the book is enjoying.

Coordinate with your printer so you can get a fast reprint if necessary. Consider reprint time, trucking time, seasonal demand, etc. Then, considering the size of your storage space, amount of money you can invest, need for future revisions, inventory tax dates, etc., print a one- to two-year supply. One great advantage of these annual printings is the ability to make revisions, keeping the text up-to-date.

DISCOUNTS must be set down in a definite policy right from the beginning. Discount structures must be clear to both you and your customers to avoid any misunderstanding.

Ultimate consumers placing individual orders usually pay the full retail price and send cash with their order (CWO). When an order is received without a check, it is best to return it with a copy of your brochure and a short note requesting payment in advance. Circle your prices and terms on the brochure; some people order asking to be billed because they don't know what the full price will be. Asking for payment in advance will lose only a very few orders but it will stop credit losses and cut billing costs. Customarily, you pay the postage on retail orders unless you have stipulated otherwise in your brochure. COD shipments necessitate too much paperwork for a small sale and the collection charges often upset the customer.

DEALER DISCOUNTS. The terms publishers extend to the trade (booksellers, etc.) vary so much from firm to firm that the American Booksellers Association publishes a loose-leaf handbook trying to list them all. Discounts are supposed to be based on the theory that there is a saving in bulk shipments. However, bookselling tradition has based the discount rate on the category of the wholesale customer, arguing that certain clients need a bigger piece of the pie to stay in business.

RETAIL BOOKSTORES. Discounts to the industry start at 40% and this comes as a shock to many new publishers. But one has to consider the high overhead retailers have in the form of rent, taxes, salaries, utilities, insurance, etc. They need at least 40% to stay in business. Incidentally, bookstore enjoy a smaller markup than gift, sporting goods and other stores which often get 50% or more. The publishing industry has been able to justify the lower discount by making the books returnable if they aren't sold. Fortunately, books are uniform in size, easy to store, simple to ship and unbreakable. The price of shipping is added to the bookstore's bill (FOB origin.)

WHOLESALERS get 50% or 55% on the theory that they purchase large quantities for resale to retailers and libraries. Often then are regional suppliers providing both one-stop-shopping and a short supply line for quick and easy restocking. In order to maintain large library accounts, they usually extend to them discounts of 20-33%. Bookstores get up to 40% depending on the size of their order but they are usually allowed to mix titles. Wholesalers pay the shipping (FOB origin) when purchasing from the publisher.

Some wholesalers will not handle a small press book unless the publisher is willing to take out a space ad in their catalog. This may be little more than a disguised bonus discount and each request must be considered on its own merits. For example, the charge for inclusion may be $250. If they agree to order $5,000 worth of books at 50% and normally you would give 55% for this large quantity, then the $250 can be justified as it is 5% of $5,000. It all

---

"Make effective use of your most important asset, your time."

works out the same to you. Sometimes these are first-time only charges to get you into the system and to test your book. Also, some wholesalers offer to give one-line listings to the rest of your books if you will pay for display space for one of them.

TEXTBOOK publishers give the college bookstores 20-25% off on the books to be sold to students. Here the quantity is often large and any books not sold after the school term begins are returned. There is very little risk as the store is just acting as an order taker. This "short discount" results in a lower price to the consuming student.

These short discounts are sometimes applied to regular books and when this is done, all sales literature should be clearly marked. The book trade will not be too enthusiastic about the poor discount but they can't complain if they are buying in ones and twos and have been informed of the short discount in advance.

LIBRARIES. Some publishers and wholesalers give libraries 20% off but they do not expect a discount because many orders will arrive with a check made out for the list price. Most small publishers are charging the libraries full list price and shipping postpaid (at library rate.)

THE FEDERAL TRADE COMMISSION (FTC) requires that the discounts you offer one dealer be offered to all dealers who are purchasing the same quantity. You are not required to extend credit, but if dealers are paying cash and want the same quantity, you must sell at the same discount.

A "UNIVERSAL DISCOUNT SCHEDULE" is being used by many publishers in deference to discriminatory tradition. It is based not on the classification of the customer but on the order quantity. The Universal schedule works well for larger publishers since they have several books and allow titles to be mixed to achieve higher discounts.

> *"In this world a man must be either an anvil or a hammer"*
> — Longfellow

1 book–no discount	50–74 books–44% off
2–4 books–20% off	75–99 books–46% off
5–9 books–30% off	100–199 books–48% off
10–24 books–40% off	200 or more books–50% off
25–49 books–42% off	

A typical universal discount schedule

The theory of the schedule is that the wholesaler will earn a better discount by buying in larger quantities. Bookstores and libraries ordering smaller quantities get a "courtesy discount." This encourages the purchasers of small quantities to order from wholesalers with a great title mix where they can get a better deal and to reduce their paperwork with one-stop shopping. Remember that these small quantity special orders from the stores are not getting your books on the shelf for all to see. The book has already been sold and will go straight to the customer.

No single plan fits all types of publishers. For example, if you have one book or a single small line of specialized books, cater primarily to a specific class of people, and expect to have several large dealers who purchase hundreds of books at a time, you may wish to consider a simplified discount schedule.

3 up	–40%
200	–50%
500	–40% – 25%

A simplified discount schedule

"Less 40 percent, less 25 percent" amounts to 55% off. First you deduct 40% and then take 25% off of what is left. Wholesalers may make 25% on their investment which is a good amount.

The simplified schedule gives every dealer the 40% they need, allows you to serve the non-book industry with large orders while not upsetting the book trade with its small orders and leaves you with just three figures to remember. Whatever discount schedule you choose, make it simple. You will have to use it to compute each order.

Prices are offered on assorted titles except where there is a great difference in price, that is, you wouldn't

148

mix a $1.50 title normally wholesaled 500 at a time with a $30 book usually purchased three at a time.

Don't confuse "discount" with "markup." A discount of 50% from $2 to $1 is the same as a 100% markup from $1 to $2.

When figuring your discounts, total the order and then subtract the discount. You will come out with a higher figure than if you figure the discount per book and then extend it out. For example, buying 200 $5.95 books at 50% off, there is one dollar difference. $5.95 x 200 - 50% = $595.00, but $5.95 - 50% = $2.97 x 200 = $594.00.

Your discounts and terms should be printed in your dealer bulletins, listed in the <u>ABA</u> <u>Book</u> <u>Buyer's</u> <u>Handbook</u> (122 East 42nd Street, NYC, <u>NY 10017</u>), etc. where they will be continually seen by your dealers.

Once you have published your prices and terms, stick to them. Besides the FTC rules, it just is not profitable to deviate from those figures which took you so long to calculate. Some dealers are always asking for a better deal and some publishers feel that any sale above their cost is a good one. But since you are the one building up the demand for the book, it will probably sell anyway--through another dealer or direct from you. You have to draw the line somewhere. Your valuable time should be used to generate additional net income not more marginal gross.

CONSIGNMENTS make you into a banker as well as a publisher. Consignment is where the dealer takes delivery on the books but doesn't pay the publisher until they are sold. The biggest problem is that since this inventory is free, the dealer may push his paid-for inventory harder. He has no incentive to move your book when he can move another he has paid for. Wholesalers are an exception; many of them operate only on consignment and pay 90 days after they ship. On the other hand, with the returns policy peculiar to the book industry, all sales really amount to "consignment.

"We are in a consignment business that pretends it is not"
— Sol Stein, President of Stein and Day.

"Delayed billings" are a little of the same thing and only constitute a loan from the publisher to the dealer. Money costs money. You can check today's price for it at your bank.

SHIPPING CHARGES are usually included in the price charged on individual retail sales. The book may be advertised at "$9.95 pp" (postpaid). While you have made an allowance for postage in the list (cover) price, the buyer feels he is getting something for nothing. Occasionally, the publisher will pay the shipping where a wholesaler has sent cash with order (CWO). Normally, however, the dealer pays the shipping (FOB origin).

Book rate postage is spiraling upwards and both publishers and booksellers are becoming very conscious of the shipping expenses. Similarly, the cost of packing materials and labor are high and some publishers try to offset some of these with a "handling charge." The term "handling charge" is sure to evoke a nasty response from the customer no matter how small it may be. If "postage" is not exactly the same as the amount on the package, you will also hear about it. So, if you do plan to tack on a little extra to pay for the invoice, its First Class mailing, envelopes and shipping supplies, call the postage and handling charge "shipping." Those dealers who object to any figures higher than the postage on the carton usually just scratch it off the invoice when paying the bill. Invoice altering becomes more frequent after each Postal rate hike.

Some publishers tack a processing charge of 50¢ onto all orders. This is a lot on a single book but is only a penny each on a carton of fifty. Processing the orders costs the same.

STOP stands for "Single Title Order Plan" and like SCOP or "Single Copy Order Plan," consists of a special multi-part order form which arrives with a check. Because the store is paying in advance, they assume a discount of 20-40%. The check may be filled in or blank and restricted to a certain maximum amount. Sometimes the order asks that the book be shipped direct to the customer and other times to the store. Part of the purchase order may be used as a shipping label. It is cheaper and easier to fill

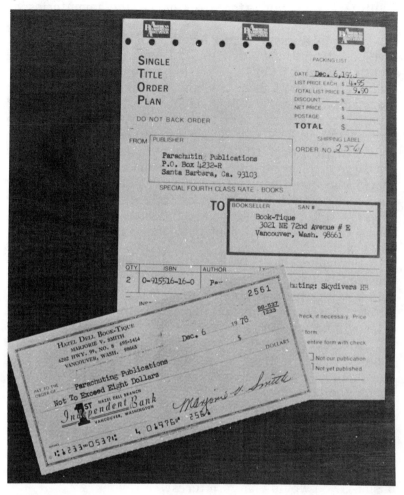

these orders than to haggle over the discount in those cases where the store has assumed too much. When filling out the form for the ABA Book Buyer's Handbook (122 East 42nd Street, NYC, NY 10017), indicate that you wish to participate in STOP. This is where the bookstores will find you.

TERMS and credit are different in the book trade. Most wholesalers and bookstores routinely take 60 days to pay, many take 90 and some get around to mailing out checks in six or eight months. This forces the publisher into a frustrating banking situation. There are very few small publishers who can afford to finance the inventories of their dealers.

The customary terms for the book industry are that invoices should be paid within 30 days of an end-of-the-month statement (30 EOM). This is up to 30 days longer than "net 30 day" terms. Some publishers, eyeing other industries, offer "2% ten day" terms, but the dealer usually pays late and still takes the 2%. Another way to get most of your money faster is to offer 5% for "cash (or check) with order" (CWO). Unfortunately, this offer is usually taken by the financially sound "good pay" customer who would pay on time anyway, not by the slow pay customer you will have to chase for months. Many of the newer small publishers don't subscribe to the 30 EOM terms or discounts for fast pay, they quote strictly "net 30 days."

"Advance dating" of invoices is sometimes done for seasonal business and catalog houses. This provides the dealer with the opportunity to get the books into stock before the rush; important where timing is critical and sales will be late.

Ship your invoices separately via First Class Mail, don't just enclose them in the carton with the books. The longer it takes the invoice to reach the customer, the longer the customer will take to pay it.

Once you have decided on your terms and have published them, stick to them religiously. Any sign of relaxation will be evidence that you don't mean what you say and some dealers will take advantage of you. You are a publisher, not a banker, and if you were in the loan business you would charge interest.

CREDIT. It is only practical to extend credit and ship quickly to new accounts. You will receive all sorts of small orders from distant bookstores and it is not worth the time and effort to run a credit check on each one. It may cost $50 or more to run a credit check even if you do it all yourself by telephone and it will take a lot of time. On one and two book orders, credit checks are not worth the effort for the occasional bad pay or bankruptcy.

If a large order out of no-where seems to good to be true, it probably is. A few people have ordered large quantities of books (200 of a title) from small publishers without ever intending to pay for them. They turn around and sell the books to stores and remainder houses.

Set a limit of say $50 for any dealer order coming in on a letterhead or purchase order. Enclose your brochure, statement of terms and return policy with the invoice. You might also like to slip in a form letter welcoming their account and explaining that you are happy to extend credit and that prompt payment of this invoice will raise their limit to $100. Beyond that you will need trade and bank references. Those who do not stand your test or who are awaiting a credit check for a large purchase may be urged to pay in advance via a "pro forma invoice" (you make out a complete invoice to include shipping charges but you don't ship the books until the invoice is paid).

Another clever trick is to ask for 50% of a large invoice in advance--then ship just 50% of the order.

Schools, libraries, state and federal governments are "good pay" but often "slow pay." They have taxing authority so it is hard to go bankrupt no matter how badly they are managed. Just make sure their request comes on their purchase order. Too often someone in the Park Department will write you on city letterhead asking for a book with no mention of money. This may well be an unauthorized order.

Join a local publishing association and meet some of the people in other book firms. If you question an account, often a call to one of your contemporaries will provide the credit information you seek. Oldden Mercantile (31-P Glen Head Road, Glen Head, NY 11545) publishes a monthly book industry delinquent list. Write for price and details.

Foreign orders may be treated in the same way as domestic ones. There will be a difference in shipping charges, sometimes higher and sometimes lower. Unless they pay in dollars drawn on a U.S. bank, there may be a check cashing charge. Foreigners have about the same payment history as U.S. customers.

COLLECTIONS. When the money does not come in on time you have to exercise your collection process. Wholesalers and bookstores are accustomed to receiving end-of-the-month statements of their account; they want a recapitulation of the many small orders they have placed.

Statements are not a requirement but they may speed payment. You can type up statement forms but initially it will be cheaper to photocopy your invoices or to use a four part invoice form saving one copy for these end-of-month statement mailings. Often the copy shops near colleges charge as little as 5¢ each for photocopies. Check the Yellow Pages and make some calls.

```
┌─────────────────────────┐
│                         │
│   (clear plastic)       │
│                         │
│                         │
├─────────────────────────┤
│  (collection message)   │
│                         │
└─────────────────────────┘
```
Collection message overlay

The quickest, easiest and most efficient way to make a statement of account is to use a photocopy machine collection overlay. Simply tape the sheet of clear plastic with your collection message to the top of the machine. Place the invoice on the overlay and make a photocopy. Then just stuff the copy into a windowed #10 envelope. The plastic sheet makes use of the bottom 1/3rd of the page which is normally wasted. This system avoids separate statements, transposition errors, small envelopes, typing and collection stickers. Hand-write your collection message on the clear plastic sheet with an overhead projector pen with permanent ink. One brand of pen is the Vis-a-Vis from Sanford. The collection messages may include:

1. Is there any reason why this past due bill has not been paid?
2. If you are unable to pay the whole bill, won't you evidence your good faith by sending us a partial payment?
3. We subscribe to Dun and Bradstreet's Commercial Collection service.

154

4.   If payment is not received within ten days, we will be forced to turn this matter over to our attorney for collection.

When typing invoices, always include the name of the person signing the order on the second line.   This focuses your claim on a specific individual where it will have more impact than if you simply send invoices and statements to the company.   Now pen a nice personal note on the bottom of the statement to this particular person.

If they go another month without responding, pen a stronger note on the bottom of the statement.   Then wait two weeks and make a telephone call.   If they don't pay in 90 days, cut them off.   You don't need customers like them.

After this, there are a couple of options.   You may arrange with your attorney to send a standard collection letter which will be typed out automatically on a mag card typewriter or word processor.   The charge may be $10 - $15 and the attorney may give you a better price on a quantity of collections.   You may also consider a collection agency.   Your local firm will have "affiliates" all over North America or you might contact a large firm with many offices such as Dun & Bradstreet.   Collection agencies usually take one-third as their collection fee and they prefer the easy cases.   They have little power and usually get their money through a personal visit which embarrasses the bookseller.   They will threaten legal action and will turn the case over to a local attorney if they fail to collect.   Generally, the older the debt, the harder it is to collect.

Whatever collection system you select, make it automatic so that you can be objective and will not allow deadbeats to negotiate delays.   Let them know you mean business.

The telephone is a powerful collection instrument and a good supplement to dunning notices.   Many callers use "guide scripts" to make sure they get their complete message across quickly.

Remember, it is better to have the books returned unsold than to have the books sold and not get paid.

If a customer has been bouncing large checks on you, put the next ones in "for collection."   Your bank will send it to the customer's bank with instructions to hold the check until there is enough money in the account to pay it.

To collect from a foreign customer, try calling the cultural attache at the nearest embassy or consulate. Often the attache will relay your message and this puts pressure on the foreign debtor.

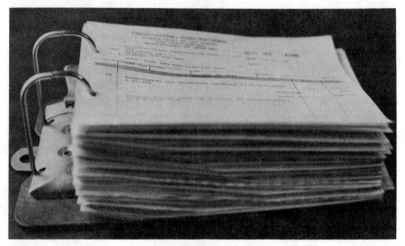

Invoices

THE ACCOUNTS RECEIVABLE OPERATION is one of the most pleasant. It is always fun to count your money. As the checks arrive to pay for due bills, match them with the invoices (if only everyone would note the invoice numbers on their checks!). Mark the invoice with a date stamp to indicate when the payment was credited. Put this pink file copy in a record storage box or binder. See the invoice handling discussion in Chapter 10.

For Deposit Only
Para Publishing
Daniel F. Poynter
098-079971

Checks will be received made out to the publishing company, the author or the name of the book. Name them all on your check cancellation stamp. Pay a little extra for a self-inking stamp, it will save you a lot of time.

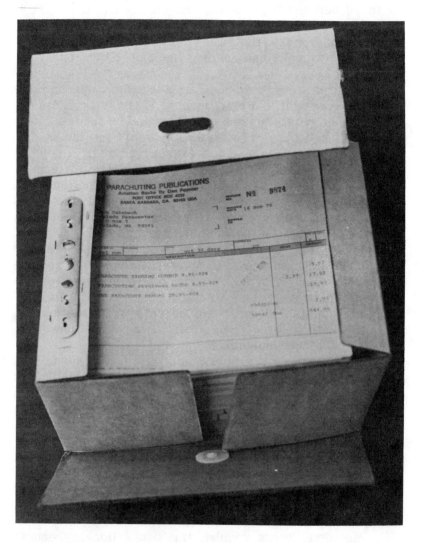

DEPOSITS may be made up every week or so. Endorse the checks with a rubber stamp and list them on an adding machine tape. If your bank wants you to list each check individually on the deposit slip, threaten to go to another bank. Big corporations do not have to do this and you won't either if you stand your ground. Keep it simple!

RETURNS are one of the biggest controversies in the book business. Both wholesalers and bookstores expect to be able to return all books they do not sell and they return 15 to 20 percent (figures for the chains are higher.) If this sounds like a lot, the figure is so high for mass market paperbacks that the dealers save shipping by stripping the books and sending back only the covers for credit.

Returns almost amount to a consignment and the publisher is caught in a bind because if the booksellers did not have the return privilege, they would be far less likely to carry his books. The publisher wants his books displayed and so has to take the chance of having a number of them come back. Therefore, there is little difference between consignment and a no-strings return policy. Returns result in zero profit transactions (ZPT's): the books went out with paperwork, came back with paperwork, everyone was busy but nothing has been sold.

From time to time, people in the book industry suggest changes to the system of returns. One recommendation which is often heard is to eliminate the returns and to pass the savings on to the bookstore in the form of higher discounts. Because we operate in a free-market economy with a lot of competition, none of these suggestions have ever caught on.

Make up a return policy and send it to anyone who requests it. Ingram and Baker & Taylor will probably ask for your return policy when they first open an account with you. Also send the policy when you reply to a return request.

Most publishers will allow returns between ninety days and twelve months of the invoice date. They specify ninety days because they want to make sure the books were given a fair trial on the shelves, but twelve months because they do not want them sitting around too long; the title may go into a new printing.

Most publishers require the bookseller to request permission and specific shipping instructions first but few do. They just ship the books back.

The paperwork with the return should identify the original invoice number under which the books were purchased. The publisher wants to credit the bookseller with the correct amount, the amount they paid. He also wants

PARA PUBLISHING

Books by Dan Poynter

BOOK RETURN POLICY

1. OUR BOOKS ARE RETURNABLE. If a title isn't moving in your market, we want to get it back before a new edition makes it obsolete. Thank you for giving it a chance on your valuable shelf space. Our return period is normally between NINETY DAYS AND ONE YEAR of the publisher's invoice date; however, we will accept the book for return after one year as long as the edition is still in print. To keep our products current, we update our titles every one and a half to two years.

2. RETURN PERMISSION MUST BE REQUESTED so that we may issue detailed packing and shipping instructions.

3. NOTICE OF SHORTAGE OR NON-RECEIPT must be made within thirty days of the shipping/invoice date for domestic shipments; sixty days for foreign.

4. BOOKS DAMAGED IN TRANSIT are not the responsibility of the publisher. Please make claim to the carrier.

5. Returns must be accompanied by your packing slip listing QUANTITY, TITLE, AUTHOR, ORIGINAL INVOICE NUMBER and INVOICE DATE. Books returned with this information will be credited with 100% of the invoice price minus shipping. Otherwise, it will be assumed the original discount was 60%. Some books have been returned to us when they should have been directed to one of our wholesalers; they should be returned to their source.

6. ROUTING: Ship book via Parcel Bost (book rate) prepaid or UPS prepaid to Para Publishing, Attn: D. Poynter, Rt 1 (Barney's Route), Goleta, CA 93117. Note, this is not the same as our order address.

7. To qualify for a refund, returned books must arrive here in good RESALABLE CONDITION. If they are not now resalable, please don't bother to return them. If you are not willing to package them properly for the return trip, please don't waste your time and postage.

To package the books so that they will survive the trip, we suggest you wrap them in the same way that they were sent to you. There are two important steps in successful book packaging: Keep them clean and immobilize them. Place the stacked books in a plastic bag. This will separate the dirty newsprint and greasy styrofoam "peanuts" or discs from the book edges and will prevent grit from creeping between the covers. To keep the books from shifting (which causes scuffing), cut a shipping carton to the right size and stuff it tightly with dunnage.

Since it has been our experience that books shipped loose in oversize "Jiffy bags" always arrive scuffed, it is now our policy to simply REFUSE them at the Post Office so that they will be returned to the bookstore. DO NOT USE JIFFY BAGS!

8. A credit memo will be issued toward future purchases.

9. Industry tells us that it now costs more than seven dollars to write a letter. Correspondence, packaging and postage cost us all a great deal in money and time (and time _is_ money). Years ago when postage was cheap, it made sense to return slow moving books. Today, however, many bookstores are finding it is far more cost effective to simply mark down the books and move them out.

Post Office Box 4232 ———— Santa Barbara, CA 93103 USA ———— Telephone: (805) 968-7277

Sample return policy statement

to make sure the books came from him. If the books were purchased from a wholesaler, they should be returned to the wholesaler.

Books must arrive back at the publisher in good, unblemished resaleable condition so that they may be returned to stock. This is the biggest failing of the bookstores. They never pack the books properly. They just throw them in a carton, often without cushioning material and send them back. During the long trip, the books chafe against each other and the carton and, consequently, they arrive in a scuffed, battered condition. The shipment has to be set aside while a letter is written asking the dealer where he wants his books shipped.

Large publishing firms usually do not send refunds on returns. They issue credits because they are dealing with the customer on a continuing basis. Small publishers, with few other titles to offer, should send a refund check.

"The worst thing that can happen to a new publisher is to have a phenominally successful first book. They think they know the secret and that publishing is easy." — Tom Drewes, Quality Books.

Chapter Seven

PROMOTING YOUR BOOK
MAKING THE PUBLIC AWARE OF
YOUR BOOK WITHOUT SPENDING
FOR ADVERTISING

As an author, whether you self-publish or go with a large publisher, you must do the promotion. If you intend to be a successful author, you will measure your success with money. To make a profit, you will depend on good promotion and marketing. This chapter covers promotion: those methods which require some time and effort but no big advertising dollars. Of course, there will be a certain amount of overlap.

Your most important reference book will be <u>Literary Market Place.</u> While you may use the copy in your local library, this reference will be used so often, you should buy one for use at your desk. Also recommended is <u>The Publicity Manual</u> by Kate Kelly.

Do not spend money on advertising when you can get publicity free. Put your time and money into less expensive review copies and news releases. Use the free publicity to find which magazines are right for your book. Then spend your advertising money there. Always test before you spend money. Too many publishers start with large ads and blow their promotion money in the wrong places.

Most small publishers receive very little publicity for their books. This lack of attention is not because of any great conspiracy between the big (New York) publishers and the media, it is simply because the neophytes do not ask for coverage. Many small publishers are good at publishing but haven't any experience in marketing. They seem to have little interest in their books beyond the editorial work and production; they do not want to sell, they just want to create. Some beginning publishers seem to feel the marketing–end of publishing is "too commercial" and this becomes their excuse for neglecting the most important part of any business: informing the buying public of your wares. For, obviously, if you cannot sell your product, you will not be able to afford to produce more editorial material.

The major differences between publicity and advertising are cost and control. Publicity is free while advertising is not. On the other hand, you may control your advertising while your publicity may be rewritten by the editor or not run at all. The public is usually more receptive to publicity as it is viewed as news. Advertising is perceived as self-serving. An industry rule–of–thumb is that editorial coverage is seven times as valuable as paid coverage.

Competition for free space is a tough proposition. Over 100 titles are published for every day the bookstores are open; the crowd is thicker in the fall than the spring. It is difficult to compete for attention in such a crowded field and against much larger, more knowledgeable firms. But you will be surprised at how successful you can be when you jump into the fray, exploiting the media through news releases, review copies, radio and TV appearances, feature stories, lectures, etc.

Large publishers are lucky if 40% of their titles make money and they have departments of experts to launch their promotion. They also have built up thousands of key contacts during their many years in the business.

"Do not spend a nickel for advertising until you have exhausted all the free publicity."

You have only one book, your first, and therefore, you have only one chance to make it. But look at the brighter side. The big firms often work through routine and without imagination. Your overhead is much lower and you are cutting out the middlemen by publishing yourself. You will do a more effective job of promotion because you have a greater interest in the book than a publisher who is looking after several titles at one time.

By doing the promotion yourself, you are avoiding the most common problem in author/publisher relationships: differing views on the amount of effort which should be invested in each area of promotion and advertising. The author cannot be objective about his product and is convinced that the book would sell better if only the publisher would promote it. The publisher, on the other hand, needs more sales to convince him it is worth investing more dollars in advertising.

Before we plan the attack, we have to analyze the current state and trend of the industry. We have to understand their approach to selling books. During the late 1970's, many of the big New York publishers were absorbed by the bigger multinational conglomerates such as ITT and Gulf & Western. Normally, the main interest of these larger companies is to serve their stockholders by generating maximum return on their investment. To do this, they employ sophisticated marketing techniques to move books. These conglomerates concentrate their efforts on sure bets and high volume, often tying in films and merchandise offers to build public interest. Their marketing dovetails perfectly with the approach by the large chains such as Walden and B. Dalton. Most of their manuscripts come from well-known celebrities or are custom written for a pre-defined audience.

Many of the small publishers, on the other hand, accept "good literature" manuscripts and then try to interest the public in the book. Because of this approach, the book often lacks a well-defined audience. The problem is compounded by a lack of resources for proper promotion.

It is nearly impossible to compete with the large publishing firms on their ground because you do not have their money. You do not want to follow the small publisher because he is not making much money. There is a lot of room for the very small independent publisher with imagination and initiative. There is no competition; it is a challenge. All you have to do is think.

ANALYZE YOUR MARKET by determining who might purchase your book and then figure the best way to reach them. If your book is on auto repair, you will want to send news releases, review copies, ads and maybe even articles to auto magazines. Since there aren't too many little old ladies who are going to purchase such a book, you don't want to waste your time pursuing them. If you are approaching book stores, college book stores, public libraries or school libraries, you want to determine their seasonal buying patterns. If you are pursuing direct mail sales, you will want to set up a system of mailings and emphasize the program in certain seasons. The keys to your promotion are market targeting and timing. More on all of these later.

As you read through the next few chapters, think about your book and its market. Make a list of, or underline, those ideas mentioned that best fit your book. Then go back and work out a promotional schedule by the week for a period of several months. List ad deadlines, dates for mailings, etc. Set a schedule so you won't lose sight of it later when you are busy typing orders and stuffing boxes.

A common complaint by those who use a Hi-Liter felt tip marker to indicate the important parts of this book is that their copy of The Self-Publishing Manual winds up completely yellow.

BINDER ORGANIZATION. Organize your thoughts and record your work by setting up a binder for your book. Use a 2" or 3" three-ring binder with dividers for five sections.

"Analyze carefully the kind of person who is a prospective purchaser of your book. This is, perhaps, the single most important thing to consider."

Section one is where you record your promotional plan. Whenever you have a new idea, turn to the first page of section one and make a note. Use the balance of this section to store every news release you write, every ad you place and every brochure you design.

Section two is for all your costing information. Store copies of all the printing, artists', trucking, etc. bills as well as all the printing quotations. With this information all in one place, even after six printings you will know exactly how many books have been printed and what each print run cost.

Section three is where you store the reviews, testimonials and other publicity you have generated. All of the good things which have been said about your book are kept in one place so that when you want to make a list of testimonials, they will be easy to find.

Section four is for any important correspondence. Here you will store some of the more interesting letters which do not fit in the other sections.

Section five is the revision section. As you come across new material or think of something that should be included, make a note and store it here. Also take one copy of the book and mark it "Correction Copy" and keep it near your desk. As you find errors or want to make changes, mark this book. Then when it comes time to return to press, all your revision information will be in these two places.

You will appreciate the promotion binders even more after you publish several books. At any time you will be able to pick up a binder and find exactly where the book promotion is and how it is doing.

RATE OF SALE. You can expect your sales to take on an airfoil shape if your prior promotion is good. Sales will climb rapidly, level out, taper off and become steady. Thereafter you will notice bumps in response to seasonal changes or when your advertising or promotional work is successful.

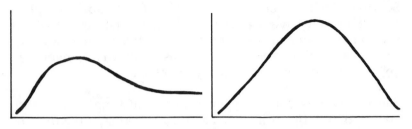

Your sales chart   Typical big firm individual book sales chart.

The big initial jump is due to your pre-publication publicity and resulting orders; they all hit at once. By contrast, the big New York publishers market books in the same way Hollywood sells a motion picture. They throw it out on the market to see if anyone likes it. If it gets a response, they dump in a lot of promotional money. Then they push it for a couple of months. When the interest cools, they bring out another product and start all over.

As a small publisher, it makes more sense to market your book like breakfast food or soap. Develop your product, pour on the promotion, carve a niche in the market and then continue to sell at the same level for years. This can be done with a non-fiction book which is revised at each printing.

"BESTSELLERS" are only a name, a myth. This is not like a gold record in the music industry or another service to the trade run by Bowker. National best seller lists (there are several and they do not often agree) are assembled from certain bookstore sales reports. Even if you move a million books via mail order distribution, you won't make a bestseller list. On the other hand, you may calculate that your book is the best selling book in its field and there is no reason why you can't mention this in your advertising.

PROMOTION IS UP TO YOU. Whether you are an author or both the author and the publisher, it is up to you to make your book a success. If you have a little of the ham in you, if you are a performer, so much the better.

"Books do not sell themselves, People sell books."

166

One of the major problems in traditional publishing is that the author assumes the publisher will take care of all the promotion. Publishers do not do much promoting and by the time the author figures this out, the book is "not new" making any promotional efforts too late. The media does not pay attention to old books. Many publishers will welcome active promotional participation from their authors. They want to sell the book as much as you do. The author can start by searching for mailing lists, sending for ad rate cards and drafting news releases (more on these later.) There is a lot to learn from this chapter even if you aren't self-publishing.

Bookstores make your book available but they do not promote it. These outlets provide availability but you must encourage people to go into the stores. If your book is a hot seller, the bookstores will want to carry it. If no one asks for it, the stores will not touch it. You must create the demand.

KEY CONTACTS are those people who can help you move the greatest volume of books with the least expenditure of time and money. These contacts must be developed if you are going to properly promote your book. The only difference between you and a professional book publicist is that the professional already has the media contacts. There are many wholesalers, TV people and subsidiary rights buyers who are just waiting to "discover" you and your book. While most are very busy, they want you; that is what their job is all about. You will meet a great number of nice, helpful people but only a few "key" contacts will do you a great amount of good. What you have to do is to locate and then carefully cultivate them. Some of the people will be listed in <u>Literary</u> <u>Market</u> <u>Place</u> and other directories available at your library. For others, you may have to call the company and ask for the name of the "small press buyer," etc. Tell the company operator who you are and ask who you should properly correspond with. Write or call this contact and field your

---

"Show me a publisher who says you never can tell which book is going to make it and I'll show you a publisher who considers manuscripts before evaluating the market."

sales pitch; establish a rapport. Maintain credibility and remember that they are everyone else's key contact, too. Do not expect them to return calls. Send review copies of your book and follow up in a few days with a telephone call asking "have you received it?" If this is a chain or a wholesaler, be bold and ask for an order.

Start files on these key contacts and fill them with letters and notes of your telephone conversations. Note their personal likes and dislikes so you can bring them up in future conversations. Treat contacts well and they will be there to help you with your next book, too.

ADDRESS CODES. Tracing each order you receive back to a specific promotional effort or paid advertisement is important business intelligence. Without this information, you may be unknowingly spending your energy and money in the wrong places. Waste becomes tragedy when you continue blind promotional spending because you are not certain which projects are paying off by bringing in book orders. Both your time and money are limited; you must spend them in those places which will bring maximum return.

Just add an extra letter or number to your street address or box. Code everything! Every brochure, ad, order blank, press release, directory listing, everything. Then, you will receive only a few orders you cannot trace. Some people will be influenced by your promotion and will seek your book through their library or bookstore. But coding will indicate the source of most of your orders.

List your address as "4759 Via Camarada, Suite 712," or in a classified where every word costs, "4759-712 Camarada." Many customers figure out the obvious codes and, knowing they aren't important to the address, leave them off. So, if you are advertising in Popular Science in August 1986, don't use "4759 Via Camarada, Dept. PS-8-6." Careful coding is even more important with press releases and those items not going directly to the general public because the media are conscious of these codes and won't repeat them. An address code is of no value to you if it doesn't get used.

"If your book fails to sell, you don't know your market.

List all the places to which you are mailing ads and other promotional material and give a short code to each. Letters are good for a start but there aren't enough of them and some can be confused when rendered in script on an envelope. Avoid "I" & "1", "u" & "v", "G" & "6", "0" & "O", etc.

Many people ask "but won't the Post Office object to all this added information?" The answer is no, as long as the essential addressing information is there so they may easily determine where to direct your mail. On the other hand, you may confuse visiting customers who drive down your street looking for a building tall enough for a "suite 712."

If you have more than one title and are advertising or promoting two or more in the same market, you will want to make a notation as to which was ordered on the envelope as you process the orders. Then total up the responses at the end of the month and record them by code letter or number on a spread sheet. Also enter on the sheet when certain advertising and promotion hit so you can better visualize the reasons for the results.

These tallies aren't hard work and can even be done spread out on the floor in front of the TV set. It is terribly revealing where some of your orders come from. How else would you know, for example, that a mention in a Changing Times article brought in 140 orders? Or that most foreign bookstores find you in Books in Print? With this information, you will be able to assess what works and where you can most effectively spend your time and money to generate more sales. After a couple of months you will wonder why address coding wasn't obvious to you from the beginning.

PROMOTIONAL MATERIALS take many forms and many are already at hand. Think of the ways you can use photocopies of your manuscript, folded and gathered pages, overruns on covers, photocopies of the boards, etc.

"Being an author is 5% writing and 95% promotion." — Russ Marano, *Hi-Tek Newsletter.*

Consider combining the jacket with a cover letter and an order blank for a mailing. Another successful and popular promotional piece is to make press kit folders with overruns of the cover. Just ask the printer to print a few hundred extra covers. Then fold them, tuck in your promotional materials and mail them out. The result is an inexpensive yet impressive, professional-looking press kit.

PROFESSIONAL BOOK PROMOTION SERVICES are available for those who haven't the time or desire to do their own work. These professionals can be a great help, especially on your first book when you are just learning the ropes. Book publicists write and place news releases, organize autograph parties and place authors on TV. Typically, they charge a flat monthly fee plus expenses for all services. For radio and TV they might ask for $750 for the first city they service such as a big one like Los Angeles and $250 plus expenses for each additional city. In each city, you might do four radio and TV shows each day for two days. If you decide to hire a professional publicist, start early. Do not wait until the pub date.

Large publishers have their own in-house promotion departments while Publishers Weekly estimates there are close to 200 independent book publicists. Some are listed in the Appendix. More may be found in Literary Market Place under "Public Relations Services."

TESTIMONIALS. Many people feel that there is no better promotion than a recommendation from a satisfied customer. The best way to collect testimonials is to ask for them. If you want to use the testimonials on the back cover of the book, you will need them early. You can send photocopies of the boards to prominent people and ask them for a few well chosen words. Or if, as suggested in Chapter Two, you have sent certain chapters of your book to various experts during the drafting stage for a critique or technical proofing, you can solicit a testimonial from them.

Unsolicited testimonials will arrive after the book is published. They should be answered and filed for future use. You will want to add them and excerpts from your reviews to a "review and testimonial" sheet. The rev/test sheet is an important piece of publicity in that it indicates that other people like your book. This sheet should be sent to later reviewers, prospective dealers and anyone else you are trying to convince the book is a winner.

Ask for permission to use testimonials and get it in writing. Most people will jump at the chance to be included. Full names and occupation are best but if you haven't time to get permission, sign the testimonial such as "J.S.H., Attorney, Denver."

NEWS RELEASES. The media are in the news gathering/publishing business; they want to hear from you. This is not expensive advertising, publicity involves the use of inexpensive news releases. News items receive a much higher degree of readership than advertising and greater readership leads to more response (sales.) News releases generate publicity and invite book reviews. Releases may be used to announce publication of your new book to newspapers, magazines, libraries, radio and TV. In fact, they should be sent to anyone who will listen.

On your first book, while you are still learning about the printing trade and your own schedules are apt to slip, it is probably best to send out your first press release when the manuscript is actually delivered to the printer. When you are writing your next book, you may start sending out the releases earlier. These early releases should contain a more generalized publication date such as "March 1986." Later it may be moved or the specific day may be added. Do not send early releases to newspapers. Publicity before your books are in the stores is wasted.

Some authors do not like to reveal their project too early and hold off on their releases. They are afraid someone might pick up on their good idea. But other writers purposely get their release out very early in the hope of scaring off the competition. Whichever approach you take, someone will call to say "Don't write it, my book is at the printer now!" "At the printer" usually means they may sit down at their typewriter soon.

The format of the release is standardized. The easiest way to design it is to simply type "NEWS RE-

171

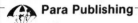 **Para Publishing** ──────────────────

news release

FOR IMMEDIATE RELEASE
Contact: Mindy Bingham
(805) 968-7277

CORRESPONDENCE OUTLINES OFFERED TO PUBLISHERS

Business Letters For Publishers is an 82 page book of sample letters especially created to be used in small and medium sized houses. The letter outlines not only save time for the older firm; they enable the newer publisher to establish company policy which conforms to current, sometimes peculiar, publishing industry standards.

Letter writing is expensive. Studies show each one now costs more than seven dollars and most of the cost is salaries. Often answering a letter is postponed because it is difficult to think of all the important elements which should be included; creating the text is usually the most difficult and time consuming part.

Cleverly drafted, these letter outlines are divided into the areas of sales, promotion, information requests, financial and general. Business Letters covers requests for use of copyrighted information, bounced checks, publication delays, price changes, reviewer letters, ad rate requests, answering various complaints, catalog submissions, shipping instructions to printers, return authorizations, drop shipments and collections; there are 75 in all. Publishers will adopt many of the outlines verbatim while using others as prompts in custom-drafting correspondence.

Business Letters was compiled by Dan Poynter, author of The Self-Publishing Manual. It is the fifth item in a line of publishing aids well known to the industry.

The 8½ x 11 softcover edition (ISBN 0-915516-28-4) is available from Para Publishing, P.O. Box 4232-59, Santa Barbara, CA 93103-0232, (805) 968-7277 for $14.95 postpaid. It is also available on a magnetic recorded disc for use in a Xerox model 860 word processor for $29.95. Satisfaction is guaranteed.

-30-

Photographs of the book and/or the author are available on request.

Sample of a news release

LEASE" on your own letterhead stationery. The release will look fancier if you use "press-on type." By using your own stationery, the important information such as company name and address will be at the top. Then just type in the release date or "For Immediate Release" and a contact name and telephone number. If your name is Tom Drewes, the book is authored by Tom Drewes and the book is published by Tom Drewes Publishing, make your company look a little larger by selecting another name for the contact person.

Type a clever and catchy headline in capital letters. Then space down and get into the body of your release. Begin with the most important information first and progress to the least important. This way, if the editors cut part of the copy, the major message will still get through. The release should begin by telling why this is an important subject; make it provocative. The release should be issue oriented; write about the "problem", not the book. Then describe the contents of the book; mention it as a resource. Continue with some background on the topic and show why your book is unique, useful and timely. Spend a paragraph on yourself and tell why you are an expert on the subject. Give the price and mention that the book is available from the publisher as well as the stores. List your address so the reader will know where to send the money. Use the fewest number of words to communicate any thought. Never use a less-common word when a familiar one will convey your meaning. Use simple sentences; complex sentences can be hard to read.

Give the editors what they want and need; deliver the information in such a way that it is useful and newsworthy. A release which starts out "Festival Publications is happy to announce..." is self-serving. There is a much better chance your release will be used if the headline begins "Breakthrough found in...." The release is being written for the readers of the periodical, it isn't an announcement for your company picnic. When drafting a news release for a specific section, such as Publishers Weekly "Back to Press" column, write it in the same format, no more and no less. Do not make the editors rewrite the release, they may round-file it instead.

Double space on 8½ x 11 paper and write in newspaper style. Begin a third of the page from the top and leave wide margins. The release may be any length but one page is usually best. If the release runs more than one page, identify the story with a header in the upper left-hand corner of the second page. End the release with the newspaper termination sign "-30-".

Take your time and compose a good release. Not all news gatherers do their own work all the time so your work may appear verbatim in print. It may even be reprinted word-for-word as a book review.

If possible, include a photograph. One from the book illustrating the point you are making in the release is best. Remember, you want the release to push your program, the book is secondary—almost subliminal.

Business editors receive a lot of news releases but use only 20 to 25% because most are so poorly written, lack relevance and significance, lack a local angle, do not say anything of interest to the readers or bury the good material. Other editors may use only one release out of ten. Do not load your release with puffery or hype. With so many junk releases out there, is should be easy to make yours better.

Type up the release and have it duplicated at the "instant print" shop by photocopy or offset depending on the number you need. Ship them off with a photo of the book and enclose a reviewer response card (below).

Send the releases to all appropriate magazines (below), book clubs (see Chapter 6), to subsidiary rights contacts (Chapter 6), wholesalers, libraries, sales representatives, hometown papers, etc. In later mailings, you will use a brochure but right now you are making an announcement. Don't forget alumni, fraternal trade or church publications with which you may have a connection. Spread them around. Follow up with a telephone call to the most important periodicals.

News releases to local periodicals may be hand-carried. Personal delivery not only receives more attention, meeting editors will be a great education for you.

Use news releases liberally. Every time you go back to press, issue a release to herald it. Magazines such as the prestigious <u>Publishers</u> <u>Weekly</u> will give you a few lines if you just let them know. Releases should also be issued

---

"While publicity, misused, can be nothing but an ego trip for the author, well used it can be a powerful sales tool" — Al Lind.

to announce speaking engagements, TV appearances, auto-graph parties and any other newsworthy event. If business slows down, think up a newsworthy event and write a release on it.

```
┌─────────────────────────────────────────────────────────────┐
│                                                             │
│  ┌───────────────────────────────────────────────────────┐ │
│  │               PLEASE ACKNOWLEDGE                      │ │
│  │                                                       │ │
│  │  We have received your News Release about (book title): ____ │ │
│  │  We will take the following action:                   │ │
│  │  ☐ Your book will be featured on (date): _____ │ │
│  │  ☐ Your book will be featured in the near future      │ │
│  │  ☐ Please send a photograph of the book               │ │
│  │  ☐ Please send a photograph of the author             │ │
│  │  ☐ Please send a complimentary copy of the book       │ │
│  └───────────────────────────────────────────────────────┘ │
│                                                             │
│  ┌───────────────────────────────────────────────────────┐ │
│  │                                                       │ │
│  │  Name:_____ │ │
│  │  Full job title:_____ │ │
│  │  Name of publication or broadcast station:_____ │ │
│  │  Mailing address: _____ │ │
│  │  _____ Zip: _____ │ │
│  │  Comments (optional): _____ │ │
│  │  _____ │ │
│  └───────────────────────────────────────────────────────┘ │
└─────────────────────────────────────────────────────────────┘
```

Release response reply card

An enclosed Release Response Reply Card will pro-vide instant feedback. The cards will tell you if you are writing good releases and if you are sending them to the right people. You won't have to wait months wondering if the articles will appear. You will be ready to collect clippings and the responses will provide leads for possible book reviews. Some people feel they receive a better return if they stamp the cards. The theory is the editor will feel obligated to reply since you have included postage. Once replying, it is nicer to say something positive. Other professionals argue that editors of most publications are employees who do not buy their own postage. They just toss the card in the out basket, so applying postage is a waste of money.

Always respond to PW's requests for information for their spring and fall announcements issues. Once you register for an ISBN, you will be on Bowker's mailing list and will receive these requests automatically. If you are going on tour, send a short release listing the places and dates to PW's "Author Publicity" column.

Remember that media people work in a pressure-cooker world. Be polite, they won't expect it. You will get a lot of mileage out of one kind word.

The best time to write your first release is before you write your book. Do not send the release out, just write it. This exercise will help you to focus on your reading audience and will guide you in your writing.

YOUR PUBLICATION DATE is a place in the future, well after your books are off the press, when your promotion hits and your books are available in the stores. The pub date is a means of focusing attention. The idea is to have the product accessible when public attention peaks in response to your promotion. You want to time book reviews, TV appearances, space advertising, autograph parties, etc. with bookstore deliveries. The big important pre-publication reviewers need 12-15 weeks lead time so you will have to pick a publication date at least four months away.

Production is always subject to delay so it is recommended that for your first book, and until you learn the problems of the printing trade, you wait until the book is on the press before you set your publication date. Set it three to four months away and then start publicizing and selling books. The publication date is a fiction for the benefit of the few, big, important pre-publication reviewers such as Publishers Weekly and only gives you a target for promotion and distribution. There is nothing to stop you from selling and shipping books.

The pub date is only for the few pre-publication reviewers. Do not use it when filling out the copyright form. The registrar wants to know when the book came off the press and went on sale.

> "The main difference between marketing a book and marketing soap is that a book is a one-shot deal...a book usually only has 90 days to make it or it's dead" — Carole Dolph, promotional director, Doubleday & Co.

If you have achieved sufficient pre-publication momentum, you should make a significant amount of sales before the printing bill arrives. It is a matter of planning, scheduling, timing and work. The big publishers expend 90% of their promotional effort by the publication date. You, of course, will keep up the pressure.

The best publication dates are probably in the first quarter of the year. Most of the big publishers aim for the second half to take advantage of the Christmas selling season. An early release also gives you maximum mileage for your copyright date. People want a new book and if you publish in December, the book becomes a "year old" in just a few weeks. If your book comes off the press after September, select a copyright and pub date in January of the next year. Mail order sales are traditionally best in the spring. There are many considerations.

If you have shipped your galleys off to the pre-publication reviewers and then find your production is snagged. You may call these magazines and tell them the pub date has been postponed.

BOOK REVIEWS sell books. Reviews are not difficult to get while they cost you very little in time and money. But there are two types of reviews. They cater to two separate markets and the approach to each is different. They can be labeled: "Pre-publication reviews (wholesale)" and "Publication date reviews (retail)."

PRE-PUBLICATION REVIEWS are directed toward the industry. Certain publications will review your book prior to publication so that the bookstores and libraries will have the opportunity to stock it before patrons start asking for it. Since 100 new titles are published for each day the stores are open, many book dealers and libraries depend on these concise summaries in making their purchasing choices. Pre-publication reviews are directed at the trade and should not be confused with the regular book reviews aimed at the ultimate consumer/reader.

"Just as a parent's responsibilities do not end with giving birth, an author's does not end with publication. The child must be raised and the book must be marketed."

Ninety or more days prior to your publication date, send bound photocopies of the pasted boards (or galleys if you are printing letterpress) with a cover letter, reply card and a news release to:

1. Publishers Weekly, Attn: Sally Lodge, Forecasts, 205 East 42nd Street, New York, NY 10017. PW is directed at bookstores. Mention your promotional plan in the cover letter. The readers want to be sure you are going to bring customers into their stores. PW also wants to know if you have sold any foreign rights.

2. Library Journal, Attn: Book Reviews, 205 East 42nd Street, New York, NY 10017. For many nonfiction books, a favorable review here will sell over 1,000 copies. Most of the library orders will come through Baker & Taylor.

3. Kirkus Reviews, Attn: Library Advance Information Service, 200 Park Avenue South, NYC, NY 10003.

4. ALA Booklist, Attn: Bill Ott, Up Front, 50 East Huron Street, Chicago, IL 60611. A review magazine directed at libraries.

5. The New York Times, Attn: Daily Book Page, 229 West 43rd Street, New York, NY 10036.

6. Forecast, Baker and Taylor Co., 6 Kirby Avenue, Somerville, NJ 08876.

7. The Washington Post, Book World, 1150 15th Street NW, Washington, DC 20071

The cover letter should be addressed to a particular person; current names can be found in Literary Market Place, available in your library. Write a paragraph on each of the following: introduce the book and its contents, tell why the book is important to today's reader, and say that you hope they like the book. Keep it short.

News releases (sample reviews) probably will not work with the above publications as they usually do their own work. But it does not hurt to try and the release will provide them with important information on the book.

"I never read a book before reviewing it, it prejudices a man so." — Sydney Smith

You may send a finished copy of the book to most regular reviewers but those listed above prefer galleys. If you send the finished book, they will think it is too late for a "pre-publication review" and they will probably ignore it. Some reviewers collect galleys feeling they offer more prestige than just books which are available to anyone. In offset printing there is often less time between typesetting and printing than there used to be with hot type. The new video screen text editing equipment allows authors to set their own type as they write, thus shortening the procedure even more. Eventually, galleys may go the way of the buggy whip. If you do elect to send the finished book only, mention in your cover letter that modern printing methods make sending the galleys impractical, then emphasize your publication date.

Most publishers photocopy the boards to make up sets of galleys while others have chopped off the spine of the book in order to submit loose pages. Still others have photocopied the printed book. All this to satisfy the idiosyncrasies of the pre-publication reviewer.

To make up sets of "bound galleys", take your pasted-up boards to a photocopy shop. The copy shops near colleges generally charge less. Check the Yellow Pages and shop around for price. Have the shop photocopy the boards, one side, on 8½ x 11 paper, add paper covers and bind with the Velo-Bind system.

On the cover of the bound galleys, list the title and subtitle, author, publication date, price, ISBN number, number of pages and illustrations and include a statement of special advertising/promotional plans and book clubs. The more promotion you list here, the better chance you will have they will review the book. Review magazines such as PW like to review books from established publishers which will get a lot of promotional backing. Many reviewers do not consider a book to be a book unless it is

"Book reviewing is one of the few activities in the world that could be said to depend largely on love" — Jack Beatty, Literary Editor, New Republic.

published in hardcover. Knowing this, some publishers note on the galleys that the book will be in hardcover even though it is coming out in soft. Other publishers have just a few hardcover books manufactured to keep the reviewers and librarians happy. Do not worry about the illustrations unless this is an art book. Pre-publication reviewers are used to reviewing books without the photographs.

Reviews in the above listed publications are the most important. Good reviews in them will bring you more reviews in other publications later.

COPYRIGHTS, LISTINGS AND EARLY REVIEWS. In anticipation of your new book coming off the press, address large envelopes to those places listed below and stuff them as appropriate with: cover letter, review sheets, photocopied ABI form, 4 x 6 or larger book photograph, etc. Then when you receive your first delivery of books, stuff them into the envelopes and send them off according to the following checklist. When mailing to the review magazines, address the package to the specific appropriate editor. Check the current names in Literary Market Place. Stuff in brochures, early reviews, etc. to convince reviewers the book has been accepted by others. Don't skimp here.

1. One copy for LC cataloging. See the discussion in Chapter 5. CIP Office, Library of Congress, Washington, DC 20559. Use their postpaid label.

2. Two copies for copyright registration, along with your check and the copyright form. See the discussion in Chapter 5. Register of Copyrights, Library of Congress, Washington, DC 20559.

3. One copy to LC Acquisition and Processing along with your brochure and discount schedule. Library of Congress, Attn: Jane Collins, Acquisitions and Processing Division, Crystal Mall Annex, Washington, DC 20540.

4. One copy to Publishers Weekly, Attn: Weekly Record, 205 East 42nd Street, New York, NY 10017.

5. One copy to Library Journal, Attn: Janet Fletcher, 205 East 42nd Street, New York, NY 10017.

6. One copy to <u>School</u> <u>Library</u> <u>Journal</u>, Attn: Trevelyn Jones, 205 East 42nd Street, New York, NY 10017.

7. One copy for listing, per the discussion in Chapter 5, to H.W. Wilson Co., Attn: <u>Cumulative</u> <u>Book</u> <u>Index</u>, 950 University Avenue, NYC, NY 10452.

8. One copy to <u>The</u> <u>New</u> <u>York</u> <u>Times</u>, Attn: Daily Book Review Section, 229 West 43rd Street, New York, NY 10036. Does not review very technical, specialized or juvenile books.

9. One copy to <u>The</u> <u>New</u> <u>York</u> <u>Times</u>, Attn: Sunday Book Review Section, 229 West 43rd Street, New York, NY 10036. This is one of the most prestigious and valuable review columns. Retail book buyers read this medium and rely on it more than any other.

10. One copy to <u>Small</u> <u>Press</u> <u>Magazine,</u> 205 East 42nd Street, New York, NY 10017

11. One copy to <u>Choice</u>, Attn: Rebecca Dixon, 100 Riverview Center, Middletown, CT 06457. <u>Choice</u> covers the undergraduate school library market.

12. Two copies to American Library Association, Attn: <u>ALA</u> <u>Booklist</u>, 50 East Huron Street, Chicago, IL 60611.

13. One copy to <u>Kirkus</u> <u>Reviews</u>, 200 Park Avenue South, NYC, NY 10003.

14. One copy to <u>The</u> <u>Horn</u> <u>Book</u> <u>Magazine</u>, Attn: Ethel L. Heins, Park Square Building, 31 St. James Avenue, Boston, MA 02116. Horn reviews books for children and young adults.

15. One copy to <u>Small</u> <u>Press</u> <u>Review</u>, P. O. Box 100-P, Paradise, CA 95969.

16. One copy to Gale Research Co., Attn: <u>Contemporary</u> <u>Authors</u>, The Book Tower, Detroit, MI 48226.

17. One copy each to some of the larger wholesalers and chain bookstore buyers. See the discussion in Chapter eight and the listings in the Appendix.

18. One copy to The Library of Congress, Exchange and Gift Division, Gift Section, Washington DC 20540

"It takes a certain brilliance to write a book but it takes a genius to sell one." — **William Rickman, Kroch's and Brentano's**

19. Send one copy to Baker & Taylor Co., Academic Library Services Selection Department, P. O. Box 4500, Somerville, NJ 08876, for their New Book Approval and Current Books for Academic Libraries plans. Enclose a copy of the ABI form (as discussed in Chapter five.)

20. Send one copy to Dan Poynter, P.O. Box 4232-P, Santa Barbara, CA 93103-0232, autographed.

21. Send one copy to Openers, American Library Association, 50 Huron Street, Chicago, IL 60611.

22. Send one copy to Book Review Digest, H.W. Wilson Company, 950 University Avenue, Bronx, NY 10452

23. Send one copy to Kliatt Book Guide, Doris Hiatt, 425 Watertown Street, Newton, MA 02158. Softcover books for young adults.

24. Send one copy to Newspaper Enterprise Assn. Carol Felsenthal, ALA, 50 Huron Avenue, Chicago, IL 60611.

25. Send one copy to each of the half-dozen most important opinion-molders in your field. If these people talk up your book, you will be off to a good start.

REVIEWS FOR THE ULTIMATE CONSUMER. Book reviews are the most effective and least expensive method of promoting your book to the retail market. While few other products can regularly approach the media for free publicity, books have always received rather special treatment. It is almost as though there were an unwritten agreement within the communications community to publicize each others' work.

Your book is a product of yourself. You poured your time, heart and soul into it. But just because you were interested enough to take the time to write it doesn't mean everyone else will be interested enough to take the time to read it. A book critic will read your book but a book reviewer will probably only check the front matter. Some reviewers write-up ten to 15 books a week. Most of the reviewer's work will come from your news release and other enclosures. Make them good.

It helps to understand the lot of the editor and/or reviewer. Whether they are full time or freelance, they have one thing in common: they are very busy. Freelancers are paid little or not at all. Neither time nor room are available to review all the books that come in and there just aren't enough book review columns to go around. Even the prestigious and prolific Sunday Supplement of the New York Times can only cover about 20% of the books. Books are not assigned, most reviewers select the ones they want to review. Most editors live in a pressure cooker world. In New York, reviews tend to be longer and deeper while in the west, reviews are usually shorter and punchier. You can't change the situation so you might as well understand and take advantage of it.

The Los Angeles Times receives some 125 review books each day; perhaps 5% are reviewed. Times editors look for books which are of general interest to their newspaper readers. Some books are sent on to the food, sports and other editors. Short books (150 pages, not 800) are preferred and the book has a better chance of review if it has been "pre-selected"--sent in by an agent.

A few years ago, this author was dropping off a load of books at the loading dock around back of the Post Office in Santa Barbara. He saw a young man (not in a Postal uniform) with a cart full of packages over near the Dumpster and his curiosity mounted. As he watched, the man ripped open the cartons, took out what appeared to be books and placed them in a large carton. Then he threw the wrappers in the trash. Unable to stand it any longer, he approached the man and asked if these were "lost-in-the-mail books. Turns out the packages were for L.A. book critic Robert Kirsch. This gigantic load of books was being received at his home address (imagine what showed up at work) and he not only didn't have time to pick up the books himself, he didn't have room for the wrappers. There is a second lesson here too: much of the material you ship with review copies is likely to become separated from the book.

If your book has special area appeal, you can greatly increase your chances for review by submitting your book to the special publications reaching that particular group. For example, if your book is on hang gliding, you would

183

send review copies to Hang Gliding magazine and Glider Rider. Then you would consider every aviation, outdoor, sport, recreation, do-it-yourself, teen, men's, etc. magazines you could find. There are some 60,000 magazines being printed in the U.S. today (and a lot more foreign). There must be some which are reaching the groups you want.

Be prepared for delays with the smaller association publications. They want to review your book but they have certain staff and budget limitations. Usually they rely on outside free help for book reviews. Typically, the editor will only scan a book before sending it off to an appropriate expert requesting him or her to review it. Often, the reviewer is very busy too. If you know the editor or reviewer, usually the case in an industry publication, give him or her some help. Offer to write the review yourself, sending it to the reviewer for additions or changes. They usually simply sign your work and send it in.

SELECTING MAGAZINES and other media for news releases and potential reviews is fun. Go to the library and search through the racks for appropriate magazines. In a large library in a major city, this could take all day. Look for book review columns and copy down the name, title and address of the reviewer. If you don't send the book to the attention of the right person, your book may get ripped-off by someone else on the staff. When this happens, you not only waste a book, you lose out on a review. Pick your publications carefully. Pay particular attention to the print media that move the most books: Newsweek, Time, People, The Wall Street Journal and The New York Times Book Review. Select only those likely to review your book because it is relative to their publication and the interests of their readership. In other words, don't send an aviation book to Solid Waste Management

---

"So long as reviewers continue to be resistent about paperbacks, we'll go on printing small hardcover runs. Reviews are so important to a first novel; you really have to do a hardcover to get reviewers' attention." — Gretchen Salisbury, Congdon & Lattes in Publishers Weekly.

---

magazine until you see garbage trucks with wings. Be objective and realistic.

Once you have a feel for the wide range of magazines and how they treat review books, visit the reference desk and ask for directories such as the Standard Periodical Directory (thousands of magazines), Ulrich's International Periodical Directory (many U.S. and foreign periodicals), Writer's Market, Literary Market Place (with many good lists such as producers of TV talk shows, news services, syndicated columnists, newspaper book reviewers, etc.), the Ayer Directory of Publications (lists newspapers and magazines), Bacon's Publicity Checker, International Yearbook (the key personnel of newspapers), Broadcast Yearbook (key radio and TV personnel), Encyclopedia of Associations and the National Trade and Professional Associations Directory (both list special interest trade and professional organizations). Address news releases and review books to the position, not just the name of the editor or reporter. If your recipient is on vacation, your mailing might be pigeon-holed for weeks-- and no longer considered news. Some people take a pocket-full of dimes for the copy machine so they won't have to hand-copy the addresses they need.

PLEASE REPLY

☐ YES, I would like to receive a review/examination copy of:

Book title: _____

☐ No, we do not feel these books are suitable for our review.

PLEASE SEND THE BOOK(S) TO:

Name of reviewer: _____

Full job title: _____

Name of publication or broadcast station: _____

Mailing address: _____

_____ Zip: _____

Comments (optional): _____

_____

Review book request post card.

185

Depending on your subject, you may find 200 to 400 potential reviewers for your book. Don't be surprised if you come up with 600. Divide the periodicals into two groups: the sure bets and the rest. Some magazines will be perfect matches for your subject and some will have such a large circulation, they cannot be ignored. Send books to the small group of sure bets but send only the literature and a reply post card to the majority of them.

When the cards come back, send out the books and the literature. You are fishing at this point; you won't hook a fish with every cast but you have narrowed your odds with the post cards.

Reviewer addresses should be typed up on 33-part labels or entered into a computer address program so they can be reproduced and used again. Save and maintain your lists, you will use them over and over.

THE REVIEW PACKAGE sent to the reviewers should include the following: a book, brochure, review slip, a sample review in the form of a news release, cover letter, reply card and some photographs. Make the reviewer's job easy by providing everything needed.

The cover letter should start by mentioning that this is the complimentary review copy they requested. Some publishers save time by just photocopying the reply card to remind the reviewer this is a requested book. Help the reviewer. Suggest an interesting or unique local angle. Introduce the book and its contents. Tell why the book is important to today's reader and ask for a review.

Sample reviews in the form of a news release (mentioned above) are worth writing. Many reviewers will use them verbatim. In fact, it won't hurt to write up two samples, a short one and a long one. For the more important magazines, check the particular publication, write an individual release and follow their style.

Use the same type of reply card you sent out for the pre-publication reviews.

Artwork will get you a lot more space and make the review more attractive resulting in a higher degree of readership. Enclose a 4 x 6 or larger black and white photographs of the book and, if the book is well illustrated, samples of the artwork.

▲▲Addison-Wesley

We are pleased to be able to
send you this review copy
and would appreciate receiving
two copies of your review.

THE INDEPENDENT SCHOLAR'S HANDBOOK

by Ronald Gross

Publication Date: June 24, 1982

$8.95 trade paperback

$16.95 hardcover

contact:

Lisa Strawbridge, Publicity Manager
General Books Division
ADDISON-WESLEY
Reading, Massachusetts 01867
(617)944-3700, ext. 2431

Book review slip

Many books are sent with book review slips listing
vital information while a lot of others also have the title,
publication date and price(s) rubber stamped on the inside
of the front cover. Some reviewers want the information
stamped on for identification in case they lose the book
review slip and many publishers stamp the book to prevent
the reviewer from selling the book to a bookstore. Some
stores find they can get more for these rubber stamped
review copies than for other used books.

Review book rubber stamp

Some publishers stamp their review copies "Professional Review Copy, Not For Resale" while others just use an address stamp. The rubber stamp will not stop the sale of review books but it will insure the book will not be returned to the publisher by a bookstore for credit.

In mid-1979, the newspaper and book industries were scandalized when ten newspaper book reviewers were accused of selling review books to the Strand bookstore in New York. Apparently, several bookstores send form letters to reviewers soliciting books. Typically, the stores buy the books at 25% of list price and resell them at 50% of list. One reviewer estimated he received 30,000 review copies in seven years. Many periodicals have a policy of donating review copies philanthropically, to hospitals, charitable book fairs, foreign libraries, etc.

Certainly the ability to sell review copies may promote the requesting of them. There is nothing wrong with a reviewer requesting a book if he or she plans to review it. But it is wrong if they plan to sell the book without first considering it for review.

Always include a self-addressed reply post card so reviewers may indicate the response they plan. You want to be ready to collect the clippings for your files and future promotion. Don't be too upset by the return rate on the reply post cards. Some cards will take a long time and others will not be returned at all. Many reviewers just don't know when the review will appear.

If you know a freelance or staff reviewer personally, send him or her a review copy. Use every possible "in" you might have. Hometown newspapers and magazines are easy. They are almost obligated to pick up local color; in a small town weekly you might even make the first page. Hit all your home towns, where you live now, where you grew up, where you went to school, all of them. Address your cover letter to the specific editor and you may not only get a nice review but a special feature story as well.

PLEASE ACKNOWLEDGE

We have received the complimentary review book or galleys you sent of
Book title: _____

☐ We expect to review this book on (date): _____
☐ Please send a photograph of the book
☐ Please send a photograph of the author
☐ We did not find this book suitable for our review.

Name of reviewer: _____
Full job title: _____
Name of publication or broadcast station: _____
Mailing address: _____
_____ Zip: _____
Comments (optional): _____
_____

Sample of reply postcard.

Some public relations people like to get very personal in review copy mailings. They jot a little personal note to the reviewer hoping to snow them into thinking they have met before or that the reviewer may have made some long forgotten promise at a cocktail party.

Reviewers are cautious people. They are more apt to review your book if it has been treated favorably in pre-publication reviews by big name reviewers. One way to convince them your book is worthy of their attention is to include copies of these early reviews. Just paste them all up on a sheet of paper and make a photocopy.

Follow through on important reviewers. If they don't respond right away, you may call "to verify that the book has been received."

Once you receive a card notifying you a review will appear in a given publication, you may like to advertise in it, too. Some publishers feel this double impact is worth

Throwing the Book at You

Journal of Aerospace Education

The New York Times Book Review

Discus plasticus. The oddest-looking book of the year has just arrived from the oddest-named publisher of the year: "The Frisbee Handbook" (Parachuting Publications, Santa Barbara, Calif., $8.95), a 187-page, circular-shaped paperback nestling within a plastic Frisbee, all of it neatly shrink-wrapped. The opus is the collaboration of Mark Danna, a young New Yorker who makes a living as a top-rated Frisbee player, and Dan Poynter, a young Californian who's into such things as parachute-jumping, hang-gliding and publishing books on aviation sports. The picture-filled, amusingly written handbook gives pointers on both solo and team Frisbee play, facts about clubs, competitions and the lore of a sport that has won several hundred thousand devotees, male and female, over the past 20 years.

And how did the Frisbee get its name? It seems that many, many years ago there was a New Haven firm named the Frisbie Baking Co., and Yale men got into the habit of using its empty pie tins to play games with under the 'elms. ∎

So catch it and get in on the action. *The Frisbee Player's Handbook* — shaped like a Frisbee — is a new and exciting book by Mark Danna (a top world ranked Frisbee player) and Dan Poynter (one of the world's foremost authorities on aviation sports). Specially die cut to a circular format, the book comes nested and shrink wrap packaged in a custom designed Frisbee disc. All this to inspire the world to think circular.

Written for easy reading by both the casual beach player and the accomplished master, this fascinating 187-page book offers a unique training method and a systematic, step-by-step approach to basic, special, and advanced Frisbee throws and catches. Other chapters cover games, competition, Frisbee lore and origin, world records, and even training methods for teaching dogs how to catch a disc. The

appendix lists Frisbee books, magazines, and clubs throughout the world in order to direct the reader to the local action. Enhancing the text are over 400 action photos — including sequential shots and overhead views — nearly all of which were staged by the authors with motorized equipment to illustrate the essential parts of every throw and catch. The *Frisbee Player's Handbook* is indeed the only complete up-to-date, how-to, where-to Frisbee manual, and the disc is sure to become a collector's item.

The price for both the circular book and the custom Frisbee disc together is just $8.95 ($9.95 foreign, Californians add 54¢ sales tax). It is available in many sporting goods, toy, and book stores or directly from the publisher: parachuting Publications, P.O. Box 4232-Y, Santa Barbara, CA 93103.

PUBLISHERS WEEKLY

A pair of illustrated frisbee books, one for each hand perhaps, are being published this month. The more unusual of the two is "Frisbee® Players' Handbook" by Mark Danna and Dan Poynter ($8.95). The difference is in the design. The April paperback from Parachuting Publications (P.O. Box 4232-Y, Santa Barbara, Calif. 93103) is round and fully packed—inside an actual frisbee. The publisher notes that there are more than 100,000 members of the International Frisbee Association and that more than 10-million frisbees are sold annually. Future converts will encounter training methods, frisbee lore, world records and such detailed in this would-be flyer. Danna is about to set out on a 13-week tour for a Coppertone/frisbee promotion.

The Frisbee Players Handbook by Mark Danna and Dan Poynter (Parachuting Publications, P.O. Box 4232, Santa Barbara, California 93103, 1978, 187 pages plus Frisbee, paperback, $8.95; Californians add 54 cents sales tax).

With the *Frisbee Players Handbook* you not only get a carefully organized and illustrated manual instructing you in basic throws, advanced throws, basic catches, simple trick catches, advanced trick catches, and special catching maneuvers; you not only learn about throwing multiple discs, about Frisbee games, the official format for Frisbee competition, records for outdoor distance, indoor distance, and maximum time aloft, records accomplished by men, women, seniors, juniors, children, and dogs; you not only find out about the lore and origin of the Frisbee, about Frisbee clubs and proficiency standards—you not only get all of this in a book that is shaped so that it can nestle unnoticeably in your Frisbee, but you also get a specially developed training model Frisbee patterned after the World Class 119 G.

GAMES

Library Journal

Danna, Mark & Dan Poynter. **Frisbee Players' Handbook.**

Parachuting Publications. 1978. 190p. illus. LC 77-79101. ISBN 0-915516-15-2. pap. $8.95

SPORTS

This is a manual for Frisbee players from beginners to potential world class masters. The authors describe simple throws and catches and more advanced techniques. Many photographs accompany the instruction. There are rules for games and competitive events, and there is a list of current record holders in various events. There is also an explanation of the certification requirements for the four levels of proficiency recognized by the International Frisbee Association. An appendix provides a regional directory of clubs and a list of magazines and books for the player. The book is awkward for libraries, however, because it is rounded to fit into the inner rim of the Frisbee that is sold with it.—*Jack Oakley, Dearborn Dept. of Libs., Mich.*

PREMIUM/INCENTIVE BUSINESS

Frisbee Packs Book In Conventional Disc

Circular 187-page book outlines step-by-step method for learning how to throw a frisbee. Written by a frisbee expert and an authority on

aviation sports, it is neatly packed in a Frisbee. Both Frisbee and book retail for $8.95. FROM: Parachuting Publications.

Circle No. 236 on product card.

Example of pasted-up pre-publication and early reviews

their while though others do not. Many like to see how the review pulls before investing in an ad. They let the review test the medium.

Some of your reviews may be bad and one reason is that some reviewers are bad. Some of these critics are frustrated writers who try to bring all other published authors down to their level. They take cheap shots or use

book is when Johnny Carson or Merv Griffin takes a personal interest. According to TV Guide, an appearance on Today will sell 3,000 copies of a book while a few minutes on Donohue can move 50,000. But these bigger shows are hard to crack. They have lots of material as they are deluged with press releases, visits and other personal contacts by the public relations departments of the big publishers. The competition is great and there just isn't enough air time to go around.

But there are ways to get on the big talk shows as well as to crack the other media; it depends on your subject. For example, if your book is on Frisbee disc play, you would approach the Wham-O Manufacturing Company which makes the Frisbee disc. Of course you already know them because they gave you a lot of the material for your book. They have a public relations firm on retainer and it is to their advantage to give your book a lot of promotion. You can use their muscle free. You are actually doing them a favor since your book gets their foot in the media door so they can promote their product. Incidentally, such a company would be a prime customer for your book. A Frisbee book would make ideal corporate gifts and could be used in promotions.

Whether or not you can crack into the big shows, do not overlook the smaller and local ones. They are much easier. Many stations have special shows for interviewing authors and most have at least one talk show. The local station will want you on its community affairs program. Depending on your subject, the station may even produce a short clip for their news broadcast. Once you have appeared on one local station, don't give up on the others. Use another interesting angle.

To get on a show, find out who the producer is. Locally, you may simply call the station and ask the switchboard operator. For other stations, consult the directories in your library.

Write to the producer enclosing a copy of the book, your news release, a reply card and photocopies of any

---

"When promoting it, speak proudly about your book. You worked hard on it and you should be proud. False Modesty will get you nowhere." — Mark Danna.

reviews you have received. Mention two or three of the most interesting aspects of yourself and your book. If one doesn't grab their attention, with luck another will. It helps if you can tie in to some topical problem of the day: local, national or international. Let the producer know, generally, when you will be available. If the station is local, you may be ready most any time. If you are on tour, you will have a tight schedule. Give as much advance warning as possible. Since radio/TV people are used to dealing with a third party, you might have someone else sign the letter.

If you do not hear from the station in a week or so, telephone the producer. Be persistent and polite and you should finally get through. Be prepared. Have a rough script and practice it. Express a positive, lively attitude and exude enthusiasm. This is almost an audition; if you come across well, you will get on the show.

A much less expensive program involves live and taped radio interviews by telephone. For a modest fee, you can be listed as available for interview in Linda Meyer's Spotlight (write to 18409-P 90th Avenue West, Edmonds, WA 98020 for details.) Then you just have to sit back and wait for the calls.

You may write directly to radio shows in your area. Make the letter short and tell them what your subject is about, why it is good for their show and when you are available. If you can't get together on a time, ask the producer to send you a list of questions. Then read off the first one into a cassette recorder and answer it. The talk show host will then ask the question on the air in his or her own voice and play your answer. It is just as though you were in the studio. Some people feel that radio sells more books on the West Coast than television. This is because people there spend so much time in their cars.

When you go on the air, be prepared. Since several months have passed since you wrote the book, reread it. Practice public speaking. Think over the best answers to the questions most likely to be asked. Rehearse the stock answers and use high-impact words. Go over the main points you want to make and slip them in no matter what the questions. The talk show host will frustrate you by bouncing from subject to subject so don't be caught with

194

nothing to say. On the morning shows, you will be lucky to have 90 seconds on the air. Later in the day you may have four to eight minutes. Radio, by the way, is much less demanding than television and, of course, the tube would not be appropriate if your wrote your book under a pseudonym. Send for "Tips on How to Talk With the Media" to Media Tours Northwest, P.O. Box 7, Northgate, Seattle, WA 98125.

Push a subject not your book. Do not mention the book at every opportunity—it turns off viewers and wears out your welcome on television. Express an interest in helping the viewer by pushing your program, tieing-in with a news event or some other "hook."

Many broadcasters have "information centers" to handle incoming calls about people and products aired on their station. Let the information center know where your book can be purchased.

Media people are busy and are under a lot of deadline pressure. While your book is the most important thing that has happened to you lately, it is just another news item to them. They are not easily impressed, they deal with newsmaking personalities all the time. Be polite, they won't expect it. Everyone around them is tough and short. A kind word from you will go a long way. A thank you note afterwards will leave a nice memory and you will receive great treatment for your second book.

Sometimes you just have to be ready for an opening. If your book is on parachuting and you hear the radio disc jockey announce that he plans to make his first jump on Saturday, call him up right then and offer to come right over. You will be on for a week.

When you go on tour, be sure to tie in with local bookshops. Carry a carload of books and visit the bookstore first. Then when you go on the air, refer the listeners to the local store. You might even like to follow up the program with an autograph party in the store.

AUTHOR'S TOURS are the way you promote your book out of town and they are very hard work. There was a time when all the author did was to deliver his manuscript to the publisher and then go home to await his royalty checks. However, with the advent of TV and more hype in the book business, the major effort on the part of the writer now is in criss-crossing the country selling the book. According to The Wall Street Journal, "For the publisher it is publicity at low cost. For the author it is an endurance test." It's a tough, grueling experience and it isn't inexpensive but there is no cheaper way of reaching so many of the book buying public.

Author tours mean going on as many radio and TV shows as possible and visiting bookstores in between. It is terribly discouraging to find that most of the stores do not have your book in stock. Some self-publishers fill their van with books so they can make deliveries before going on the air.

Mail your itinerary to ABA Newswire several weeks before you are scheduled to leave. The American Booksellers Association publishes this newsletter for the bookstores. Then when you call, they will have heard of you.

You may try to book the shows yourself or hire one of the publicists listed in the Appendix. Most book publicists feel Los Angeles is the most cost-effective city for a touring author.

TV GIVEAWAY PROGRAMS will provide you with great exposure and all you have to do is donate a book. These programs are presented to raise funds for charitable organizations. Be on the lookout for them.

NEWS CONFERENCES are often staged by big firms by hosting a lavish party for the press. But there is nothing wrong with a small gathering. If you have something provocative to say on a timely subject, if it would normally be mentioned as a news item, you may be able to draw out the media. You do not have to rent a hotel suite or serve food. Press people just want the information as quickly as possible. Cater to them.

FEATURED ARTICLES ON YOURSELF are another way to gain publicity. Local papers, company magazines, alumni publications, etc. are always looking for interest-

---

> *"The secret to successful publishing is not to produce more books but to effectively market those books already published."*

ing news about their people. Let them do a story on you and they will mention your greatest accomplishment-- your book. You are now an expert, an interesting person just because you are a published author.

Mail off the same package you sent to the talk show producers. After several days, call to ask if you may come in for an interview. You are news to every publication with which you are connected, from a national association to a local newspaper. Take advantage of them. Remember, book reviews sell books but featured stories sell more books.

BOOK PROMOTION THROUGH MAGAZINE ARTICLES is another way to gain publicity for your book while further- ing your writing career. It is easy to spin off articles from the chapters of your book. You can sell the articles, build your reputation and help to sell the book, too.

First of all, you will be quite pleased to find that you have less difficulty selling to magazines now that you are a published author. You are an expert and magazines want authoritative articles. Of course, you will want to end the article with "Editor's note: Jan Nathan is the author of. . .which is available from..." and type it in just as you want it, do not leave this up to the editor. Those who read the article will be interested in the subject or they wouldn't be reading about it. Many will want to know more and will seek your book. So, while you are making sales on books, you might as well get paid for the article.

Most national magazines do not pay a great deal for articles—usually just a couple of hundred dollars. How- ever, the exposure is more important to you than the money. You even might like to consider that if you offer the article free, you have a better chance of its seeing print. Write to the editor, enclosing a few applicable pages from your book, and offer to write an article with the magazine's editorial slant. Offer to send an outline or include it with this first mailing. If your book is in a word processor, it will be easy to extract a section, add an introduction and a conclusion and edit it slightly.

SPEAKING ENGAGEMENTS are another way to publicize your book. As an expert on your subject, you are in demand by service organizations, adult education programs, church groups, PTA's, in the Chamber of Commerce and others. Many of these groups feature a guest speaker at every meeting. Sometimes they rotate the responsibility among the membership to find a speaker. Your call to them may actually get someone off the hook.

The possibilities will become obvious once you begin to think of your topic from the marketing standpoint. If yours is a carpentry how-to book, a hardware store or lumber yard might like to build a seminar around you. It might turn into an annual affair. Think of the nurseries which hold pruning classes every spring. You will make good contacts as well as developing new ideas; it is stimulating.

When you make your appearance, always mention your book. Have one on display and make several copies available for sale and autographs. Prepare a short, powerful speech on one small, very interesting, related item and leave plenty of time for questions and answers. Always write out your introduction so the host won't stumble around trying to explain how important you are.

Speaking engagements will do three things for you; they promote your book, you may receive a fee for speaking and they add to your professional portfolio. Now, in addition to being an author and a publisher, you are a lecturer, too. You must be an expert!

SEMINARS are speaking engagements you organize yourself. You set up the day-long program and collect the admissions. A General Motors study found approximately 40,000 seminars are given in North America each year and generate revenues of $100 to $160 million.

Use your book as a text for the seminar and include it in the admission fee. Display related books in the back of the room and sell tapes of your lecture. If you have an idea, you can get $20 for the book, $50 for the tape and $120 for the seminar. For information on setting up seminars, write Communications Unlimited, Gordon Burgett, P.O. Box 1001-P, Carpinteria, CA 93013.

AUTOGRAPH PARTIES are a good ego trip when successful and can help to make your other advertising more effective. Normally these events are scheduled by the publisher for the benefit of the author. However, unless the author is well-known, the autograph party rarely pays. The best scheduling is to tie in with a radio or TV appearance and some local advertising.

Contact a local bookstore and ask if you may set up a table, erect a sign and provide some refreshment. The bookstore may be reluctant to sponsor such an event unless you are willing to underwrite some of the cost. The expense won't be small because in addition to the refreshments and sign, you will have to consider a good deal of advertising via mail and space ads. But the store should pay at least half. Even if they fail to sell a lot of your books, this "event" you are staging will bring new customers into their shop. Once introduced to the bookstore, they are more likely to return in the future.

Once you know a local paper is going to review your book or do a feature article on you, visit the bookstores. Suggest they might like to place an ad in the same edition to draw readers into their store. Offer to stage an autograph party, another fine tie-in.

Don't overlook fund-raising event autograph parties. Here, you would do the selling and would donate part to the club or organization.

To make an autograph party successful, you must pour on the publicity. Send out large numbers of news releases and invitations. Make the event sound big and important. Make everyone in town think that everyone else is going, that if they don't go they will be the only one not there.

AUTOGRAPHING BOOKS is something you will be asked to do both in person and by mail. It is surprising how many prolific authors have never given much thought as to how they might autograph a book. Confronted with an admiring fan, they are suddenly at a loss for words. Most authors simply sign: "To Kathy with best wishes," add their signature and sometimes the date. At times you want to be more personal such as thanking a contributor for his or her help and support on the book. If there is

> "To autograph your book to a stranger is easy, to autograph for a friend is difficult." — Rex Alan Smith.

something special about the buyer, include it in your autograph. Often, there is a question of time. On a mail order book, you can dream up something special while at a well attended autograph party it is difficult to think about a few well chosen words while trying to give witty answers. And, by the way, especially when rushed, make sure you spell their name correctly. In all the hustle, it is easy to draw a blank and misspell the simplest name or word, ruining a book.

BOOK AWARDS. There is probably no greater satisfaction to a writer than having his book selected for an award. Some book awards are big and well known and some are small. Most are for fiction. There are those that are general while others are quite specialized, but all are awards and just being nominated for one looks good in your advertising.

Awards may be mentioned in advertising and announcement stickers may be applied to the books. These stickers are a bit of extra work but they get attention. In later printings, the "sticker" may be printed on.

Book awards, contests and grants are listed in Literary Market Place and Writer's Market available at your library and in a pamphlet entitled Grants and Awards Available To American Writers published by P.E.N. American Center. See the Appendix.

RELATED BOOK LISTS can be used to plug your other books. Each of your books should carry a list of all your books and these lists should be updated at each reprinting. The list may appear on the rear jacket flap or inside the text of the book. This is a way to get your sales message to potential buyers in the same field at little cost.

BE PREPARED to move when your book takes off. Have your promotional plan organized so you will be able to gain maximum mileage from your publicity. Capitalize on each piece of publicity. Have your releases, ads and letters drafted.

Take advantage of every possible market. Pursue the most lucrative but don't overlook the marginal ones. It costs very little to service more markets once you have done the initial organization.

Chapter Eight

WHO WILL BUY YOUR BOOK? FINDING CUSTOMERS (MARKETS)

Your marketing effort is vital to the success of your book. Yours may be the greatest tome ever written but if it fails to reach its intended customer, it won't sell. People will not line up automatically to purchase your book. You have already expended a great deal of effort in writing and publishing your book but it is the energy you expend now that will make your earlier effort pay off.

Unfortunately, many creative people recoil at the thought of selling their own product. But they must promote their book even when they have elected to go with an established publisher rather than publish themselves.

The role of marketing is to return maximum sales on minimum promotional investment, "to get more bang for your buck." You want to invest your money where you will get the best return. This means placing promotion and advertising where you receive the best response per dollar invested.

An often heard rule of thumb for response percentages--for example, the number of orders received for a mailing—is 2% and there are many entertaining stories of much better returns. What really counts is the return in sales on the advertising investment. A cheap ad becomes expensive if it fails to bring in any sales. To determine your results, you must total your alternatives before you sign up. The woods are full of ad salespeople and their primary mission, like yours, is staying in business. They will promise you anything to get into your advertising budget.

Consider the amount of work which will go into the promotion. Total up your office expenses ("licking and sticking") and the direct costs such as stamps and envelopes or ad bills and balance these against the selling price (if to wholesalers, you will get less per book) and the expected response. Total these up and make the decision, but try to be objective. Run small tests before rolling out in a large investment. Code your address in all marketing efforts as described in Chapter Seven, so you can trace the source of your orders.

THE SIZE OF THE INDUSTRY. Book publishing is a $8 billion industry. Each year some 47,000 books are published in the United States. Nearly 4,000 are mass market paperbacks while some 13,000 are softcover. The percentage in softcover is increasing. The balance of 30,000 titles are hardcover. Roughly 30,000 titles are new and 17,000 are reprints. There are some 9,000 retail bookstores where the shelf life for a book averages six months.

In adult trade hardcover sales during a recent year, 46.6% were sold through retailers, 39.6% through wholesalers, 7.9% directly to libraries and institutions, 3% through special sales and 2.5% directly to customers. Over 5% were exported, about half to Canada. But professional books, those including technical, professional, scientific, medical and business titles, went directly to consumers 30% of the time. There is also other evidence that the number of books sold direct to the consumer via mail order has been on the increase in recent years.

In Canada, some 65% of the books sold are imports, 25% are Canadian published and the rest are foreign books adapted and manufactured for the Canadian market.

In a Publishers Weekly article, a poll revealed that only 5% of the population buys six or more books per year (hardcover and paperback) and most buyers were between 18 and 45 years old. Women buy more books than men and prefer fiction while men buy more nonfiction. The better educated buy more nonfiction and the lesser educated more fiction. While 40% would consider a book as a gift, they weren't sure a book was appropriate and thought it would be difficult to choose one the recipient might like. They did feel, however, that books are very personal.

Research and experience will help you select the best places to spend your advertising money. Some of these markets are obvious and you should start planning around them. Then you will want to branch out into the non-traditional markets where the competition is often less. For example, Warner Publishing cracked a new market in 1978 when Karen Lustgarten's Disco Dancing was sold in record stores. Your options are so numerous and varied that it is difficult to concentrate on the important areas.

AUDIENCE SPECIALIZATION is concentrating your efforts on the best areas. Before you wrote your book, you analyzed your potential audience and then you slanted your text toward them. In producing your book, you considered how it might be marketed and made your product attractive in this medium. Perhaps you put extra effort into the cover. The selection of your marketing channels is very important. For example, the chains seem to concentrate on fast moving books. If your book does not have a wide audience, you do not want to be in the chains. The unsold books will only come back. Even if you get your book into a non-book market where there aren't any returns, you want them to sell, not to sit on the shelves forever. So consider who patronizes each of the various outlets and be objective in considering whether they are your audience.

There has been little market research in the general segment of the book industry. Most of the sales effort is based on past personal experience. In analyzing the market, you will consider your principal marketing con-

---

"The writing of a best seller represents only a fraction of the total effort required to create one" — Ted Nicholas

cerns, your customers (individuals, schools, libraries, international markets, subsidiary rights, industry, government, etc.) and your distribution channels (mass market outlets, wholesalers, bookstores and book clubs). Your marketing tools are space ads, direct mail advertising, sales representation, etc.

With a specialized nonfiction book you can avoid the expensive traditional big publisher methods of marketing to everyone and concentrate on the more profitable areas. Work smarter, not harder. Define your core audience and then get to work. Select your special audience and find a way to reach them. You will find your target group is served by magazines, stores, catalogs, broadcast interviewers, specialized book clubs, columnists and others. For example, if your book is on skydiving, you know you can reach your customers through the U.S. Parachute Association, the Para-Gear catalog, Parachutist magazine and at the national championships.

You do not have to attack the whole group, you can go after just the cream off the top. Mail to the libraries with the biggest budgets, visit the buyers of the larger chain stores, and select the wealthiest of the direct mail purchasers. Ads and mailing lists can be purchased selectively by region; you do not have to buy the whole country.

Hedge your bets by balancing your markets. Put most of your energy into selling your target group. Sell to the rest, too, but don't spend a lot of time courting them. Invest your time wisely.

REPETITIVE AUDIENCE CONTACT is the key once you have identified your marketing area. A repeated promotion in direct mail advertising, space ads, etc. will normally bring the same response as it did the first time. Naturally the returns will drop off if done too often but many agree that six weeks is sufficient spacing. And, there is some value to repetitive exposure; after a while, people begin to recognize you. It is wise to change your

> *"There's no secret formula. It's simply a good item for which there is a need, at the right price, offered to the right market."*

204

message occasionally as some in your audience will pass over it having seen it before. But don't change for the sake of change. Repeat what works, go with a winner. You must test each type of advertising on a small sample of the group you are trying to reach. One initial ad rarely produces a bonanza. But each customer who bites is a prime target for similar books on the same subject. People who buy how-to books on a specialized subject collect them all. Slowly build your clientele and your product line.

MULTIPLE MARKETS will cost more in time and money but will stabilize your financial position by smoothing out the peaks and valleys. It is wise not to have all your eggs in one basket. With a how-to nonfiction book, you will probably concentrate on wholesalers, catalogs, space ads and direct mail. Some of your effort will depend on you. If you like personal contact, you might do more talk shows and visit more bookstores. If you like your privacy, you might concentrate on direct mail. Book promotion should be fun so do what you enjoy most.

SEASONS will affect your sales and you should plan your major marketing efforts around them. The big publishers bring out most of their new titles in the fall targeting them at Christmas. There is a good gift market but the competition is rough. June graduates are a good market. Business books are best moved in the late spring and late fall, not during the summer. Mail order and outdoor books do best in late winter when people are confined indoors and thinking about the activities of the coming summer. Travel books will do well a few months before the applicable travel season.

THE PUBLIC, or ultimate consumer, may be approached directly. Books have been sold door-to-door, hawked on street corners, at street fairs and flea markets. The advantage of selling direct is the elimination of the

"The fact is, do-it-yourself books have never been more popular than they are now, and their popularity is growing steadily — Arnold F. Logan of Petersen Publishing Co.

middlemen, you keep the entire list price for yourself. But approaching the ultimate consumer requires greater effort and the books are sold one at a time.

The other method of reaching the public is by mail. It is not so personal and the work is different; it appeals to many authors. Direct mail advertising and mail order distribution are discussed in detail in the next two chapters.

Your Christmas card list of friends, acquaintances and relatives provides a ready market for your book. They will buy no matter what the subject just because they know you. Be sure to send them a brochure and it will help if you will include a short, personal note.

EXCLUSIVES. Some book dealers, usually wholesalers, may request an exclusive. They argue they need this protection for all the sales effort they plan to put into your book. The problem is that exclusives usually make people lazy. They don't have to work because they are receiving credit for all the sales anyway.

MICROFICHE SYSTEMS. Some of the larger distributors such as Ingram, Baker & Taylor and Bookpeople have instituted microfiche systems. They ship these 4 x 6 film negative "fiche" inventory lists to the stores each week. Now when a customer asks for a book not on the shelf, the bookstore can look it up, verify that it is available, make a toll-free call and have it delivered on UPS in a couple of days. The customer may pay for the book then and return to pick it up or have the book delivered to his or her home. Bookstores like making sales when they do not have to inventory books. Even the chains use the system because it is sure and fast.

While you cannot place your book in every bookstore, you can make it available to every store through these microfiche systems. Some distributors want a larger discount to include you in their system but this investment is well-worth the added exposure. Visit a bookstore and ask to use their microfiche reader.

DIVISIONS OF THE INDUSTRY. The industry has divided itself by concentrating on certain areas of the product, marketing areas and marketing methods. The balance of this chapter will concentrate on the various marketing channels.

As you read about the industry, you will come to the conclusion that the best way to handle the book trade (bookstores and libraries) is through various distributors. Distributors consolidate shipments to bookstores providing a lower per-unit shipping cost, they recycle returns back into stock and sweat the collections. The last thing you want is an order from 600 Walden stores. It would take weeks to invoice and ship three to five books to each store. Often the cost of the shipping supplies alone will be more than the difference in discount. It takes just as long to ship one book as it does a carton. Better to ship cartons to a distributor than many small parcels to individual stores.

MASS MARKET PAPERBACK DISTRIBUTORS, about 450 in number, merchandise the smaller pocket-sized paperbacks along with magazines. No more than ten independent distributors ("ID's") account for 90% of the total volume. They service some 80,000 outlets including newsstands, drugstores, department and college stores. In 1982, they sold over 500 million books at a median price of $2.93 each. At 4000 to 5000 new titles each year, there are just too many for the rack space available. Print runs usually begin at 50,000 and paperbacks are treated like magazines. If the books do not sell, the covers are ripped off and returned for credit (to save postage). It is estimated that 36% of all mass market paperbacks are returned but 50% on a particular title is not unusual.

Mass market paperbacks are treated like magazines even though they do not have a date. They are distributed by the same people who handle magazines. These jobbers own their racks and refill them each week. There is no buying decision by the store. If the books do not sell in two weeks, they are pulled and replaced. If they do sell out, the space is filled with something new; the title is not reordered. Again, these books are treated just like magazines.

It would be nice to have your book in every supermarket in the country but the gamble of low price, high return rate and high print run is too great. To be successful in this market, your book must have vast general appeal.

WHOLESALERS AND DISTRIBUTORS. 30% of the book-stores and 70% of the libraries buy from distributors. These wholesalers ask for a 50-55% discount from you and sell to their customers at 20-40% depending upon quantity (titles may be mixed.) With regional warehouses, whole-salers offer fast service and one-stop shopping. Even the big chains make use of wholesalers when they run out and are desperate for a book. Often with a call and UPS service they can get the books in a couple of days. Many wholesalers cater only to libraries. They provide a valuable service by combining orders and saving the librarian from thousands of single title orders.

There are a lot of people in the book business who have visualized the big buck and have gone into whole-saling. While the gross may be big, the net is small and it takes a very large and highly efficient operation to be profitable. A number of distributors have folded.

With wholesalers, the important mission is to get into their system with a large stocking order. This does not mean you should oversell them. They will return what they can't move so it is always safer to go low. This approach also maintains your credibility with the buyer who is more likely to take your suggestion for an initial stocking order next time.

Selling to wholesalers is most effective with a personal visit but you can often make a sale by mail. With a single book, your first, it won't pay to fly across the continent but some wholesalers may be close by and you might be able to get to others while on a business trip or vacation. The best months are January and July in anticipation of the peak selling seasons.

You will find these contacts very educational; these visits shouldn't be left to sales reps. Make an appoint-ment so your trip isn't made only to find the buyer on vacation. Be prepared. Take copies of your book, in both softcover and hard if available, your dealer price list, copies of your reviews, your return policy, photographs of the book, everything. Prepare a summary of recent purchases and returns if they have ordered from you already. A lot of small orders may indicate a demand requiring a larger single order. Remember that the buyer is not there to help you and won't be judging your book on its literary merits. He or she is thinking about whether the buying public will care; will it move and if so, how many.

A good reorder rule of thumb is to take half the quantity the distributor has sold during the last three months. If you make the suggestion, it will ease the decision making. Don't shoot too high or the buyer will have to lower the number. If the buyer can get a discount break by adding a few more books to the order, mention it. Don't forget to offer any catalog or display materials you may have such as photographs, posters or dumps (shipping cartons that become display stands.)

Familiarize the wholesaler with your terms and return policy and have an order blank ready with his name and address already filled in to save time. Get a purchase order number and always leave a carbon of the order.

Make up a "call report" just as you would demand one from a salesrep working for you. It is a good working habit and, filed away until you next have to contact that buyer, will provide revealing information which has slipped your mind.

Then follow through by mailing your brochure, etc. to the buyer with a note. Follow up later with a telephone call to ask if they are ready to reorder. Look up the buyer at book shows, establish a person-to-person contact. Whenever you receive major television or print coverage, send the information to the buyer. Let them know if you are going on a major talk show. Let them prepare for the demand. Some publishers make monthly mailings to their distributors.

If the distributor has purchased from you before, check their stock. They may even let you into the warehouse. Some wholesalers have very poor inventory feedback systems and aren't even aware that they are out of your book until you mention it. You will build a lot of good will by suggesting they return stock that isn't moving.

Wholesalers don't often return books since when one is returned by one bookstore, it simply gets recycled off to another one. Your book may fail in one store because of its unusual clientele or because the book was "lost" under counter and not displayed.

Many distributors operate on consignment inventory and pay ninety days after they sell the books to the bookstore. This means they have very little invested in their operation. While publishers should avoid selling to small accounts on consignment, there are good arguments for these terms with distributors. Book manufacture requires large print runs so the inventory might just as well sit in a few other warehouses as your own. Remember, however, title to the books is still yours. If the books are lost or damaged, if the wholesaler does not have insurance, the loss could be yours.

Most of your volume will be through a half dozen wholesale accounts if you have a general interest book. These distributors move quantity; that's maximum books for minimum processing paperwork. Accordingly, they are very important to you. In fact, if your dealer price list requires a large number of books for a discount, it will force more stores to order from wholesalers which may simplify your business. Remember that wholesalers only fill orders, they don't create demand. Even if you don't contact them, they will order from you sooner or later. Then you will know that your promotional efforts have encouraged one of their clients to order. But single copies are not enough, you must get into their system. Once they place a number of small orders, bring this to their attention and suggest a larger stocking order.

Wholesalers are often reluctant to open accounts with a publisher with only one book. Therefore, you must be persistent. You must convince them this is the first book of many and that this book will move.

The two big stocking wholesalers are Baker & Taylor and Ingram. Smaller stocking wholesalers are Bookpeople, Publishers Group West, Inland, the distributors and Pacific Pipeline. The many other library wholesalers rarely stock books. Coutts, Blackwell, Bro Dart, Ballen, EBS, Midwest, Key, and Scholarly only respond to orders from libraries. You can find these wholesalers listed along with others in the Appendix and in Literary Market Place. The American Book Trade Directory also has a list and even provides contact names. Here are brief profiles of some of the wholesalers.

INGRAM BOOK CO. Ingram is headquartered in Nashville, Tennessee, with regional warehouses in City of Industry, California, and Jessup, Maryland. Ingram stocks fewer titles (some 70,000) than Baker & Taylor but stocks the books in greater depth. Ingram does not promote books, they make them available. They are business oriented: they want to know about your promotion. You must convince them there will be demand for your books. Be prepared to answer their questions about what you plan to do to make your book sell. Their decision to buy or not to buy your book will be based on your promotional plans as much as the quality of the book itself. Most of the buying is controlled from Nashville. There are several buyers, each responsible for a particular area. Try to get to the computer books buyer, the trade nonfiction buyer, etc. as applicable or you may wind up with the small press buyer. Ingram wants a 50% discount and pays the freight though some new publishers have been unable to negotiate a deal better than 55%, FOB destination.

Ingram mails its microfiche listings to over 8,000 bookstores each week. Getting on the fiche is a respected accomplishment but staying on it through backorders is more difficult and a more accurate measure of your book's success. Ingram also publishes Advance magazine and Paperback Advance.

Ingram runs special promotions. For a price, your book can be featured in a circular mailed with the monthly statements or microfiche mailings (cost was about $900. in 1984) or it can be mentioned by the order operators.

BAKER & TAYLOR is headquartered in Somerville, New Jersey, with nearly autonomous branches in Reno, Nevada, Momence, Illinois, and Commerce, Georgia. While the company is education oriented and much of their effort is directed toward finding books for libraries, the bookstore market is serviced with a microfiche system. Baker & Taylor is a mirror of library demand. If you receive a good review in Library Journal, some 75% of your library orders will come through B&T.

Baker & Taylor stocks more than 110,000 different titles. They will require a 50% discount (they pay the freight) to put your books into their system as a "stock publisher." Agreements vary; some publishers give B&T 55%, FOB destination. If you do not choose to be in the system, you may allow Baker & Taylor any discount you wish. Since they are usually waiting for your book to complete a large order, they won't quibble over the discount and will even pay a pro forma invoice (in advance.) Being a stock publisher with a listing on the microfiche makes your books available to many more buyers; this is easily worth the 50%.

Write Baker & Taylor (Publisher Contact Section, 6 Kirby Avenue, Somerville, NJ 08876) and ask for a copy of Information Outline For Publishers. This multi-page document explains all of the Baker & Taylor programs. Fill out and return their "vendor profile questionnaire" and their "new book information" form. Work with the Publisher Contact Section in Somerville but also contact the facilities in Commerce, Momence and Reno for a stocking order.

PUBLISHERS GROUP WEST accepts your books on consignment, FOB destination (You pay the shipping) takes a 55% discount and pays you ninety days after they ship to the stores. Sales reports are sent to publishers each month. Located in Emeryville, California, they have several reps and cover the west very well. They are very selective, run a tight ship and pay on time. The only thing wrong with Publishers Group West is that there is no Publishers Group East!

PGW will represent your book to Walden and Dalton. They make semi-annual treks east to pitch books to both major chains. Selling the chains can be a major coup but the last thing you want is direct sales. Shipping three to five books to each store in the chain could take weeks of typing, licking and sticking. It is well-worth 15% to ship the books by carton to PGW. Let them slip your books in with those from other publishers when they ship the chains.

Write to PGW (5855 Beaudry Street, Emeryville, CA 94608) for their "book information sheet." Fill it out and return it with a review copy.

BOOKPEOPLE started with the small press in 1968 and is known throughout the industry for small press titles.

They carry some 8,000 titles from more than 800 publishers to service over 4000 bookstores, health food outlets and women's stores around the world. 50% of their customers are on the west coast, 35% in the east and 15% outside the U.S. Bookpeople has a microfiche system, publishes a catalog and issues a monthly listing of new titles named Bookpaper.

Bookpeople accepts books on consignment, FOB Berkeley, takes a 52% discount and pays ninety days after the books are shipped. Sales reports are sent to publishers each month.

Send a news release or brochure on your book to Bookpeople and follow up with a review copy.

OTHER DISTRIBUTORS such as Inland, the distributors, New Leaf and Pacific Pipeline operate much like Bookpeople. Find their addresses in the appendix and write for details.

CHAIN BOOKSTORES. Chains are run by marketing people, not the booklovers who operate the independent shops. Chains concentrate on the fastest moving books rather than the specialized. Waldenbooks, B. Dalton, Barnes & Noble and Crown together do about 20% of the $4-billion retail book trade; Walden (over 800 stores in 1983) and Dalton (almost 700 stores in 1983) alone account for 16%. B. Dalton, and discounter Pickwick are owned by Dayton-Hudson Corporation while Walden is part of Carter Hawley Hales stores. Crown is a discounter (125 stores in 1983) owned by Dart Drug and Thrifty. Walden, Dalton and Crown are growing rapidly. There are some sixty other smaller chains.

According to Publishers Weekly, Dalton is the largest hardcover retailer in the U.S. and they have the lowest unsold book return rate in the industry. Their operations are computerized so they know what is selling and can plan reorders. They purchase by category, matching books to the store's clientele.

Many of the chain stores have their cash registers tied into the central computer to monitor sales. Often the computer will throw a large number of books out to a store as a test only to be sent back if unsold after a period of time. This instant access to sales information enables the headquarters to stay on top of fast-breaking books. They can reorder sooner to maintain inventory levels.

An order from a chain means a lot of books going out the door. If the books sell quickly, the title will be listed on that chain's bestseller list. This publicity will encourage other retailers to stock the book.

Most chains learn of new titles from personal sales visits to their headquarters and many publishers feel this is by far the best way to close a sale. But they also respond to direct mail promotion, reviews and space advertising in Publishers Weekly. Walden and Dalton buy books by subject area. That is, their buyers specialize by field: cooking, photography, computers, hardcover fiction, etc. Make sure you contact the right one or let a wholesaler such as the distributors or Publishers Group West do the pitching. Most chains would rather buy from a few wholesalers than from many individual publishers.

Establish and maintain key contacts at the chain headquarters but don't overlook sales visits to their individual stores. Most local outlets are authorized to make small purchases and they are especially receptive to regional books.

Most chains expect a 40% discount, FOB origin and many pay in 60-90 days. A listing of chains can be found at your library in the American Book Trade Directory.

BOOKSTORES, individual but not necessarily independent, are a diverse group of retailers. They include the downtown bookstore, the college store, the local member of a chain, the religious bookstore and others. Over 9,000 in number, they come in all sizes: some sell books exclusively while others carry books as a sideline, some stores are general and some specialized, and some are attached to museums or libraries. With the introduction of new marketing techniques, the stores are proliferating but their quality is dropping as some confine their selections only to the fast moving titles. They do not stock in depth.

> "If selling books to bookstores was good business, the stores might be paying their bills."

The patron profile of the bookstore consists of the regularly purchasing book addict and the occasional buyer. Then there are those who never come in. 50% of the customers in a bookstore are looking for a particular book. These particular book seekers are more likely to be younger and female. 47% are looking for a nonfiction title, 27% for a particular book of fiction and 28% want textbooks. While 20% do not find the book they are looking for, 54% buy one or more books before they leave.

Modern booksellers are faced with trying to attract and sell to all these people. To do so, they have to locate in high rent, heavy-traffic areas and they carry too many titles. Stores report an inventory turnover of 2 to 5 times a year with the average about 3.3 times. If a book hasn't moved in six months on the shelf, it is usually returned. The new author/publisher is trapped between the Scylla of wide exposure and the Charybdis of massive returns.

Many small publishers tolerate but don't pursue small individual bookstores. The major problems with stores are that they order just a few books at a time, complain about the 40% discount, seldom pay in 30 days and often return the books for a refund--damaged. If you hire a sales rep group to show your books to stores, you will process a lot of paperwork for many small orders and make very few sales. The best approach is to let the wholesalers handle the stores. Once they make your book available, you may spend your energy creating a demand. Remember, bookstores only make your book available for sale; you still have to do the promoting.

Publishers reach the bookstore market through personal sales visits, direct mail and space ads, particularly in Publishers Weekly. But a lot of orders are generated by customer requests from those influenced by an ad, a television appearance or other promotion.

Large publishers with many titles send their sales representatives to call on bookstores. With one or two titles, it is hardly worth your time. But, these sales calls can be a good learning experience. The big publishing reps carry only the (lighter weight) dust jackets of new books to show the buyer. You have an advantage by

---

"Bookstores are a lousey place to sell books."

carrying in the actual book. You can also offer to drop off the books and save them the postage. The best time to visit a store is between 3:30 and 4:30 in the afternoon when there are the fewest customers. Always call for an appointment, buyers usually do not have time for drop-ins. Ask to speak with the store manager or paperback buyer.

Bookstores rely on sales reps for recommendations so the buyer should be receptive. He or she may ask about your promotion plans. Tell them you are a local author and, therefore, local people will be interested in your book. Mention any local publicity such as talk shows which are planned. Stores want to know if the book will be promoted. Reviews and author appearances are more important than advertising. If the book is professionally produced, a sale should not be difficult. Be ready with the stock phrase: "I can offer you the books at a full 40% discount, without delivery charges and they are fully returnable, of course." The whole pitch will probably run five to ten minutes.

If you still can't persuade the buyer, you might like to try "consignment." Here the store pays for the books only after they are sold, that is, when they need more of them. With consignment, the discount should be dropped to 25-35%. Keep the initial order small. It won't help to overload the store only to get the shelf-worn books back in a few months. It is better to keep the inventory turning over.

You might like to try offering posters, displays and racks but most stores won't have room for them. Experiment with your local store.

You might try sending a free sample copy to a few more distant stores. It will get their attention and is cheaper than a visit. Be sure to stamp the book "Review copy, not for resale" so you don't get it back as a return.

College, school and textbook stores also respond best to face-to-face sales calls. There are some 2,800 college stores serving 2,200 U.S. colleges and universities

> *"Booksellers as a group have not been aggressive enough. There are too many individuals just selling books and constantly crying to publishers, 'Give us a better discount'"*
> — David Cioffi, Dartmouth Bookstore.

with over 11-million students. These stores are on their own schedule depending upon whether they are on the semester, quarter or early semester system. Don't put too much energy into college stores. Students don't spend money on much more than assigned texts, stereos and beer. About one-third of school store orders are through wholesalers, so they may be a better way to reach this market.

If you like personal contact, load up the car and visit the stores. If you would rather stay home, you can hit more bookstores via direct mail advertising. A list of stores can be found in your library in the American Book Trade Directory. Once you have established an account, you can use the telephone for a certain amount of restocking but you can't beat a personal visit for keeping your book on the shelf.

During your visit, help the store to put your book on the proper shelves. If your book is poetry or fiction, place some copies in those areas and more in the subject matter area. For example, if your poetry is about the outdoors, place a few copies with the outdoor books.

LIBRARIES come in several types: public, private, special, school, government, etc. There are almost 15,000 public libraries, 3,000 more can be found in colleges, 15,000 are special, there are around 20,000 in high schools and 50,000 in elementary schools. Libraries spend around $450-million a year for books, buying some 14% of those published. Many of their purchases are for books with press runs under 5,000 which would not get published without their support.

Even though orders are for smaller quantities, libraries offer greater potential to the small publisher than bookstores. The size of the market is hard to verify, however. Some 76% of the libraries that respond to your mailings will order from a wholesaler and 75% of those orders go to Baker & Taylor. Rather than place thousands of orders with individual publishers for single titles, libraries save time by sending all orders to a wholesaler.

> *"Librarians view the publisher as being the money grubber between the author and the reader."*

They are extended a 20-33% discount so they are receiving both price and service. Their problem is money. The cost of ordering and processing a new title can cost as much as the book itself. In many libraries, personnel expenses make up half the budget. Many libraries are spreading their already tight budgets even thinner now by adding audio-visual and other non-print items.

If libraries bought one copy of every book published in the United States, they would need a budget of over $2-million per year. Yet less than 1,000 libraries have an annual book budget of $25,000 or more and most have much less. They have to be selective in their purchases. Many libraries buy more for topic than quality. They have to justify their budgets to the community (if public) and try to get something for everyone. Whether the book is good, covering the topic adequately, is less important. It is said that better judgment is shown in the purchasing of childrens' books and fiction. One librarian recently explained: "When material is scarce on a topic and interest is high, we will often buy any reasonably priced new book through an ad in Library Journal or even a flyer. However, we usually don't buy if it receives a bad review."

> Some publishers will not sell to libraries on the theory that one sale will kill several others when many people read the book free. Other publishers find the libraries are show-casing their book--and are paying to do it. At least four orders for The Self-Publishing Manual are received each week with a letter starting "The library will not let me check the book out again so I guess I'll have to buy my own copy." Libraries may hurt sales of fiction but not reference books.

Many wholesalers serve their library accounts automatically by sending blocks of books "on approval" allowing the library to reject the unwanted titles. Because the wholesaler has "pre-screened" the books and matched them to special collections, few are returned. Obviously, it is to your great advantage to have your book included in these computer matched offerings, especially the Baker & Taylor system.

Libraries tend to do most of their ordering around the beginning/ends of their fiscal year (usually December 31 or June 30) when they try to use up their old budget or break into a new one. This is when they show less buying discrimination. Your book might be selected at this time even if it is an afterthought, not a first choice. At the three-quarter point in their fiscal year libraries are usually out of funds. School libraries usually use the slow summer months to work on ordering.

Some libraries have acquisition librarians while in others title selection is done by committee. Because more than one person is often involved in acquisitions in the larger libraries, it is wise to send more than one copy of each piece of literature. It helps if you build consumer demand as most libraries respond when a title is requested. School libraries are responsive to the wishes of their faculties. As could be expected, childrens' books and fiction aren't of any great interest to college libraries.

Do not send your promotional material to the "head" or "acquisition" librarian. In large libraries, it is best to direct mailings to the subject area supervisor who makes the actual buying decisions. These supervisors are in charge of areas such as: "childrens' books," "adult fiction," "reference," etc. For names, consult Bowker's American Library Directory.

Many communities have both city and county libraries; hit them all. Large library systems will need copies of your book for every branch and these multiple orders are very nice.

Books wear out, they can be loaned out only so many times. The life span of most books is 1½-2 years. Unless a worn out title has seen a lot of recent use, it usually doesn't get reordered. On the other hand, if it has been very popular, the library may order several copies. Books are also stolen—some 20% of the collection per year. So many books are kept past the due date that librarians do not have time to look up their price. Many libraries have a flat fee, say $10, for any overdue book.

In 1979, when The Self-Publishing Manual was first presented to a librarian in Santa Barbara, she said "We will have to order several of these. This is the

219

type of book our patrons keep." During the next four years, the library went through some fifteen copies and this is despite the fact the book is available in several bookstores, instant print shops and office supply stores around town.

Book reviews are very important in library selection decisions. Librarians just do not have the time to read and evaluate the some 100 new titles available each day. Librarians rely mostly on Publishers Weekly, Library Journal, ALA Booklist, Kirkus Reviews, Choice and The New York Times Book Review. A good review of a nonfiction book in LJ will move about 1,200 books. 94% of the librarians rely on reviews in Library Journal while 91% read the reviews in ALA Booklist. Only 44% believe the ads in LJ and 35% use the ads in Booklist. The figures for Publishers Weekly are 75% and 53%. Your brochure is also very effective in selling libraries even if it isn't as objective as a review.

While only 24% of the public libraries and 55% of the school libraries deal directly with publishers, they will buy from you if your offer looks good. One of the most effective means of promotion is to send them quotes from reviews.

Library mailing lists may be rented from the R.R. Bowker Mailing List Department and The Educational Directory (see the Appendix). The lists can be broken down according to book budget, etc., so you can reach just the libraries that can afford your book. Look for special libraries or those with special collections. If yours is an aviation book, send brochures to libraries with aviation collections. After drafting your brochure, show it to a local librarian for a critique.

While librarians don't throw out as much mail as bookstores, most will only buy one book. It is hard to justify a mailing when more often than not, the library will order it through a wholesaler to whom you give 40-50%.

When you receive an order direct from a library, add the name to your list and include the contact name. Send periodic mailings. Librarians react like any other clients to your direct mail advertising.

To reach libraries, the best magazines for space advertising are Library Journal and ALA Booklist and the best places to exhibit are at the annual American Library Association Book Fair and the state library association conventions.

Your local library should buy your book just because of the proximity of the author. Some even have a special private room for books by indigenous writers. If so, it may be appropriate for you to donate a copy to this reference section. If you do make such a donation, be sure the local paper is notified with a news release so you can get some mileage out of your largesse.

Some publishers say price is not a major consideration because the librarian is not spending his or her own money. The librarians say they buy to cover a subject; they will buy a high priced book if it meets the need and is the only one available. Libraries do not expect a discount (in fact, many magazines charge them more on the theory that more people will read the periodical) unless they order several copies. Some publishers follow a universal discount schedule giving 10% for an order of five, 20% for 20, etc.

The best way to handle the library market is to become a stock publisher with Baker & Taylor, to let all the library wholesalers know where to find you by sending them a brochure, prepare a great review package for Library Journal and strike a deal with Quality books.

QUALITY BOOKS uses sales reps to sell books to special libraries. In the business over 20 years, they have some 6,000 active accounts. Quality offers a choice of plans: 55% off, consignment, returnable and 90 days or 60% off, no returns and 30 days. 60% may sound like a lot but Quality buys by the carton, doesn't interfere with other sales and pays on time. They are very selective, they do not accept every book sent. Write to Quality (Tom Drewes, 400 Anthony Trail, Northbrook, IL 60062) for a "New Book Consideration" form.

Quality Books moves a lot of copies of Parachuting, The Skydiver's Handbook. The rate of sale was unexpected because the book is aimed at a small target audience. Quality was handling a number of

221

the authors other books and elected to try the handbook soon after Tom Drewes took up skydiving in 1983.

The Quality Books Selection Committee looks for the following when evaluating a book:

1. Good title and subtitle. Must be informative, not cute.
2. Index. Librarians like to fill information gaps.
3. Cataloging in Publication data to help in cataloging the book.
4. ISBN to aid identification of the book.
5. Binding. 34% of the books purchased by libraries today are softcover. The less expensive edition allows librarians to order more books from the same budget. Must have a spine to display the title. Must be shaped to fit a library shelf, not long, low or round.
6. A topical subject.
7. Sales aids. The publisher should supply extra covers for the reps to show the libraries.

THE SCHOOL MARKET spends over a billion dollars each year for text books and while most of these books are developed especially for certain courses, many are regular books developed for other markets but adapted as supplementary educational aids. While educators want the very latest information, they are leery of being experimental. Teachers need to be assured that the book is up-to-date and as been accepted by experts elsewhere. Educators are the most price-conscious of all the book markets even though they aren't spending their own money. Under pressure from the schools to keep the price of texts down, publishers can only extend a 20% ("short") discount to school book stores and this is what is expected.

ELEMENTARY AND SECONDARY SCHOOLS. In the U.S. there are some 64,000 public elementary, 24,000 public high and 1,800 combined schools in 18,000 school districts. Additionally, there are some 14,000 private elementary and 4,000 private high schools. Together they employ 2.3-million teachers.

222

In 22 states, schools purchase texts under a state adoption system where titles are approved by a board for a five-year period. State adoption is a hunting license and allows the salespeople to try and sell the book to the schools. Even where there is no state adoption system, planning seems to follow a five-year cycle. In some areas, publishers have to ship to central depositories where the schools draw on books as needed. This usually means a consignment inventory and the books aren't paid for until requisitioned by the schools. The school market is tough and very competitive.

In recent years, publishers have had to use larger type in their school texts—not for the students but for the teachers. The median age for teachers in the United States is 40 years, 49 in California.

COLLEGES AND UNIVERSITIES. Colleges are changing. There are more students over 25; more women are going back to school; and more people are turning to continuing education courses in their specialty.

Publishers concentrate on wooing the instructors who must select books for their courses in more than 3,000 schools. This decision is easy for some professors as they pen their own. Normally the purchasing is done by the local bookstore and the instructor notifies them as to his or her choice by April for the fall term. Of course, there are problems. The choice is made late and the estimate of the number to be needed is frequently off. Then some students avoid buying the text by sharing or making repeated visits to the school library. The result is a return rate on textbooks of more than 20%.

There are three types of college bookstores. Some are owned by the institution, some are private and some are college stores with a private lessee. Those connected with the institution may take advantage of "library rate" postage schedules.

Teachers expect to get free examination copies of books and while some treat this privilege with respect, others just collect books or sell them to the bookstore. The bookstore, in turn, sells the book to a student or returns it to the publisher for a refund. The bookstores even supply the educators with blank "Desk Copy Request Forms" designed to be sent to the publisher. Often the younger instructors are trying to build up their libraries. The older professors who have more say in book selection do much less collecting. Some publishers like to request more information about the size of the course, the requester's academic position, etc. Sol Marshall of Creative Books answers desk copy requests with a form letter offering the book at a greatly reduced price. This way he at least covers his costs.

During the last five years, this publisher has sent out several dozen requested "desk copies" and so far no more than one has resulted in a large bookstore order.

To attack the college market, analyze your book's subject and determine what course might find it useful. The educators are easy to find and direct mail advertising is the most effective method of reaching them. In fact, some publishers find the lists so specialized that they use them to send free examination copies unsolicited.

Mailing list information can be found in your library. See the Standard Rate and Data Service's directories, An Advertiser's Guide to Scholarly Periodicals and Direct Marketing magazine. Also check the Yellow Pages for local list brokers.

Another way to reach the educational market is through book exhibits at book fairs and conventions. With only a title or two, you may like to share a booth with someone else or turn your book over to a firm which will represent you for a small fee. These exhibit services are listed in the Appendix and Literary Market Place. See the paragraph on book fairs.

College buying patterns are affected by school schedules depending on whether they are on the semester, quarter or early semester system. The best months to make mailings to colleges are February, April, July and October. Once you make contact with an instructor, add him or her to your mailing list, they are valuable. Once a professor has adopted one of your books, some say he or she is twice as likely to do it again.

PRE-PUBLICATION SALES will bring in some money early and help you pay the printing bill. But it isn't wise to start too soon on the pre-publication publicity for your first book. The first time around is a learning experience and there will be countless delays. You do not want to find yourself spending all your time answering the questions: "where is the book?" With the first book, wait until it is on the press. The next time, adjust and start earlier.

Write up a press release, send in your ads and make a mailing. Offer an early wholesale deal ("to be shipped direct from the printer") to associations and specialty dealers. It is nice to have a pile of orders on the desk when the book comes off the press. But timing is important; these orders must not pour in too early or too late.

If your book is specialized and you are able to find an appropriate mailing list, you should consider a pre-publication retail offer. Tell them the book is being printed and if they want one hot off the press, to send their money now, that you will be shipping on a first come, first served basis. Include an early order deal such as "postage free if you order from this ad." This mailing should be sent to all your friends and acquaintances; many will respond and be pleased that you thought of them. If a prospect is mentioned in the text or the acknowledgments, he is sure to buy one.

SPECIALTY (NON-BOOK) OUTLETS offer many non-fiction publishers with their largest market. For example, a book on mountain climbing may sell better in back-packing shops than bookstores and the size of the store's purchases will be larger. Many potential book buyers do not realize they need a book and do not frequent book-stores. They visit a backpacking or SCUBA shop for information on the sport. Once inside they discover that a book will fulfill their mission and they make an "impulse purchase." Once you have written a book on a specialized activity, you should know the field well enough that such outlets will immediately come to mind. Finding non-traditional book outlets only takes some imagination.

> *The smallest houses were relatively more successful in using non-book retail outlets than the largest houses were."*
> — Judith Appelbaum in *Publishers Weekly*

These non-book outlets usually feel 40% is a good discount, buy in large quantities, pay promptly and haven't heard of returns. Consequently, many publishers aim for these outlets and service the book trade only secondarily.

The author's parachute books are sold to parachute lofts, skydiving clubs, parachute equipment catalog houses and to the United States Parachute Association for resale to their members. He sold to this non-book trade for more than five years before visiting a bookfair and finding out he was a publisher.

In these specialty shops it is very important to establish, cultivate and maintain a close personal relationship with the management. It is of the utmost importance that they like you and your book so they will promote it at every opportunity. Selling them the first time often requires a personal visit to demonstrate the sales potential of the book. When making a direct mail promotion to these firms, remember their peak selling seasons and the required lead time.

One of the very few good book marketers is Bruce Lansky of Meadowbrook Press. He is good because he markets books the way he used to market candy. His (then) wife Vicki wrote a book on nutrition for babies called Feed Me, I'm Yours and the Lanskys decided to publish it themselves. First Bruce tried a local children's clothing store. They bought so he approached a wholesaler of infant items but was turned down flat. He had to offer consignment and counter racks to let the wholesaler prove to himself the books would move. The wholesaler called three days later and ordered 12 dozen more--they were in business. Next Lansky created a mailing stuffer for the wholesaler to put in with the statements sent to his 1,000 accounts. Sales soared. Lansky's secrets are:

1.   Play dumb. Visit the account and learn all about terms, key accounts and trade reps in that field.
2.   Don't act like a publisher, act like you are in the same business. Bruce was in "infant accessories" that day.

3. Use success to breed more success. Do your re-
    search, run small tests and learn the industry.
    Subscribe to their magazines, join their associations,
    exhibit at their trade shows. Make a mailing to
    distributors and retailers and follow up with calls.

Other non-book retail channels include gift shops,
hardware stores, garden shops, sporting goods stores, etc.
Many are establishing book corners to lend prestige to
their line. Some good sales possibilities are not immediately obvious.

A few years ago, the author was in a local instant
print shop when the owner began asking about The
Self-Publishing Manual. 40% off sounded good and
the printer wanted to put some books on the
counter. The author doubted the books would sell
but brought in eight copies to humor the printer.
Three days later, the printer called for more. Apparently, the type of people who frequent copy
shops are the type who work with the written word--
a good market after all. This lesson resulted in
expansion into other instant print shops and to a
book on how-to paste up.

Run a test in a few local shops. Develop your
approach (posters, dumps, price, etc.) before rolling out in
a wider promotion. Just as there are wholesalers servic-
ing the bookstores, there are those who cater to the non-
book outlets. Check these stores and look for books. Find
out who distributes them to the store. If books are not
being carried, ask for names of hot rep groups who handle
other lines of products.
If you receive an inquiry from a market you never
thought would be interested in your book, draft a letter to
similar groups saying "this group ordered the book and we
thought you might be interested too." The mailing may be
just 100 pieces--no great investment--and there is a good
chance of a payoff. If the Appendix of the book has a
source directory, make a mailing to each firm saying "you
are mentioned in the book; thought you would like to
know; and we think you might like to offer this book to
your customers." Though fiction is harder to move in

these non-book outlets, sometimes you can find a good tie-in. It is fun to move book that ordinarily has a short shelf life.

SELLING TO THE U.S. GOVERNMENT. There are 2,300 libraries in the federal government library system and 80 agencies which purchase books according to Publishers Weekly. Most of the libraries come under the Defense Department and have funding problems. Some of the Army's libraries must be approached through central offices while others deal direct. The Office of the Director of the Army Library Program procures hardbound books for Army libraries around the world and paperbacks for distribution in the field. Of the about 60 clothbound titles chosen monthly, some 60% are nonfiction. About 100 paperbound titles are procured each month and distributed in 900 kits; selections are highly recreational. Centralized purchases are made under annual contracts with wholesalers. Navy libraries spend over $3-million each year. The International Communications Agency, formerly the U.S. Information Agency, runs 129 libraries in 110 countries with 6,000 to 25,000 volumes each and devotes about $2-million each year to procurement. They like to see brochures and review copies. The Veterans Administration operates 392 libraries with a budget of more than $2-million. See the listings in the Appendix.

The U.S. Government Purchasing and Sales Directory ($4) and Selling to the Government ($1.80) are two publications you will want. They may be purchased at Government bookstores in the major cities or from the Superintendent of Documents, U.S. Government Printing Office, Washington, DC 20402.

Another source of orders is from special groups within the government or military services. For example, a manual on parachute rigging would be of interest to parachute riggers both civilian and military. A mailing to all military parachute lofts might generate some private sales and/or the brochure might be passed on to the procurement office so that a book could be ordered for the library or the loft.

SUBSIDIARY RIGHTS may produce fame and fortune far beyond the regular sales of your book. Essentially, subsidiary rights give someone else permission to reproduce (repackage) your material. Subsidiary rights include book clubs, mass market paperback, film rights, translations, premiums, etc. and they are so important to the big publishers that the rights are often auctioned off before the original book is printed. See <u>Literary</u> <u>Market</u> <u>Place</u> for subsidiary rights possibilities.

Some subsidiary rights require only a continuation of the same printing (quality paper back, premiums, etc.) but don't let your customer get away with just paying for the additional press time. They should pay for all of your setup and overhead costs. If you aren't very familiar with negotiating rights, get an attorney who understands the publishing business or a literary agent. The agent will get 10% of whatever he brings in while the lawyer will work for a percentage or a straight fee for checking the contract. Agents are listed in <u>Literary</u> <u>Market</u> <u>Place</u>.

Most people feel that selling subsidiary rights helps to sell the original version of the book by generating additional publicity for it. Such a sale is also a great morale booster for both the author and the publisher not only for the money but because someone else obviously likes the book. Write to likely prospects well in advance of publication and ask if they would like to see photocopies of the manuscript. Then follow with a telephone call. Mail out a lot of inquiries simultaneously, don't go at them one at a time. There isn't enough time for this luxury.

SELLING OUT. Those self-publishers who do sell their book to the big publishers usually sell too cheap. Editors from major houses make the rounds of the booths at bookfairs such as the American Booksellers Association Book Fair in the spring. These acquisition editors are hunting for good books to add to their lines. Small publishers are usually thrilled to be courted by a big house and often make the mistake of selling for the same 10%

> *"A publisher's attitude toward a manuscript ought to be similar to a coal mine operator's attitude toward coal: get every last bit of value out of it."* — Sol Stein, President of Stein and Day.

royalty an author gets for a manuscript. Ten percent of the cover price is small reward after expending so much time and money to package and promote a book as well as to test the market. The big publisher is exploiting the little publisher at 10% because all the risk has been removed. Successful books should cost more. The large publisher must understand the book is coming from another publisher; this is not just a manuscript from an author. A fee should be paid to the small publisher for packaging and market exploration as well as a royalty to the author.

When a large publisher buys a book from a small publisher, the price should be for two-times or three-times the production costs plus 10% of projected sales. They should pay for all your time, work and financial risk. The deal should be made "royalty inclusive" which means receiving your money up front—not waiting until months after the books are sold.

Sell only the North American Rights to the book trade. Retain all rights except to sell the bookstores and libraries in the U.S. and Canada. Always keep the non-exclusive mail order rights. The big publisher will not be interested in individual sales anyway. Make sure you can buy books for the printing cost plus ten percent. Normally you will be required to buy in lots of 1,000 or more but this is a great deal for you. Make sure all rights revert back to you once the publisher lets the book go out of print. In evaluating a contract, consider the royalty, advance, when you will get paid, who gets what part of other subsidiary rights, the duration of the contract and free copies to the author.

Small publishers and self-publishers would be better off to cut a distribution deal than a co-publishing deal. In a distribution arrangement, the big publisher would buy several thousand books for 60%-70% off list price on a non-returnable basis with payment in 30 days and would have an exclusive in the book trade: bookstores and libraries. Insist on a large quantity so the large publisher is in deep and has to promote the books. With the

> *"Without subsidiary rights, publishers would operate in the hole"* — John Dessauer.

booktrade covered, the author/publisher is now free to concentrate on the retail mail order sales and the non-book markets. But be forewarned, if you do sell out, you will probably make less money while losing control of your book.

"PAPERBACK RIGHTS" usually refer to the production of a "quality paperback" (softcover) edition after the hardcover has been in the stores for several months. It isn't likely you published in hardcover only but if you did, you will want to explore the softcover market. Since the distribution for hardcover and softcover books is the same, it will be easy for you to publish in softcover and plug it into the system.

If you want someone else to handle the paperback edition, they may want a 7-year contract with a right to renew. Royalties range from 7% to 9% with the lower amount until sales reach 12,000 and the higher amount after that (as mentioned above in "Selling Out," these figures should be higher.) Advances against royalties may be a few to several thousand dollars with half paid on signing the contract and the balance due on publication. It is always wise to get as large an advance as possible as this investment is good insurance against the reprint publisher's losing interest and never going to press. When evaluating an offer, compare the number they plan to print (5-15,000) and the list (cover) price they intend for the book in addition to the royalty and advance; all these figures greatly affect your income.

MASS MARKET RIGHTS are for those pocket-sized books selling from $1-4.50 in the supermarkets. They are different from the quality paperback primarily because of the distribution system. Since they are treated like magazines, it would be very difficult to break into this market by yourself. Unless you have a very popular book, the mass market firms won't be interested.

> *"The bottom line makes it abundantly clear; subsidiary rights have become less and less subsidiary."* — Nancy Evans

Mass market rights are one market where it is easier to sell fiction than nonfiction. They like 7-year contracts with renewal options and initial print runs of 30,000 to 50,000 copies. Mass market publishers offer 4% to 7½% in royalties but the cover price is low and the scale does not slide up until sales reach 150,000 copies. Advances are usually just a few thousand dollars.

SERIALIZATIONS and excerpts by magazines and newspapers may be "first serializations" if before publication or "second serialization" if afterward. Both generate a lot of good publicity. Big publications pay more and the first rights are more valuable than second. The subject matter has to be of great interest to the publication's readers. Serializations help generate sales for the original book. Always request the periodical to print ordering information for your book. Such a notice will generate a lot of individual mail order sales. See the discussion in Writer's Market.

BOOK CONDENSATIONS in magazines do not normally pay a lot but the publicity they provide will sell more books. Condensations lend further credibility to your self-published work since someone else has "approved" of the material by purchasing it. Make sure the magazine is a quality product, one you will be proud to be associated with. Check their past condensation work and call the publishers of the subject books. Ask if they are happy with the way they were treated, with the quality of the condensation and compare the price they were paid with the one you have been offered. The name and number of the person in charge of subsidiary rights at each publishing house can be found in section one of Literary Market Place.

The magazine normally farms out the rewrite and the work should be a condensation, not a reprint of the two meaty chapters. You can expect them to offer a couple of hundred dollars up to several thousand depending upon the publication. Sell on a non-exclusive basis; they will be first in print but you want to retain the right to sell again to other publications. Always obtain "text approval". They could completely miss your point in making the condensation. Read the draft over carefully and make corrections; your name is on the piece and the condensation will be a major sales tool for your book. You want it to be right. Make sure the condensation includes information where the original book may be purchased complete with price and address.

COLLECTIONS, particularly for school use, pay small amounts for parts of books.

CO-PUBLISHING is a way for two firms to spread the risk and reward in a new book. Usually one publisher is large and the other small or the two concentrate on different ends of the business such as editorial and distribution.

EXCHANGE TITLE PROMOTION. Mail order customers interested in a certain subject tend to purchase every book which covers the area. Unfortunately many small publishers do not have titles in any depth on any particular topic. When two or more publishers of like material handle each other's books, their customers get a wider range of choices and the publishers get an improved response rate to their advertising. This cross-distribution, formerly common only in other sales channels, is now becoming more familiar in mail order book marketing.

Approach publishers with books that compliment yours. Buy the books wholesale and add them to your brochure. If you do not wish to take on products from other publishers, at least make an agreement to stuff each other's brochures into outgoing packages.

RECORDINGS AND BRAILLE editions are published for the blind. If your book is well-received, you may be approached by a library for permission to translate your book into Braille or to put it on tape.

BOOK CLUBS offer you some money and a great deal of prestige. Since they were established in the mid-twenties, the Book-of-the-Month-Club (BOMC) and the Literary Guild have been helping their members by selecting the best books of the thousands available at lower than normal prices. Now there are more than 170 book clubs, most of which cater to highly specialized groups.

Normally, selections are made before the book is printed so that the book club edition costs less to produce; it only requires more press time. Sometimes, the clubs economize more by specifying cheaper paper, narrower margins, less costly bindings, etc. Smaller clubs and some alternate selections will not require a separate club edition; they just buy from the original run.

Approach book clubs when you have galleys to show them. If they don't respond, write them again after publication and enclose photocopies of your reviews. They have to be convinced it is a desirable book and that is where clippings of reviews can help. The best time to strike a deal with a book club is before you go (or go back to) press as their order enables you to enlarge the print run which achieves a lower per-unit cost.

The usual book club royalty is 10% of the list price plus production expenses (roughly the print bill plus a dollar.) If they invest in the printing, you get 10% of the list price. The larger clubs usually want an exclusive; they don't want other clubs to carry the book too. Smaller clubs aren't so particular.

Offer your book to the Small Press Book Club (P.O. Box 100-P, Paradise, CA 95969) and look through Literary Market Place for other possibilities.

THE INTERNATIONAL MARKET. Foreign sales of books exceeded $650-million in 1982 with most going to Canada (37%), Great Britain and Australia. About 3.5% of the U.S. adult hardcover books are exported along with just over 5% of the adult softcover. Other export figures are better: 20% for professional books, 14% for university press sales, almost 10% for college texts, 9% for elementary and high school texts and almost 10% for mass market paperback. Since English is the commercial and aviation language of the world as well as one of the most used tongues in the fields of science and technology, there is a good demand for books in our language.

Be advised that adding a country will not double your sales. For example, expanding from the U.S. to Canada may increase sales 7% to 10%. You must compare the sizes of the English-speaking populations.

The most common way to cater to the international market is to fill and mail foreign orders in the same way you fill domestic ones. Most of your export sales will come with the daily mail. They will be just like your domestic orders but for their lighter weight stationery, strange addresses and pretty stamps. Most of these foreign bookstores will get your address from Bowker's Books In Print.

Postal rates for foreign shipments may be higher or lower than domestic rates depending on which rate has been raised most recently. There is a 5 kg. (11 lb.) weight limit for books but if you are shipping more than 15 lbs., you may qualify for "Direct Sacks of Prints" at 43 cents per pound. Since it is so inexpensive to export, it makes little sense to print the book abroad unless the press run is huge. One exception is translations; see below.

One way to reach foreign bookstores and libraries is by renting a mailing list from Bowker (see the Appendix.)

Many small firms use an export agent. These distributors usually want 55-65% off and then handle all the distribution and debt collection. A list of export agents may be found in Literary Market Place.

TRANSLATIONS offer good possibilities and here you will want to deal with a foreign publisher. If you have a terribly popular book, it should even be translated into "British English" for the commonwealth countries. These foreign publishers will pay you a royalty and take care of everything. Normally you supply the photos and a couple of copies of the book with late changes noted. They translate the text, change the measurements to metric and take care of all the printing, distribution, etc. Royalties may be 5-7% for hardcover rights and 5-10% for paperbacks. Some countries impose a tax on exported royalties; Japan, for example, charges 10% of the remitted amount.

Over 30,000 titles were published in Spanish in 1982 and 4,000 of these books were translations from English. One way to reach over 500 publishers in Spain and Latin America is through Contacto newsletter (165 West 20th Street, #3H, New York, NY 10011.) Foreign publishers and foreign rights representatives are listed in Literary Market Place.

When negotiating a contract, consider the number of copies to be printed, the printing schedule, cover price, royalties for both hardbound and softcover editions, the advance and the government tax, if any. If you are printing in a country with a currency harder than the U.S. dollar, such as Germany or Switzerland, you might ask to get paid in their money and to have it deposited in one of their banks. The investment may appreciate against the inflating dollar and could be worth more to you on your next visit abroad.

FILM RIGHTS will be somewhat unusual for a nonfiction book but it does happen. The usual rate is 15% of the **net** and this is a very bad deal. Film companies are notorious for their unusual accounting procedures which result in a very small net; they write off everything against the film. Always get a (smaller) percentage of the **gross.** The gross figure is much more objective.

PREMIUMS are big business and there is a lot of room for books. premiums are products which are given away or sold at a discount to promote business. They may be given away by a store to attract customers or to sales people as prizes for achieving sales goals. Books make especially good premiums as they may be customized by printing a special cover and because they are held in higher esteem than some other premium trinkets. In fact, in some areas, regulated industries such as banks are prohibited from giving away certain items or the value of the items they may consider is limited.

If your book covers a regional topic, try local businesses. Small quantities of books may be rubber stamped with "Compliments of Lin Sayre Insurance Co." as an example. If you cover a subject with wider appeal such as a book on beer can collecting, contact the beer, aluminum, steel and can companies. Such a book would make an ideal corporate gift or might be worked into a promotion. A tour guide book might be sold to a motel chain. The possibilities are endless. Think of firms which might like to identify with your book or subject. For more ideas, send for a sample copy of Premium Incentive Business magazine (1515 Broadway, New York, NY 10036). If your book is right for the premium market, you will want to send this magazine a review copy too.

Premium orders are large, usually 1,000 or more books, and the customer may ask for 60% off. Such a discount can be justified for a large order which eliminates the problems of financing, storage and individual shipping. A typical premium discount schedule might look like this:

Number of copies	Discounts
25-99	20%
100-499	40%
500-999	50%
1,000-14,999	60%
15,000 up	Cost plus 10% of list price

If you can strike some premium deals before going to (or back to) press, you may increase your press run and achieve a smaller per-unit cost. Early sales are also a great help in paying the first printing bill. Be prepared to do a lot of leg work. Premium sales are tough and time-consuming but the payoff is big.

SPONSORED BOOKS are those you are almost commissioned to write. There may be an institution which wants your book printed badly enough to give you a large advance order. For example, if you wrote a book on the Frisbee disc and there were no others on the subject, the Wham-O Manufacturing Company which makes discs might want the book to be published because the publicity would help their sales. With this sponsorship, they might want some sort of cover credit, such as: "Published in association with Wham-O." Such an endorsement is to your advantage as it would only lend credibility to the book.

Some industries need favorable publicity and find that sponsoring a book is much less expensive than placing full page ads. A book is also much more effective promotion as it appears to be more objective.

NONPROFIT ORGANIZATIONS are always running sales to raise money for their cause. These flea markets, bake sales, etc. promoted by church and civic groups can provide you with an opportunity to move some books. Try approaching some local organizations first to get a feel for the way they operate. If you are successful, consider a mailing list to similar groups. Don't forget to tell them of your past good track record for sales and assure them that the unsold books may be returned. Local clubs and local chapters of national organizations raise funds too. If your book is appropriate, you might strike a deal. A gardening book might be sold by a gardening club, for example. By making the nonprofit organization a dealer, they raise money for their group and you gain access to a new audience.

SPECIALTY SHOWS such as sport and boat exhibitions and trade shows are rarely worthwhile for a small author/publisher. However, you can make sure that your book is carried and offered for sale by someone in the show. Find a booth with related merchandise and offer them some books on consignment. Give them a carton of books and an examination copy for the table. They get a piece of the action and you get the exposure while moving books. If you make up a little poster, you won't have to be concerned about their lack of sales concentration on your book.

EDUCATIONAL CAMPAIGNS conducted by special in-terest groups offer another market for books. These people range from helpful social agencies to business interests promoting their side of an issue. Be careful to remain objective to maintain your credibility. You don't want to become too closely associated with either side; you want the use of their name, you don't want to let them use yours. After all, you will sell your book to anyone and your control over it ends with the sale.

"Publishers might be well advised to shift away from the concepts of the backlist and the frontlist and toward the concept of the active list, on which some books are new and some books are old, but each book has a life cycle of its own, so that with sensible planning every title can be made to yield maximum profits over time." — Judith Appelbaum in *Publishers Weekly*

To find organizations with "causes," consult National Trade & Professional Associations of the U.S. and Canada and Gale's Encyclopedia of Associations available at your library. Write to these organizations enclosing your brochure, press release, etc. Tell them why your book would be valuable to them. Hold off on the price until you get a bite. The price will depend on the number they want and it could be thousands.

BOOK FAIRS provide important exposure to your book. The major national U.S. shows are sponsored by:

- The American Booksellers Association, 122 East 42 nd Street, New York, NY 10168 (often in late May and attended primarily by bookstore managers)

- The American Library Association, 50 East Huron Street, Chicago, IL 60611 (Late June and attended primarily by librarians)

- The National Association of College Stores, 528 East Lorain Street, Oberlin, OH 44074. (Usually mid-spring and attended by college bookstore managers)

write to the listed organizations regarding the fairs and then attend a nearby one yourself to assess how you might fit in to your advantage. The big associations also sponsor regional and local book fairs.

International book fairs are held all over the world with the most important being in London and Frankfurt. They can give good exposure and may lead to subsidiary rights but probably are not worth your own exhibiting effort.

Conventions and conferences of professional, academic and trade associations will present you with a "qualified" audience for your books if you match your subject matter to the show. Educational books do well at educational exhibits and these conferences are especially fun as they provide an opportunity to meet with authors as well as customers. For more ideas, consult National Trade & Professional Associations of the U.S. and Canada

Directory and Gale's Encyclopedia of Associations available in your library.

Exhibiting at a book fair is often an inspiring experience; it will recharge your batteries. You will learn more about the industry, meet some great people, make valuable contacts, sell a few books and, perhaps, even some subsidiary rights. Typically, the show's management provides a space measuring about 8' x 10', a draped table, curtained side and back panels, a sign, carpet, and a chair or two. Check their brochure closely. Take a good supply of books and brochures. Get some book stands or bend-up some bookends to prop up your books and brochures.

Shows cost. Booth space at the big American Booksellers Association fair runs $450 to $1,200. The ALA is much higher. But they also have a small press section at $175. In addition to booth expense, you must consider your personal travel, book shipping, hotels, meals, etc. You can spend $500 exhibiting but $2,000 is not unusual.

Exhibiting services will put your books on display with those of other publishers very inexpensively and some do a very good job of representing your wares. Write to several of them to compare prices and see which fairs they plan to attend; some offer package deals if you sign up for the whole season. There is a list of exhibiting services in the Appendix.

For more information on book fairs, read Book Fairs, An Exhibiting Guide for Publishers by the author.

"Quality often becomes diluted if you publish a lot, whereas to a small publisher each publishing decision is a crucial one — you commit everything to each book, without hoping to counterbalance a wrong choice with a more successful one." — Glen Johns of Rodale Press.

Chapter Nine

SELLING YOUR BOOK
REACHING CUSTOMERS
THROUGH ADVERTISING

ADVERTISING may be used to create an awareness of your new book and even to stimulate an interest in it. But advertising is expensive and must be approached slowly. Nonproductive ads will deplete your bank account fast. It is a cold, hard fact that most advertising doesn't pay. This is often because the approach is wrong. So, feel out each of the many areas and test them before you jump in with lots of money.

It is said that advertising will make a good book sell better but it can't turn a poor one into a success. We will have to assume that more people besides just you see some value in your book.

First we will talk about advertising in general and then we will discuss the details of your brochure, direct mail advertising, classifieds, space ads and radio/TV. Much of the information is overlapping and may be

---

"It is cheaper to advertise one book twice than to write a second book.

241

applied to more than one area of advertising. For example, the coding of addresses in advertisements applies to all, so, it is advisable to read the entire chapter.

The success of your advertising campaign will depend upon the sales potential of your book, whether you contact the right market and whether your ad is effective. You must select your markets (buyers) and then find the least expensive way to reach them. Target your primary market but do not overlook the secondary ones. Concentrate on one medium of advertising (e.g., direct mail) but do not dismiss the others (e.g., space ads).

In each ad campaign, figure the cost of the campaign "per sale" (how many books did this ad sell?) The cost "per contract" is interesting but it is the cost per sale that tells you if you are winning or losing. Ads placed in magazines to promote bookstore sales (wholesale) must generate sales of five times their cost to be worth your while. For example, a $10 ad must sell $50 worth of books. Ads directing the orders to you (mail order) must produce 2.2 times the cost of the ad, minimum. The difference is because you are also giving the bookstore 40% of the list (cover) price. These figures are quoted by the industry and may vary depending on the original production cost of your book. Keep them in mind as you plan your ad strategy. Do not run unprofitable ads! They waste money and make you work for nothing.

Determining an ad's potential profitability is not the place for wishful thinking. You have to calculate all the possibilities, the types of advertising and the places it might be put; this comparison will help you to choose where to place your money.

Your consumer ads should be concentrated and timed to appear in the few weeks just after the publication date. By concentrating your ads and generating other publicity with tours and reviews, the campaign will appear to be much bigger than it really is.

The people selling advertising talk about the "number of impressions" and "accumulative impact" when they try to get you to spend more on promotion (or try to

> *"I know that half of my advertising is wasted but I do not know which half."* — William Wrigley

explain why your ad wasn't successful.) A series of good, consistent ads may be of some help as a prospect may remember that he has heard of the book before, but remember that you are selling a $5 or $10 book, not a $5,000 or $10,000 automobile. You have to sell a lot more product to pay for the ad and you can't even justify as much need.

If you are pushing bookstore sales and your book is on a popular subject, space ads may be best while if your subject is normally sold to business, professional and/or educational markets, direct mail should get more of your attention. In fact, many small publishers put most of their efforts into direct mail.

Ted Nicholas (Peterson), author of several money books, describes his advertising system as pyramiding revenue derived from sales. He suggests putting up a small amount of money for advertising, running good space ads (and he tells you how to write them), waiting for the money to come in and then reinvesting it in ever greater amounts of advertising.

If you have a good method, don't deviate. Creativity for creativity's sake is dumb. Whatever worked before will almost certainly work again. All marketing methods must be tested, not just direct mail advertising. Once you find a good system, stick with it.

The two most recommended books in this area are How to Start and Operate a Mail-Order Business by Julian Simon and Successful Direct Marketing Methods by Bob Stone.

CREATING AD COPY. You will need a good basic description of the book that will appeal to the consumer; this material, altered as required, will then be used over and over. Come up with a very few words to describe the book. This becomes its "handle" and might even be the subtitle for the book. This handle will be expanded for brochures and catalogs while it is directed toward the intended audience. Some small ads will only have space

> *"When you are ready to draft an ad, stimulate your creative juices by reading a couple of articles or a couple of chapters on copy writing."*

for the handle and a small amount of hard hitting copy. Once this is done, the future copy writing is easier as you are not starting from scratch each time.

ADVERTISING AGENCIES can be a great help if you are not particularly interested in plugging your own book or if you plan a lot of promotion. If your account is large enough, or the agency is small enough, there is no charge for most of the service. Advertising agencies get a 15% commission from the magazine or TV station. They will prepare the ads, place them, pay for them and may even do some testing. You will still have to do most of the copywriting. All the agency can do is put your creativity into correct form. Classified ads are not commissionable, however, and agencies will charge you extra for artwork and other special services, too. But whether you employ an agency or do the job yourself, it will be valuable to understand what happens in advertising.

Advertising agencies are in business to stay in business just as you are. While they want to do a good job for you, their primary motivation is to keep the cash flowing in. Keep this in mind when they are trying to sell you more space or time. Don't believe everything you hear or read from advertising people.

YOUR BROCHURE lies at the heart of your promotional campaign and it may be produced long before your book is off the press. The brochure should describe the book, tell about you and answer most of the recipient's potential questions. The basics are the book's measurements, number of pages, type and number of illustrations, binding and price. The contents should be summarized to provide a clear understanding of the book's coverage. Do not use too much detail or the buyer may find too much material he or she does not want--sell the sizzle, not the steak. Excerpts from reviews will demonstrate that others like your book, too. Follow the proven, standard formats.

The brochure will be stuffed into most of the letters you send out daily to friends, associates and relatives, used with your other pre- and post-publication mailings and sent to those who respond to your ads which invite them to "send for a free descriptive brochure." Yes, your brochure is more important than a business card and has a lot more information.

The best way to answer inquiries is with your brochure. If the writer asks particular questions, the simplest way to answer is by circling the appropriate parts of the mailing piece. Many publishers like to return the inquiry letter with the brochure to remind the writer that he asked for this advertising matter. If you aren't over the postage limit yet, it is nice to stuff in other related information. For example, if the inquiry is about hang gliding, enclose a membership application from the hang gliding association. You will build valuable good will.

Brochures provide you with an opportunity to say nice things about yourself that you can't say in face-to-face selling. It is almost as though someone else wrote the copy. Be direct, clear and give the reader as much information as possible. Because you will use this brochure for your bookstore and library sales, too, include the ISBN's, LC numbers, etc.

Your local instant print shop can give you the best deal on 8½ x 11 brochures. If you need more space, they can handle 8½ x 14 and you can fold it four times to fit a standard #10 envelope. If you still need more space, you may have to go to a regular printer for an 11 x 17 sheet, folded down the middle and then into thirds.

Every pass through the press costs more money so some people like to use colored paper and another color ink. This gives the appearance of a lot of color but it is still a one-color print job. Use good materials and make the brochure slick. If you send out a mimeographed brochure, people will assume you are selling a mimeographed book. Ask the print shop where you can get some type set. And ask your printer; he just might throw the brochure in free because he is doing your book and has an interest in it.

Some publishers have produced very nice brochures by printing their ad copy on the back of book cover overruns. This is nice but it isn't cheap. There are the extra trips through the press and the additional mailing weight of the cover stock to be considered. Ask your printer for any "overs" and/or ask him to print a few hundred extra covers.

People like to see what they are buying so a photo of the book should appear in the brochure. You don't have to wait for your book to be printed to take a photograph of it, however. Ask your printer to run the covers while the type is being set on the manuscript. Then make a dummy by wrapping one around another book. Take several photos with different settings and from several angles. Then select the best print and have some 5 x 7's made up. At this point, you won't know exactly how many pages the book will have but you can estimate and then use a description like: "over 180 jam-packed pages."

To make the photo reproduce well, the instant printer will have to make a metal plate rather than the usual cheaper plastic ones. The plate should be saved for the next time you run the brochure.

Once the brochures arrive, use them everywhere. Stuff them in every package, letter, press release, mailing, etc. Carry some in the car, leave them at the barbershop, in the seatback pocket on the airplane, at the dentist office, etc. and carry some with you at all times. Pack one in with every book you mail out. A brochure has to be distributed to do any good.

DIRECT MAIL ADVERTISING is one very effective way to contact potential buyers for your book. The mailing usually includes a cover letter, brochure, order form and a reply envelope but it may also direct the addressee to a nearby store. The literature may be sent to your friends and acquaintances, to your list of past customers or you may rent a mailing list from a list company. The list is the heart of a direct mail advertising campaign. Don't confuse direct mail with "mail order" which is a form of distribution. Sales through bookstores would be another way to distribute your book to the ultimate consumer.

Direct mail advertising is one of the most effective ways of reaching the technical, scientific and medical book markets. Direct mail allows you to pinpoint your market. Your message has little or no competition when it reaches the recipient. Direct mail provides flexibility

"Direct mail compares with a sniper attack whereas display ads are a shotgun approach."

in design and format and it allows you to trace and analyze the results through simple address coding.

ESTIMATING YOUR DIRECT MAIL ADVERTISING COSTS

Use this budget outline to estimate the cost of your proposed promotion.

OPERATION	COST PER 1.000	TOTAL COST
1. Artwork and Creation	_____	_____
2. Mailing Lists (Rental)	_____	_____
3. Printing Brochure	_____	_____
4. Printing Letter	_____	_____
5. Printing Business Reply Card	_____	_____
6. Printing Business Reply Envelope	_____	_____
7. Printing Outer Envelope	_____	_____
8. Folding Brochure	_____	_____
9. Folding Letter	_____	_____
10. Labeling	_____	_____
11. Inserting	_____	_____
12. Tie, Bag, Mail	_____	_____
13. Postage	_____	_____
14. Postage First Class	_____	_____
15. Postage Third Class	_____	_____
16. Total Cost	$_____	$_____
		TOTAL COST

17. Cost of Product _____
18. Fulfillment, Shipping, Postage Cost _____

19. Total Fulfillment, Product Cost Per Order —
Line 17 Plus Line 18 $_____
20. Number of Orders Received   _____
21. Total Cost for Orders Received
Line 19 Multiply Line 20   _____
22. Total Mailing Promotion Costs
Line 16   _____
22A. Overhead — Salaries, Phone, Rent, Etc.   _____
23. Total Cost for Refunds   _____
24. Total Uncollectables/Selling Price   _____
25. Grand Total Mailing Programs Costs
Add Lines 21, 22, 22A, 23, 24   _____
26. Number of Inquiries   _____
27. Per Order or Inquiry Costs
Line 25 Divided by Line 20 or 26 $_____
28. Cash Received per Order   _____
29. Total Cash Received
Line 20 Times Line 28   _____
30. Total Mailing Program Costs
Line 25   _____
31. Net Profit for Mailing Program
Subtract Line 30 from Line 29 $_____

Most people like to receive mail and one book out of four is sold via direct mail advertising. Most of this volume goes to book clubs but they don't get all the business; there are about a half billion dollars left. Direct mail offers the small publisher an opportunity to sell the customer without competing with the big publishers. Mail provides equal treatment, something you can't get in the bookshops.

People associate books with their authors; they don't remember the publishers. Therefore, you have as much clout as the big firms. What counts is your mailing piece, not your firm name. Since you have written about an area you know, you are more familiar with the people in it than someone's marketing department. You know who the customers are and why they might buy. No doubt, a significant portion of your sales will be to a specific category of buyers. You have the advantage.

Some of the big publishers make regular elaborate mailings. But be advised that they are mailing millions of pieces and this lowers their per-unit cost of fancy four-color printing and multiple inserts. Further, the books are usually priced very high and are often part of a series. You will have to be much more conservative.

Direct mail advertising often benefits from the "echo" effect. Some people find it easier or faster to buy your product somewhere else such as dropping by a retailer. Since over 75% of libraries deal with whole-salers, most of the orders from a mailing to libraries will come to you through Baker & Taylor. Sometimes, publishers even help the potential customers in this direction and, in effect, give him a choice of purchasing by mail or visiting a bookstore. The brochure might say: "Available at your local Walden Bookstore or direct from the publisher." Some publishers imprint circulars for bookstores to be mailed to the bookstore's mailing list. Then there are millions of people who live in the sticks and don't have a bookstore handy who are best reached by mail.

One must understand the economics to put direct mail advertising of books into perspective. If you tell enough people about your book, a certain percentage will buy it. The challenge is to keep costs down by telling just that certain percentage. A general interest book advertised to a general consumer audience will usually generate a return of 1.5 to 2 percent. In fact, only ten percent of the recipients will even remember the mailing piece. That is just 15-20 orders per 1,000 pieces mailed. The cost, on the other hand, may be quite high. It all depends upon the price of the list (the more selective ones cost more), the postage, the type and number of inserts and other expenses.

Due to the nature of the pricing of books, it is generally accepted that the return on a direct mail solicitation must be at least 2.2 times the cost. This means you need good literature, a good list and a high-priced book. Highly specialized lists may cost more but they bring more results. A lot depends on whether the book is highly specialized or of general interest. Normally it costs more to sell books by mail than it does through a store. While your other advertising might cost you 20% of sales, your direct mail effort may run 50%. However, the resulting sales are at retail, 40% isn't being given to the bookseller. And, of course, mail orders come with checks enclosed; you don't have to wait 60 or 90 days for your money and expend effort to make the collection.

98% of the responses to a mailing will come within 13 weeks, so you can total your results at that time. But about half the return will come in the first four weeks. Use this period if you need comparative data sooner. One way to increase your return on a mailing list is to promote more than one book but don't confuse the customer with a cluttered brochure. Concentrate on those books in a single interest area. Don't bury the gems in garbage. The recipients may not be able to dig out the books they want.

Mailings often outpull space ads in magazines sent to the same people—probably because the ad wasn't noticed. The magazines use mailings themselves. Where you have obtained a good response in a magazine through a space ad or a review, it is worth renting their mailing list.

Finally, direct mail advertising is no place to be innovative. The margin for error is slim; you cannot afford mistakes. Do what everyone else is doing. Advance into direct mail advertising slowly by exercising the less expensive options and then begin to test the more expensive ones.

249

REPETITION is the key to direct mail. Remailing to the same list anytime after 30 days will result in the same response as the first try. You have to hit people at the right time, when they feel a need for your product. Many marketing people use a list four times a year and if it fails to draw 2% each time, it is time to change the list. They say that repetitive mailings have a cumulative effect and the message is strengthened.

If you are committed to marketing your book by direct mail, you will need a continuous program, one that can be constantly adjusted as needed. When a test list works, expand its use. When it fails, get rid of it.

It is a good idea to remain flexible by continually testing your mailing piece with small changes. Never make two significant changes at once or you won't know which one is responsible for the change in response.

TIME your mail to arrive on a Tuesday, Wednesday or Thursday. A lot of mail arrives on Mondays and the day after holidays and your piece could be lost in the clutter. Friday's mail is often put aside as the recipient is about to leave for the weekend.

The best times of year for slow Bulk Rate mailing, according to some experts, are post-Christmas to January, July and August to September. They say that March to April (income tax time?) and May to June are the worst. Other experts warn against the summer months when people are away and the mail piles up. Most agree December is bad because the Post Office is jammed and the potential customer is thinking about Christmas. All factors must be considered in relation to your specialized subject and audience.

FOREIGN mailing lists are available though, generally, they aren't as sophisticated. The problems in mailing outside the U.S. aren't any greater, they are simply different. With the increase in both the standard of living and purchasing power in many other countries, the potential for book sales is increasingly good. While French has been considered the diplomatic language of the world, English is the aviation and commercial language. English, in fact, is the second language of more people in the world than any other. In Europe, there is a whole new generation who are fluent in English. Leading European business executives consider English language publications their most essential reading matter right behind their local newspapers. Naturally, books in English should be promoted with brochures in English and prices should be quoted in dollars as it is customary to settle international accounts in U.S. currency.

In Germany, direct mail accounts for 30% of the advertising expenditures. In the Netherlands, 32.5% of the advertisers use direct mail. Both Italy and France have Post Office problems but direct mail is growing. The U.S. Post Office doesn't have a perfect record either.

Check the postal regulations for foreign mailings. For example, there is a cheap surface mail printed matter rate and you are allowed to seal the envelope if you use a postage meter, permit imprint or precanceled stamps. If you are mailing just a few hundred, it pays to talk to your postmaster about "precans."

In the book industry, direct mail is the most under-used marketing technique. It has great potential and is waiting to be properly exploited.

CO-OP MAILINGS. One way to reduce mailing costs is through cooperative mailings. Several publishers may share a list by stuffing their flyer into one envelope. This system works when publishers of like books are approaching the same market. Co-op mailing is offered by a number of companies which combine your brochure with other related solicitations and mail them to a selected list in a single envelope. The postage savings can be considerable. Each firm operates differently and uses different lists, so you should write to them all and compare their deals. One firm that makes periodic mailings to libraries is Direct Mail Promotions (342 Madison Avenue, New York, NY 10017.)

Eight publishers with books on publishing rented the R.R. Bowker list of 12,000 publishers and joined in a cooperative mailing. In effect, they were able to reach their audience for one-eighth of the cost of the postage, list rental and envelope. The only fixed cost was their brochure.

251

LETTER SHOPS will do your printing, envelope stuffing and mailing very inexpensively. Check the Yellow Pages and call a few for prices. If you deal with a mailing house, they will deliver the stuffed and addressed envelopes to the Post Office. The mailing house will send you a photocopy of the Post Office receiving form, detailing the quantity delivered, with your bill. Make sure you get copies of both sides of the form. They fill out the front but the Post Office personnel fills out the back. Make sure the numbers are the same.

Whenever you make a large mailing, send a few pieces to yourself in order to time the delivery and to make sure the Post Office has processed the mailing.

MAILING LISTS make the difference between success and failure in direct mail marketing. The list must target the appropriate group and be up-to-date. Posting your offer to the wrong person is a waste you cannot afford; the margin is just too slim. You want quality, not quantity. People get new jobs, move, die, lose interest in certain fads and trends, forget hobbies, etc. Yesterday's prime prospect may have other interests today or may have moved.

The highest quality list is normally your own. Your house list should pull two to ten times better than any you might rent. The people on your list know you and your product, they look to you as an old friend. To your list of past customers, you will want to add more qualified names. These may come from various directories depending on the subject of your book. Some firms have used contests to generate interest and more names while others have sold merchandise at a loss to attract attention. The common way to add to a list is to rent another one, make a mailing and then add the names of those who respond to your own list.

You may begin assembling your own mailing list by going through your Christmas card list. Include all family, friends and acquaintances. Include anyone who might conceivably purchase your book.

Also start your commercial lists: bookstores, libraries, magazines, newspapers, radio and TV stations. Use the addresses in the Appendix and then check references such as Literary Market Place.

Keep your lists for your second book so you will be prepared when it comes time to send out pre-publication announcements.

Lists must be kept up to date if they are to keep up with our mobile society and remain valid. This means keeping the list in mind and continually being alert for address changes and returned mail. Periodically, you will want to make a "list cleaner" mailing by using the Post Office Form 3547 "Address Correction Requested" service or asking people for more information about themselves.

Some publishers just clean out the list every couple of years and start over. Even though a name was well qualified as a former customer, if he hasn't responded again in a couple of years, he probably never will.

Should you address your labels to the individual or the company? This depends upon the product and your approach. The question is whether you want the offer to go to the individual or the person in that particular job. People change jobs quite often these days. The Post Office now likes to have the "attention" part of the address on the second, rather than the last, line. For example:

Ad-Lib Publications
John Kremer
P.O. Box 1102
Fairfield, IA 52556

If you mail via First Class, the letter will be forwarded, and if it can't be delivered, it will be returned. The problems are that First Class costs more and you won't get a new address to update your file. Third Class isn't forwarded or returned. If your prospect has moved, the letter is discarded. If, however, you mark the envelopes "Forwarding and return postage guaranteed," your Third Class or Fourth Class piece will be handled much like First Class. The economics depend on the size of the list, the weight of the pieces, the quality of the list, etc.

There are several ways to keep your list and the most important consideration is its size. If you have just a handful of highly qualified names, you could use a card file. For a thousand or so, use self-adhesive address labels. They come 33 to the page in three columns of eleven. Once typed out, they can be reproduced on many of the plain paper photocopy machines. The Avery #5351 labels, for example, are made for this and reproduce cleaner than some of the other label systems. When typing the list, leave the bottom row of labels blank so you can add new or changed addresses later. To delete a name, simply remove a label from your master. This will work until the list grows very large making it difficult to find the names to be updated or deleted. About once a year, cut the masters apart and sort labels into Zip Code order. Preparing the new list this way will help you to find the duplicates. Some people have more than one address or get mail at work addressed different ways. You might be sending two pieces to "Richard Adams, Zeller Mfg. Co." and "Zeller Mfg. Co., Attn: Richard Adams."

The best way to handle a list is with a personal computer and a mailing list or data base program. A computer will allow you to code, sort and print out the names in any order. If you are using a computer to write your book, you should also use it to maintain your list.

A name is not just a name. Saturation lists compiled from common directories are just about worthless. You want "qualified" people. These are people who have purchased products similar to yours by mail. It is possible to get specialized mailing lists for just about every human grouping imaginable. There are many unusual categories. Rental lists are "target" or "related" depending upon whether or not they are composed of people for whom your book was written. Target lists may cost more to rent.

Lists and list brokers can be found in Direct Marketing magazine, the Standard Rate and Data Service Directories, Klein's Directory and your local Yellow Pages. See the Appendix.

There are two ways to rent a list. One is to arrange for the list you want, forward your stuffed envelopes with

> *"It is a good rule to have your name and address on every piece of a mailing package. One piece alone sometimes makes the sale."*

a check for the postage and the service to the list owner who then addresses and mails the pieces. The stuffed envelopes may be shipped at your Post Office or his but in either case, you will receive a receipt showing the number of pieces that were sent. The other way to rent a list is get it on pressure sensitive labels, Cheshire labels or even on magnetic tape for automatic processing. These rentals are for one time use only and you are obligated not to add the names to your file. Copying lists violates the rental agreement, normal business ethics and is against the law. The list owner guards against second usage by sprinkling it with decoy names. Stealing a name from a list will only dilute the quality of your own house list. You are, however, authorized to add a name to your list once you have qualified it, once it has resulted in an order.

Lists go out of date fast. There is a 25% turnover in the addresses of our gypsy-like population each year and address changes are even higher with younger people. For this reason, many firms like to leave the list maintenance to the experts so they rent the cleanest list possible for every mailing.

Many names appear on several lists as people have more than one interest. It is wise not to use several lists in one mailing unless they are computerized and the duplicates are automatically pulled. When buying more than one list from a broker, ask that it be culled and arranged in Zip Code order.

You don't have to rent the entire list. Why send to all libraries when you are liable to get a better return from those with a higher book acquisition budget? The cost of the list may run $35 to $45 per thousand depending on how difficult it was to compile and its potential market. Highly qualified lists run higher. Unless the list is very small or you are very sure of it, test it first. This is done by renting just part of the list and sending your mailing to every "nth" (e.g. tenth) name. Some lists are old or watered down and you want only the best. A minimum sample should be 1,000 names and remember that you are testing the mailing package as well as the list; they both affect the results. Keep working with the small quantities until you are satisfied that you will get a good return if you use the whole list. If a mailing to a sample group produces a 2% response, statistics show that a mailing to the entire list will result in a 1.4% to 2.6% response. Realizing these probability limits will help you to evaluate a list and make the decision whether to risk a big mailing.

A lot of things can go wrong with a test mailing. A list can be non-representative or out of date. Or your book could be bad and the word may have circulated between the test and the big mailing. Keep good records; only with statistics can you effectively evaluate a mailing. Note all your costs. If a test is inconclusive, run another test. Most tests fail; expect it. When one fails, be thankful you didn't mail to the whole list. Then drop that list and don't try it again.

Consider a post card with a photo of you and your book as an inexpensive way to reach prospects. Post cards are not as expensive to print as a full mailing package and they cost less to mail.

Scores of books have been written on the many facets of direct mail advertising. We have touched on just some of the more important points here. See the Appendix for a list of some of these books and write for a sample copy of Galen Stilson's newsletter, Mail Order Connection (P.O. Box 2505-P, Bonita Springs, FL 33923.)

SELL YOUR MAILING LIST. Your list may be worth some $25 per thousand names to list-brokers who will sell it to others. If you maintain your mailing list by noting which book (subject area) the customer purchased, it becomes very selective and quite valuable. These are people who have taken the time to sit down, get out the check book and mail away for a book. They are very good prospects for similar offers:

See Direct Mail List Rates and Data and write to a few of the firms listed who seem to maintain similar lists and ask what they are paying. Generally they want lists of 5,000 names, minimum.

THE OFFER OR "ORDER FORM," while it usually comes last in the direct mail package, should be written first as it is the cornerstone around which the rest of the mailing is built. The purpose of your mailing may be to solicit an order or to request some descriptive literature and you must guide the recipient to take the specific action you want. By preparing the order form first, you will assure coordination of all the parts of the mailing and will keep the copy headed in the same direction. Make the offer simple, clear and easy.

Many people don't read the whole brochure, they are sold early in the package and turn straight to the order form. If you have more than one title, print a check-off list. Don't ask the customer to write the title in; he may lose interest. If you use the words "I enclosed $_____ for:" you are making it easy for him. If the order form is printed on colored paper, it will be easier to locate.

Make the order form easily detachable or on a separate card. Note the deadline, shipping costs and sales tax, if any. Always include a money-back guarantee, an unconditional one. The form should have enough room for the customer to write in his or her name and address; make this area big so you will be able to read the handwriting. If the form is not "business reply" make sure your name and address appear on the front, back or both. The cost of business reply has increased so much that it probably is no longer worth the expense. Pre-addressed envelopes are also expensive but they are probably worth sending to non-business people. Some advertisers like to call their order form a "trial order card." Refer to it in the text of your letter to remind the customer that it is there.

If you are offering air mail delivery for an additional charge, add a box where the customer may make a check mark. Note on the form that "Book Rate" may take three to four weeks while an air shipment will be three to four days.

Check with your bank about offering Master Card and VISA. Charge cards make buying much easier and will bring in some impulse sales, but they increase your paperwork and cost about $15 to set up plus 3 to 4% of your sales.

Code your address, not only on the order form, but on the other literature in the package. Customers don't

> *"If you want a response, you have to ask for it"* — John Huenefeld.

257

always use the coupons and you want to know where the order is coming from.

YOUR LETTERHEAD is you. It is a matter of image since your customers and suppliers never see you in the flesh. A nice design costs little more to print than a poor one and you want to instill trust and confidence. If you wish to appear successful, you might like expensive paper and an engraved letterhead.

If you use the same list very often, it is a good idea to change your letterhead and package so that the offer doesn't get stale. You don't want the recipient to take one look, recognize it and toss it out unopened. You can give the impression of color by using ink of one color and paper of another and still pay for only one press run. There are a lot of types of paper and you should look through the catalogs at your print shop. The letterhead to promote a carpentry book might be printed on a wood grain paper and you can even add scent. How about cedar?

THE ENVELOPE is often used to arouse the recipient, inviting him to open it by exciting him with some printing on the outside. This is "teaser" copy.

Doesn't this message make you curious?

To get the recipient's attention, your envelope must stand out from all the rest. Many things affect whether the envelope will be opened, such as color, artwork, size, stock, etc. Ask yourself what your reaction would be to various possibilities. To be cost effective, a minimum print run of 5,000 envelopes is required.

Self-mailers are brochures mailed without envelopes. While less expensive to produce, they usually don't pull as well as offers arriving in envelopes. Self-mailers should have their teaser copy adjacent to the address label.

POSTAGE amounts and forms vary for each class of service and some mailers feel that it affects whether an envelope will be opened or discarded. Some say to use First Class mail and to apply stamps rather than use a postage meter or a postage permit imprint. People like to receive mail, however, and your offer is quite a bit different so you should get good readership no matter how you mail your offer.

If you are going into direct mail advertising in a serious way, investigate "Bulk Rate"; ask your postmaster for a brochure. Do not use slow moving Bulk Rate, however, whenever time is important.

CIRCULARS are introduced by your cover letter and both pieces work together. Until you get into big mailings with specially designed packages, you may use your regular brochure with a cover letter. In a big mailing, it won't cost any more to print up a specific circular for that mailing and it will bring greater results. Remember that the circular has a photo of the book while the letter does not—and photos sell. Circulars are more likely to be filed for future action whereas letters have a more limited life. So don't send a letter without a circular.

To lay out the circular, start with a blank folded dummy and plot the location of each part of it: the teaser copy, order form, photos, etc. Set up the brochure and then write the copy to fit.

The "AIDA" formula is the oldest and most widely used method of reader motivation. It is designed to lead the recipient to the offer and impel him to take action. " AIDA" stands for: get ATTENTION, arouse INTEREST, stimulate DESIRE, ask for ACTION. AIDA is just as effective today as it has always been.

The circular should have big impelling headlines that give the recipient a chance to see himself in the mailing. He will respond favorably if he identifies subconsciously with the product. Always include a photo of the book so he can see how big and nice it looks. Make the copy easy to read: one thought to a sentence, short words, short paragraphs and don't overdo it. Make the type big and bold and use the layout to lead the reader from start to finish in one logical, flowing sequence. Special emphasis may be given to the more important paragraphs by setting them in italics, bold face or by indenting them. Use subheads. Use all the information necessary and end with an order form. Look over the slick promotions you receive in the mail every day and analyze them.

Most mailings succeed or fail within about ten seconds after they are opened. If they don't catch the recipient's attention in that time, they go into the round file. We are bombarded with hundreds of advertising messages from the mail, billboards, TV, etc. and we tend to build up a defense toward them.

"Teaser" copy by way of words, photos, etc. is used to suggest a strong and clear relevance to an immediate need. To be effective, the teaser must be directed to the type of people in the specific list. Individuals want to know what the book can do for them, librarians want to know what it can do for their patrons and a bookstore owner wants to know why it will sell (as opposed to why it may be a good book.)

The teaser copy may be located on the outside of the envelope or self mailer but it should also be repeated on the inside to help the recipient find the place to start reading and to reassure that you are going to deliver on your promise. Even if the recipient keeps the contents, he or she will surely discard the envelope and you don't want to lose the teaser.

Little grabbers can also help. Words like "you" and "new" and "save" and "free" still work. And gimmicks like offering to pay postage "if they order today from this form" invite action, even though it may be your policy to ship all retail sales postpaid anyway.

Highlight the important aspects of the book in the rest of the copy. Relate to the reader and use testimonials, which are more objective, if you have them. Keep the message brief or the reader will get lost in the copy and give up. He feels his time is valuable so don't insult him by wasting it. Give details on the number of pages, illustrations, chapter titles, etc. Facts, not words, sell books.

If your circular is mixed-up and illogical, what will he think you are capable of doing in a book? Be specific. If yours is a technical manual directed at a select audience, the package doesn't have to be terribly fancy but it should be very detailed.

TESTIMONIALS may be placed in the circular or on a separate sheet. You never know which part of the mailing may catch the eye of the recipient first and these objective endorsements do help. Collect the testimonials from your "happy letters" and book reviews. Use them when writing up your next mailing. Be sure to get permission if you use their full name or enough information so they could be identified.

THE DIRECT MAIL LETTER introduces the circular. It should be interesting and easy to read. As with any personal message, it should be friendly but not insincere or disrespectful. Sincerity is hard to define but insincerity can be spotted instantly. Make sure the letter is clear and complete by having a friend read it both to himself and aloud. Write as you talk, don't search for big words. The letter may run one to four or even more pages, whatever it takes to make the pitch. Be concise and don't use any more space than necessary. Keep the paragraphs short; five sentences should be the limit. Sentences should be short and simple; ten to twelve words are enough.

Your letter should have a date so it will look like a letter. Use wide margins; the eye is trained to handle narrow newspaper columns. Small margins make a letter look too detailed, too much of a project to read. It is nice to address the recipient such as "Dear Ms. Hartmann" but this requires time and some automatic equipment. A "Dear Friend" or "Dear Fellow Skydiver" may be printed on. Some people like to use a headline to grab attention even though it is much less personal. Important points may be set off from the body of the letter with indented paragraphs, underlining, or italicized type. But don't overdo it or the value becomes diluted. If your audience tends to be older, be sure to use a typewriter with larger pica (10 characters to the inch) type rather than elite with 12 to the inch. If you run the letter in two colors, say black and blue, you may use the blue for your

> *"If you use a FREE offer, be sure there are no strings attached. Folks get mightily fed up with 'free' offers that cost them money."*

signature and while you're at it, include a personal P.S. Many feel the P.S. is second in importance only to the headline.

If you print on both sides of the letterhead, put "Please turn over" at the bottom. It is surprising how many people never think to turn the paper over. Don't end a sentence at the bottom of a page. Keep the reader "hanging." Carry him over to the next page with some provocative copy.

The "second chance letter" increases sales. It is the one which says: "Don't read this unless you have decided not to order." You get mailings with second chance letters every day.

Type out your letter and have it reproduced offset at your local instant print shop. Don't have it typeset, it won't look like a letter. Don't use a mimeograph, you want quality. Fold the letter printed side out so the recipient doesn't have to unfold it.

Always include a letter in your direct mail advertising package. There is an old saying: "Let the flyer do the telling and the letter do the selling."

THE GUARANTEE CARD may be separate, part of the brochure or part of the order card but the guarantee itself should be mentioned several times. Some publishers leave their address off the guarantee card to make it more difficult to find (the address is on the order card and that was mailed). Some ask for insured Parcel Post which is more expensive than "book rate" and makes the customer go to the Post Office to mail the book back. A general "satisfaction guaranteed" is preferable. Unless your book is worthless, you will experience few returns.

THE ORDER OF INSERTION will be the way you want the recipient to read the material. The most logical way is: cover letter, circular, testimonial sheet, order card and return envelope. And remember, people open envelopes from the back, not the front. In foreign mailings, check the local custom. Do their envelopes close on the top or the side?

MAGAZINE AND NEWSPAPER ADVERTISING can be broken down into two subgroups: classified and space (display). Unless you are covering a very broad or strictly local subject, you probably won't consider newspapers. Their audience is too general and the life of the paper is too short. Most new entrepreneurs start with the cheaper magazine classified and then graduate to space advertising as their business expands and their expertise increases. Space ads cost more but pull better: greater risk, greater potential reward. Your problem is that a book is a low-priced item. You have to sell a bunch to make an ad pay.

Bookstores respond to face-to-face approaches by sales people, not ads. Librarians rely on reviews. But space ads can work with proper direction. The last few years have seen a great proliferation of highly specialized magazines which cater to particular groups. The costs are usually lower and the response is ordinarily higher. If your book is on parachuting, you would want a monthly ad in Parachutist magazine. If your book is about left-handed people, advertise in their magazine. Since 10-12% of the population are lefties, an ad in any other magazine will be wasted on 88-90% of the readers.

"TIL FORBID" is abbreviated "T.F." and it means you want the ad to run continuously until you tell them to stop. The magazine will bill you upon publication of each edition and may even charge the fee to your Master Card or VISA account. Make sure you get your 2% for "cash" (paid in advance) if they bill one of your cards.

TEST YOUR AD in inexpensive publications and compare the response with your total cost. Using the ABC circulation figures and the demographics, consider (but don't rely) what you might get from other similar magazines.

Start with magazines with "short term closing dates," where the lead time between placing your order and its appearance in the magazine is less. In the beginning, you will want some test numbers as soon as possible. The bigger national magazines may have closing dates three months earlier than their cover date.

If your ad does well in one publication, stick with it. If it bombs, pull it and spend your ad money elsewhere. Don't be overwhelmed by the high price of large ads; they are cheap if they pull in sufficient orders. But don't jump right in. Work your way up to them slowly.

TIME your ads for the best time of year. A how-to book on skiing won't sell well in June. Group your exposures and concentrate on the best periods rather than advertise everywhere. Try a magazine with one ad and wait to check the results. If results are good, try every-other-month. If the ad still pulls, try monthly. Big ads pull better than small ones and you might do better with a half page in alternate months than a quarter page every month.

Time your ads for the prime months unless your book is seasonal. Christmas books should be advertised in October and November editions. Most magazines pre-date their covers; i.e., the March issue may go on the stands early in February. This provides them with more exposure time on the stands. No one wants to buy last month's magazine.

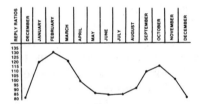

Traditional advertising reply ratios by month.

Don't run newspaper ads on any holidays or just before one. Your potential readers will be out of town just like you.

AD FREQUENCY. Some ad people talk of the "number of impressions": they say that you must repeat an ad to make it stick. What they don't say is that their commission is 15% of what they sell you. They want you to advertise as much and as often as possible. Most small publishers will tell you that an ad pulls best the first time out. So if it fails to pay its own way the first time, don't try it again. When the responses taper off, pull out and wait awhile. On the other hand if an ad is working, continue to use it. To quote the master John Caples: "Clients get tired of an ad before the public does." If the ad is pulling well, don't change a thing. One word could make the difference.

ROTATE YOUR ADS between publications. Keep half of them in old magazines where you have been before and half in testing new ones. When one ad fails to pay its own way, pull out and go elsewhere. Some publishers like to add a new magazine each month while dropping the poorest one no matter how well it has been pulling. Don't just advertise anywhere. Some books have wider general interest and, therefore, a greater number of magazines in which they might do well.

SELECTING MAGAZINES in which to advertise begins back at the library. Look through the magazine files. In a big city there are hundreds, and this could take days. There are magazines for every possible group and subject. Make a list of the magazine names and addresses. Next, consult any or all of the following references: Standard Rate and Data, Ulrich's and Ayer's. Request these references from your reference librarian. They list every magazine by subject along with circulation figures and other information. Send for the Chicago Advertising Agency's Ad Guide, listed in the Appendix.

Make up a form letter and mail one off to every magazine which shows potential. Just type the letter on your letterhead and photocopy a number of them. It is then a simple matter to fill in the address, date and signature before slipping it into a #10 windowed envelope.

To consider a magazine for your advertising, you not only need prices and circulation information, you want to look over the magazine to decide if it is the place for you, what location is best, and whether you should go for space or classified. Also look for book review sections and, if the magazine is appropriate, send off a review copy.

The circulation figures come in a pink folder marked "Audit Bureau of Circulation" (ABC). Don't confuse the ABC's "circulation" figures with the ad rep's "readership" number. He is talking about "pass on" or the number of people who may see the publication and this number may be estimated to be three or four times higher than the circulation figure. What you want are the actual circulation figures so you may compare the rates in similar magazines.

Also check the ratio of newsstand sales to subscriptions. Those who go to the trouble of purchasing the magazine might read it more thoroughly. They may also be new, fresh names for your mailing list.

(Letterhead)

February 31, 1985

Exciting Magazine
Attention: Advertising Department
123 Media Street
Communication City, NY 10000

Ladies & Gentlemen:

Your publication is being considered as an advertising medium for some of our books. Please forward a media package to include:

1. Display advertising rate card
2. Classified advertising rate card
3. Current circulation figures (ABC statement)
4. Schedule of "special editions"
5. Two different sample copies of your publication so that we may determine the best size and placement for our advertising.

Do you provide discounts or special rates for (1) book publishers, (2) mail order, (3) new advertisers?

We would appreciate being placed on file to be notified of any future rate or policy changes.

Please pass the enclosed press information on to your New Book/Product Editor. Review copies of our books are available and we maintain a large file of photographs on these subjects.

Sincerely,

YOUR COMPANY NAME

Henry M. Goodfellow
Marketing Manager

HMG/ms
Enclosure: Brochure

A media package request letter

Advertise first in those magazines where your book reviews pulled well. They wouldn't have reviewed the book if they didn't feel it fit the interests of their readership. Look at the ads in the rest of the magazine and you will get a good idea of their readership profile. Check the demographics in the media packet.

Be careful of newspapers with circulations below 100,000. Their cost per reader is usually too high. "Free circulation" (throwaway) shopping news type papers don't pull well.

Once you begin to advertise, other publications will respond with ad rate material. These low circulation publications are rarely worth your while.

CLASSIFIED ADS. The little magazines with small classified sections can be very good and these sections are often underpriced. The editors probably haven't given much thought to this section lately. The experts feel that classifieds must be limited to items with a price of $2 or less. To ask more, they recommend a "display classified" (words and photo, and often in a box but located in the classified section.) They reason that it is not possible to describe the product sufficiently in a couple of lines of type to justify the higher amount. Recent inflation may have moved this $2 figure higher to, say, $4 and/or books may be an exception. If your subject is a hot one, people will send even $10 just to get more information.

Classifieds are normally run to generate a mailing list ("two step") rather than to move a product but there are many exceptions. Many classifieds for expensive items simply offer a brochure with more details or a choice of the product or a brochure. This establishes a very good mailing list almost guaranteeing a higher than average response rate to a direct mail campaign. Interestingly enough, many advertising people feel that classifieds reach different people than space ads so they take out both in the same edition.

Some people suffer from "freebee-itis" and will send for anything offered without charge. They waste your

> *"They all want the same thing — a magic button to push that will make then thinner, more beautiful, richer."*

time and money while cluttering up your mailing list. It is a good idea to charge something for your "information kit."

The above discussion is terribly discouraging to someone with a single book to offer but many authors are marketing their books through classifieds successfully. It takes a lot of sales to justify a 15 word, $120 ad in Popular Science and they must be making money or they wouldn't be there more than a couple of months. One secret is placing your book in the best classification. Don't advertise in the "book" section. If it is a hang gliding book, stick it under "aviation." These people are air-minded and want to fly, they would never think to look for a book. But they will soon find that a book will bring them the information they seek. If you were the consumer, where would you look? You can test your locations by advertising in two different sections in the same edition. Be wary when comparing ads appearing in different issues, however. Traditionally, classifieds pull better in some months than in others.

If your classified isn't pulling as well as it once did, it could be due to the season, a saturated market or competition from other ads near it. Don't hesitate to stop an ad that isn't paying its own way. Advertise only in the best months. Books sell best in February through April because people are confined to their homes by the weather. They are planning the Summer's activities. A few months later they are outdoors and don't have time for books. If the market seems saturated, try running the ad for every other month for awhile. If you have competition from other advertisers, see if you can't word a better offer. Repetition seems to work in classifieds, especially in some rural publications. It takes several months to become "established" so that the readers become used to seeing your ad.

Always code your address and then keep accurate records of the response by month. Plot your own chart; it will be a great help in your ad planning next year. Knowing your response to each ad and knowing your costs

---

"Show how your book solves problems and enhances the stature of the user among his or her contemporaries."

will help you to determine whether you should continue to advertise in that magazine. Many ad writers prefer a street address to a P.O. Box. See the discussion in Chapter Three.

It is generally agreed that you should use your personal or company name in an ad rather than an abbreviation such as initials. People like to know who they are dealing with.

If the magazine makes an error in your ad, don't be afraid to ask for a credit. Make a photocopy of the ad and your ad insertion letter and, depending on the severity of the difference, request a refund, another ad or a partial credit on a new ad. Quite often they are very quick to volunteer a free ad in the next edition.

Some magazines will send you a copy of the issue featuring your ad while others will send "tear sheets" of the page only. Keep these ads in a filing folder along with all your correspondence to the magazine.

DRAFTING YOUR CLASSIFIED AD. Remember that people respond to classifieds and order by mail for three reasons: convenience (no driving, parking or crowds), novelty (can't find it locally) and price. Since your book might be in the reader's local bookstore and because you aren't giving the book away, your best case is novelty. Think about this as you draft your ad. Your message must be brief because you are paying for each word but it must be sufficiently descriptive to encourage the reader to buy. You have to write the winning classified.

In many magazines it costs just a little more for bold face or all caps and you should use these in your first few words. Be specific by offering a recognizable product or a benefit. For example, if your book is on coin collecting, start the ad with "COINS" or "MAKE MONEY collecting coins." Now that you have their attention, develop your concept. Stress uniqueness and personal benefits. Be brief, every word costs, but be complete. Tell the reader what you have and why he or she should want it. Don't use large, flowery, technical or cute

"Revlon makes cosmetics in the factory and sells hope in the drugstore." — Charles Revson

words. Stick to the small words which are easy to grasp; those which are easy to understand. Close with the price and your address. Avoid using verbs, articles and unnecessary adjectives; they cost while adding little. If a word doesn't make a direct point, don't use it, don't waste your money. Remember that eight-word copy will sell better than 800 word copy if you can make a case in eight words. Benson Barrett has used his winner for years without change: "Make money writing short paragraphs at home." Seven beautiful, well-chosen words.

If you want the reader to send for more information because you can't make your pitch in a few words, use the word: "details" rather than "free information." Then follow up with a powerful sales letter.

You will pay by the word in some ads and by the line in others. In some you may like to use "ppd" and in others the ad will cost no more and will look bigger if you use "postpaid." If you are paying by the line, you may wish to add some words to fill out the last one. Unused white space is called a "widow." If you abbreviate your address, try it out on your postman first; you want to receive every check.

Before mailing off the ad, try it out on a friend or relative to make sure it is understandable and interesting.

You can make big money from small classified ads. While you may take in only a few dollars on one ad, you may take in fifty times as much with fifty ads.

SPACE ADVERTISING consists of a regular word and picture message. It gets its name because what you are buying is "space." You may put most anything you want into it.

Space advertising in newspapers and magazines may both sell books and build your mailing list. But this display advertising is very expensive and may not be hitting the right audience. Prices for a full page may range from $100 for a local paper to $60,000 in Fortune or Business Week; in any case you will have to move a lot of

---

"The ad worked because it attracted the right audience...because it aroused curiosity and because it offered a reward" — John Caples.

books to pay for the ad. While space ads might give the best rate PER EXPOSURE, they don't necessarily provide the best rate PER RESPONSE. The big publishers take out book list announcement ads in publications such as Publishers Weekly, Choice, ALA Booklist and Library Journal mainly because all this clutter is an industry custom; its sort of a birthright. Display ads are often placed only to prove to the author that they are supporting his title. It takes a lot of repetitious advertising like this to generate any response and it may not be cost effective. One industry rule of thumb is that for every 100 exposures, 1% will remember they saw the ad and .01 to .12% will respond. Most won't even notice the ad.

So the big publishers may be placing those big space ads because they are too big to adjust or for other specific reasons. They may be supporting their bookstores trying to direct traffic there, they may be investing to build up a special mailing list or they may be after "door openers" for their salesmen. Whatever their motives, the chances are slim that the same type of space advertising will work for you.

Space ad size may be sold by the part of a page: $\frac{1}{2}$, $\frac{1}{4}$, 1/8, 1/16, etc. Or, it may be sold by the "column inch": $\frac{1}{2}$", 1", 2", etc. by one column wide. Often, space is sold by the "line." There are 14 lines to the inch and the width would be that of a column. One inch is often the minimum. Check the width of the columns, by the way. Some magazines run three columns while others run four to the page.

The size of your ad should be as big as you can justify through past testing. The larger the ad, the more stable you look. Small firms can't afford full page ads.

Magazines are printed offset today so they can accept ads pasted up just as your book was. Many will accept your rough copy and will lay out your ad for a small charge. However, you may wish to have the layout done by your local graphic artist so you'll know what you're getting.

ADVERTORIALS are large ads made to look like a regular article. Reader's Digest always has a couple. The only way to tell they aren't articles is by the word "advertisement" at the top or bottom of the page. Advertorials are very effective as many people start reading them without realizing what they are.

THE POSITION of your ad in magazines should be on the outside of a right-hand page in the first third of the issue. The bigger the ad you buy, the more leverage you will have regarding position. It is best to be the only ad on the page and a full page ad insures it. Vertical half pages seem to pull better than horizontal half pages. In a monthly you can expect 60% of your response within 30 days after the magazine reaches its readers.

In newspapers, your ad should be positioned above the fold, on a right-hand page and in the correct section. If your book isn't appropriate to the financial page, sports pages, etc., try the TV page, the best read of all. The next best place is the general news section, up front. If you place your ad in the TV section of the Sunday paper, put it toward the back so it will have a longer life. In a weekly, you can figure on 60% of your responses the first week and they will drop off fast after that.

MAIL ORDER RATES are offered by most magazines and these may be half the price of the regular rates. Always ask and make sure you get the right rate card; most magazines issue more than one. Just call the space rep listed on the card and ask. Most reps are authorized to make deals, so it never hurts to ask for a better price on the assumption that you are small, just starting out and that if the ad pulls, you will be back for more. Try asking for your first "trial" ad at the twelve time rate.

REMNANT SPACE occurs when advertisers purchase certain regional areas in a national publication. Picking up the rest on a fill-in basis can result in considerable savings. The magazine has to fill this space with something. It never hurts to ask.

BULK BUYERS are people who purchase a large amount of ad space at greater discounts. They use some of it to

---

"It is important to have a book that is appealing enough to its audience that little or no advertising is necessary."

move their own products and they sell off the rest of the space. You probably won't be dealing with these people for a while.

ANOTHER COUPON may be on the back side of your ad and clipping it will destroy your message. Always specify that your ad is not to "back up" a coupon.

FAVORS FROM EDITORS come to advertisers who ask for them. Try for some editorial coverage by sending in press releases, book review copies, and articles by yourself which reference your book. The smaller the magazine, the more they can wheel and deal.

HEADLINES make ads work. They must stop your prospect as he pages through the magazine, arouse his curiosity and persuade him to start reading the ad. The headline will be in large bold face type and may be the title of your book. The best headlines give news or appeal to one's self interest. Use provocative words such as "secrets of. . . reveals." The headline must stop the prospect with a believable promise.

SUBHEADS amplify the headline and may run above or below in smaller type. They get more specific but are usually more intriguing and do more selling. They whet the appetite for the text of the ad.

A PHOTOGRAPH of the book is a requirement. Sure, all books look the same but a photo is some proof that the book exists. The reader wants to be assured he isn't buying a few mimeographed sheets. The photograph helps the prospect to focus on something; help him to know what you are selling. Photos cost a little more but they are worth a lot more.

THE BODY COPY is where you tell the major features of the book. Select three or four objective facts and work on them. The body copy should take as long as necessary to tell the story. Keep the copy conversational as if you were leveling with a friend about something that has you enthusiastic. You have to excite the reader too, so much that he or she will want to act. The copy should be clear, simple, direct and logical. Make it personal, appeal to his self interest and tie him to it. Tell a compelling, dramatic but credible story using simple vivid language. Repeat the important points. List the special features and advantages of the book; a list of chapter titles might be the best way.

Overwrite your text and trim it back. Facts are interesting and they sell. Put your best benefit first. If you save it until last, he may never read far enough to see it. Avoid humor; this is a serious sales deal. Use simple words your whole audience can understand. Demonstrate why your book is unique, useful, timely. Don't be afraid to use the proven words: you, new, free and save. Some other good ones are: benefit, comfort, economy, effective, lasting, practical, service, thrifty, truth, money, help, discover, proven, guarantee, how-to, safety, love and results.

Victor Schwab used the title of Dale Carnegie's famous book How To Win Friends And Influence People as an ad headline. Using the old formula: a failure to success story followed by the promise that the same can happen to the reader, the book caught on. It sold 100,000 copies by mail and generated over $5 million in bookstore sales.

A time limit, at the top of the ad or set off in bold type, will stimulate action.

TESTIMONIALS are the subjective, emotional part of your ad and they come next. Show what people are saying about your book. Of course, it helps to have testimonials from people who are recognized in the field covered by the book. Many copy writers like to put the testimonials in a box to the side of the body copy.

SOME AUTHOR BACKGROUND information will lend a bit of credibility to the book. Concentrate on only those parts of your background that affect the book. Include a photo of yourself doing what you do: if the book is about skydiving, you should be in freefall, if it's about law you

---

"Good judgement comes from experience, and experience — well, that comes from poor judgement."

should be in court or in a library. Project the proper image.

THE GUARANTEE is particularly important in a mail order book ad. Offer a full refund if not satisfied. Of course, the book must be returned in good resaleable condition. Yes, the customer could read and even photocopy the pages he wants to retain and then return the book but this rarely happens.

THE COUPON is your contract with the purchaser and it must be large enough so that you will be able to read the name and address when filled in. You might like to precede the coupon with a line saying: "At your bookstore or direct from:." It doesn't hurt to have people ask for the book in the store.

Always code your ad so you know where the order is coming from. You might like to offer an early order bonus or say at least: "We pay the postage when you order from this ad." Normally, you would pay the postage anyway.

COLOR sells better than black and white, some say 70% better. Color also costs a lot more. Once you work your way up to full page ads you can start thinking about color. If your black and white ad pulls well, color may attract more readers to it. If your black and white ad bombs, color won't help.

RADIO AND TELEVISION advertising has great potential in book marketing and the big publishers have tried it sparingly only in the last few years. While everyone seems to agree that TV can move books, the expense is so great that air time usually isn't recommended unless you have an ad budget totaling $100,000. To succeed, you need the right book and the right approach. There usually are not enough book buyers to support such an inexpensive product.

Small author/publishers should test the medium by trying for a free talk show and measuring the results before venturing any ad money. If the book is regional, you might be successful in a local broadcast.

When buying radio and TV time, ask for the "local" rate, it is much lower than the "general" or "national" rate.

PIGGYBACK PROMOTION consists of adding information on additional books to your regular promotional work. While not a major part of your promotional effort, this element is worth constant consideration as it leads to bonus sales; it moves more books at little additional cost or effort.

Add brochures and flyers to your outgoing mail. Postage is priced by the even ounce (or half ounce for foreign air mail) so use the rate to the limit by filling up each envelope. Calibrate your postage scale easily with nine new (pre-1983, all-copper) pennies. Add the pennies and set the scale on one ounce. This is much more accurate than setting an empty scale to zero.

Filling up the monthly statement envelopes may have less value. Some of these people are "slow pay" and it is questionable whether you want to encourage any more of their business. Secondly, the statements go to the business office not to the buyers. So unless you have an office procedures type book, the brochure may never get to the right person. Some accounts are with small firms where one person handles everything; here a stuffer will get to the right one.

Exchanging brochures with other firms works well. This operates on the theory that once you have sold a customer your book, you have nothing more to offer. But you and another small author/publisher with a similar book can pat each other on the back and give each other a hand by each stuffing the other's brochure. It is like exchanging mailing lists except that it is easier and cheaper (no licking, postage or envelopes). When a brochure arrives in a mailing from another publisher, it is an implied endorsement of your book.

Dustbooks (P. O. Box 100-P, Paradise, CA 95969) will pay you $3.40 for each copy of their International Directory of Little Magazines and Small Presses which is sold via their piggyback stuffer.

Bookstores are sometimes receptive to stuffing your brochures in their outgoing mail. They will want their address on the flyers and if you are printing up thousands

276

for many stores they may agree to use a rubber stamp. To make a rubber stamp imprint look nice, it must be clean and used firmly, often slowly. So you might offer to do it. When your printer is running your brochures, have him run a batch for you with your address and then opaque out the address and run the rest blank.

Direct mail advertising is the most obvious place to piggyback. You want to be sure the extras don't detract from and dilute the main offer. Many do this by simply including a brief backlist of other books rather than another fancy brochure. If you are offering a lot of books, all in your own line or jointly with other firms, they will get more individual attention if they are offered on separate slips of paper. You can get a #10 envelope, four sheets of paper, a stamp and a label under the one ounce limit, and more if you are going for the two-ounce Bulk Rate. Be careful, staples and stamps add to the weight, too. But you can get twelve or thirteen 3 5/8 x 8½ slips into the envelope. They provide the recipient with an easy reading/sorting format. He or she is more likely to look over each offer when it is presented separately than to inspect a page with several offers jumbled together. To get the maximum out of your postage, weigh up several stuffed envelopes at the same time. Ten should be just barely under 10 ounces on the scale, for example. That is cutting it close!

Your brochure and other promotional materials should be stuffed into every package you ship out. Your customers are your best bet for repeat business. The Post Office limits this activity to "incidental announcements" when using Book Rate and this means a few flyers, not heavy catalogs. Again, you might strike a deal with another publisher to stuff each other's brochures.

Blank backmatter pages may be used to announce your other titles. Book copy and signatures rarely come out even, there are usually a few blank pages at the end. These pages may be put to work rather than wasted. This principle is so common in Germany that the last section of many books looks like a catalog. When the book is being pasted up, be prepared to add some additional promotional copy to fill up the last signature. This will also add to your mailing list since it will bring in sales from those who have purchased books before, not directly from you, but from bookstores and other indirect outlets.

"Pass along" approaches work well in large organizations such as libraries and schools, particularly when you aren't sure who you should be contacting or if more than one person is involved in the decision-making process. Just send two or three pieces of the same brochure (consider postage again) and ask the recipient to pass the others on to someone else.

Envelopes can be used for piggybacking by printing teaser ads on the outside. Some firms use their envelopes to promote "hot" forthcoming books with an exciting blurb. Then they use these envelopes for all their mail. When you grow big enough for a postage meter, you can order your message on an imprint slug.

Remember that the piggyback principle is an "add on" to other promotion only. While it will generate more business from existing customers, it will not bring in new clients. Every time you make a contact with a potential customer, you want to show him everything you have to offer. Chances are, at least one will appeal to him. But remember that stuffers cost money and must not be wasted. Send them only when there is a chance of an order.

CO-OP ADVERTISING is a popular way the big publishers direct sales to bookstores with local space ads. Typically, the publisher pays 75% of the ad cost (but no more than 10% of the value of the books shipped to the store) and the bookstore pays 25%. If the store is a regular advertiser in the local papers, they usually get a slightly better rate. The procedure is to have the store place the ads but the tear sheets and bills go to the publisher. Then the publisher credits the store with 75% of the bill toward book purchases.

To justify co-op advertising you have to anticipate that the store will move a lot of books. And, while the stores may be the major outlet for the big publisher, it may be a minor one for a small firm which concentrates on mail order sales.

The Federal Trade Commission (FTC) regulations insist that any deal offered to one dealer must be made available to all. A small publisher who tests co-op ads with one store could find himself in great financial difficulty being obligated to advertise for everyone else. Many small firms feel that co-op advertising is just too complicated and too time-consuming and they routinely answer all inquiries in the negative. They save time, money and stay away from the FTC.

AD PARTICIPATION may be worked to benefit both you and another firm with a similar book or product. It allows you greater flexibility while your participant gets a sure bet. You place your own ads and then supply him with a mailing list of those who responded but at a higher per-name price. This is not just another random mailing list. These are people who have sent for a related product lately. For example, if you are routinely offering a hang gliding book in general magazine ads, you are attracting customers from outside the sport and you are selling them on the activity with your book. A list of these prime prospects would be very valuable to a hang glider manufacturer and he should be willing to spend 50¢ a name for them. It is a good idea for him because he doesn't spend time on this part of his advertising program and he pays only for results. It is a good deal for you because it allows you to advertise in more places and to continue with marginal return ads. Some marginal sales are better than no sales.

BE YOUR OWN AD AGENCY and save over 15% on your space ads. Advertising firms make their money through the 15% commission they get on all the space they write for a magazine or newspaper. Normally commissions apply only to space ads, not to classifieds. And if you place your own ads, you can get even more. For example:

Cost of ad	$100.00
Ad commission (15%)	-15.00
Cash with order (2%)	-1.70
Total ad cost	$83.30

Being a new account, the periodical probably won't extend credit anyway, so simply write up your ad insertion order like the one above and take the 2% deduction for cash and enclose your check. It is very unlikely that they will reject your terms.

INSERTION ORDER

AGENCY:

A.M. FURMAN ASSOCIATES

527 Madison Avenue
New York City, NY 10022
(212) 421-3707

PRODUCT: DATE:

ADVERTISER: THIS ORDER APPLIES TO OUR CONTRACT
                                            NO.

TO:

Dates of Insertion	Times	Caption	Key	Space Ordered	Position

Special Instructions:

RATE _____   LESS FREQ. DISC. _____ PERCENT
    _____   LESS AGENCY COMMISSION _____ PERCENT OF GROSS
    _____   LESS CASH DISCOUNT _____ PERCENT ON NET
                        NET AMOUNT THIS ORDER $ _____
BY: _____

Example of an advertising insertion order.

Check to see if the magazine offers Master Card or VISA. By charging your advertising, you won't be billed until the magazine appears. This can give you use of your money between then and when you placed the ad order.

As the writer/publisher of your book, you are in a much better position to write ad copy for it than a copy writer who isn't familiar with the product. You will write better and work harder. You will be more alert to special deals and package prices than they.

When wearing your other hat as an ad agency, you will be in a better position to promote the author and the publisher. All this "hype" sounds better coming from a more objective, outside source.

To establish your own ad agency, there will be a small investment necessary to give the appearance of a completely separate entity. You will need a different firm name, letterhead, telephone, check book, etc., make sure that all are signed by people outside of your publishing company. Many publications such as The National Enquirer will not allow commissions to "in house" ad agencies. Some will even spend quite a bit of time trying to match up telephone numbers, signatures, etc.

"PER INQUIRY" ads require no investment and are a good way for you to try out new advertising media. Many smaller newspapers, magazines, radio and television stations will run your ad for a share of the results. The orders are sent to them with the checks made out to you, thus giving you both a check on the other. Their cut is usually 33% to 50% of the order, about what you would give any retailer. The reason they do this is to fill unused space or time, making blank areas generate some income.

Normally you have to prepare the ad. This means nice "camera ready" artwork for newspapers and magazines or tapes for radio and TV A one minute videotape may run $100 and about $25 for each duplicate. Many authors (and other entrepreneurs) prefer to do their own shows to hiring an actor at $50 or more. An author is very much a part of his book and the personal touch can go a long way.

The best approach is to write the station, paper, etc. describing your book and asking if they accept Per Inquiry advertising. They want sure deals so if you have done this before, recite your good track record.

If you have already tested a medium and experienced a good return, it would not be worth your while to offer them a P.I. deal. It is better to pay for your ads and get all the money than to go P.I. and take only part.

Even free advertising is wasted if it fails to generate business; it is a waste of your time and energy.

POINT-OF-PURCHASE SALES AIDS include bookmarks, dumps, posters, etc. Posters can be very useful in specialty shops and booths but there just isn't any room for them in a bookstore. Librarians like posters but they do not buy many books. Free bookmarks with advertising are used 30 to 38% of the time by bookstores. Dumps are special shipping cartons/display units which are used by 38 to 40% of the stores depending on the available counter and floor space. Many larger stores suggest and request them. Some clever publishers have designed small dumps with directions for detecting counterfeit bills on the back. This assures premium display space on the counter near the cash register.

CATALOGS, whether for books or related specialty goods, offer a prime market to publishers. Some catalogs list general interest books, some concentrate on a line of special titles (for example, business and finance) while others may carry a line of merchandise and a section on related books. Catalog orders are large and the mail order firm is committed to your product for (usually) a full year.

Special merchandise catalogs are those featuring a line of merchandise but which devote a page or two to related books. Since you are already in the field (having written about it), you probably know who they are.

For more, go through the ads in related field magazines. After you send for a few, you will find yourself on the mailing lists for most of them. For a list of over 10,000 mail order companies and ideas on how to approach them, see The Fifty Billion Dollar Directory (Publishers Services, 6318-P Vesper Avenue, Van Nuys, CA 91411.)

A brochure may get you into a catalog sooner. For example, if you have a book on sport parachuting, the mail order parachute supply firms will want to carry it. However, your publication dates rarely coincide with their catalog deadlines. If you supply them with a brochure which they may insert into all catalogs, outgoing mail and packages, they will be offering your book immediately. Again, of course, they will want their name imprinted on the brochure. This approach may be used in certain cases as a sneaky sales tool. Sometimes you can't convince a firm to handle your book. But if you take them a bunch of free brochures to stuff, the orders will come in. Soon they will become convinced of the book's sales potential and forced to add it to their line.

YOUR CATALOG is probably a long way off. After you have published ten books, you will need a catalog just to maintain organization. A catalog is a good reference and a public relations tool. With just a few books, a much cheaper brochure is all you will need. Flyers on individual books will usually out-pull a catalog which is too big and takes too much time to read through.

The big publishers separate their catalogs into two distinct sections: the new titles and the "backlist." The catalog may be titled "Books for Spring" and will feature all the current offerings up front. Last season's titles which are still available will be in the less prominent backlist in back.

If you want to publish a catalog but have only a few titles, you might consider carrying related titles from other publishers.

COMMISSION SALES REPS offer to do for the smaller publisher what the sales force does for the larger ones. Their job is to call on bookstores to brief the buyers on new titles, straighten up the stock, take orders and otherwise service the account. The orders are sent to you, the reps do not stock books.

Commission reps get 10% of the amount of the sales to retailers and 5% of the sales to wholesalers and they will ask for more. The first thing they will want, though, is a protected territory, an exclusive. Since most bookstore sales are made because of consumer demand in response to outside promotion, the only value in the rep is that he tries to get your book on the shelf. However, he gets his 10% even if he stays home and doesn't visit the store. The rep has many books and too little time in the bookstores. He will push only the sure-fire sellers in order to maintain credibility with the book buyer. If you want to better understand what a commission rep can do for you, visit a bookstore yourself and give selling a try. Compared to direct mail, reps are quite a luxury; many publishers don't feel they are worthwhile.

Even if you have a line of a half-dozen titles, most of the bookstore orders generated by the sales reps will be around $25. Since many books will be returned by the stores, it costs a lot of money to service these small accounts. There is a lot of paperwork and book counting.

When you get a telephone call from a sales rep, don't be snowed by his offer for "world distribution rights." Tell him you won't give exclusive territories explaining that if you had given an exclusive to someone last week, you couldn't consider his offer. Don't make any deals over the telephone, you are under too much pressure. Always ask for the offer in writing. Then you will have several days to evaluate it.

The author tried sales reps for a year and a half. While sales increased some 20%, over $2,500 was virtually uncollectable. When he let the sales reps go, his sales dropped 20% but his headaches dropped 80%.

If you are still interested in locating commission salespeople, there is a good list in Literary Market Place. Also check the classified ads in Publishers Weekly and look for reps at book fairs.

TELEPHONE SELLING may be used to complement your other promotion. It should be used aggressively on both incoming as well as outgoing calls to stimulate business. Time is money and travel takes a lot of time. While the important wholesale accounts almost have to be sold in a face-to-face presentation, there are others which may be handled by telephone. And with the telephone, those important accounts may not have to be visited so often. This approach is particularly important to the small author/publisher who is pushing a single title. Many buyers appreciate a call instead of a visit as it uses less of their valuable time.

Plan your call. What is your objective? What do you plan to accomplish? If you want to make a sale, get organized.

A written script is the best way to start. Write it up the same way you would an ad by starting with the most important point to get their attention. In calls to the trade, emphasize how well the book is selling and invite them to get in on the action. Offer to send a review copy, tell them about your return policy, get it all in there. Say: "Shouldn't I put you down for ten copies at 40%, fully returnable?" Then practice your delivery until it becomes smooth and natural. You don't want to stay on the line longer than necessary to get what you want.

Make a written record of every call incoming and outgoing. Keep a pad near the telephone and write down who, the date and what. Keep these slips on file. Before calling an account, pull their file and review your past contacts. This will make the contact more personal.

Always call the same person. Look them up when making a visit or touring a book show. If you establish your credibility and treat them right on your first book, they will probably take the second book sight unseen.

Important book reviewers should be contacted by telephone after you send the complimentary copy. A good opening line is "have you received the book?" They are more apt to review books by authors they know and the telephone is an easy way to reach them.

Subsidiary rights, remainder offers, etc., may be negotiated over the telephone but always ask to get their offer in writing. This delay of a few days will provide you with some breathing room to think it over and, perhaps, even to find a better deal.

When customers call to order one title, use this opportunity and their telephone money for an add-on; tell them about other related titles which are new and they might want.

Check your telephone directory for the rates for both intrastate and interstate calls. Clip out the charts and stick them on the wall next to the telephone. A 7:30 a.m. call from California is much cheaper than one made a half hour later and it reaches New York at an ideal 10:30 a.m. East coast publishers can use the reverse by calling the west coast after 5 p.m. when the rates drop again.

Many large firms have toll-free 800 numbers. To find whether the company you are calling has one, simply dial: (800) 555-1212 and give the operator the company name and address. There is no charge for the directory assistance call and it never hurts to ask.

Used properly, the telephone can be a great sales tool without greatly increasing the communications bill. Telephoning is much cheaper and easier than travel.

REMAINDERS are overstock books which are sold off to remainder dealers at greatly reduced prices. The big publishers are only interested in books while they are maintaining a certain level of sales. When the demand drops to the point where the books fail to pay for their storage costs, out they go. Your situation is different because you are storing the books at home, have a lower overhead, like the prestige of having a current book and can get by on the occasional sales. Initially, each book in your brochure adds to your size. You will have to have a number of titles before you will be interested in dropping any. In fact, since you have the plates, you can always run off another 1,000 copies. There is no reason to go out of print. If it is a good how-to book and you have kept it up-to-date with revisions at each printing, it should continue to sell.

John Huenefeld offers this rule of thumb for determining when to dump a title: Multiply the quantity on hand by the list price. Then divide by 20 to get 5% of the list price value of the stock. Now compare this 5% figure with the net sales for the last 12 months. If the sales were not greater than this 5% figure, it's time to call the truck.

You might be able to move the books more profitably with a sale via your own mailing list at, say, 50% off. Try the big chains, over 65% of them purchase remainder stock.

Remaindering is big business. 20,000 titles go out of print each year and some 25-million copies are remaindered. A lot of big firms are in this business; many wholesalers carry remainders and they may account for one-third of a bookstore's gross. Some books see their sales pick up once remaindered. The new price and marketing effort has turned books completely around. Remaindered books have sold out and have gone back on the press.

Notify your wholesalers before remaindering a book and offer to take their stock back. Wholesalers are needed customers and are too valuable to upset and lose. You might start by offering them a special buy on the books for, say, 60 to 70% off.

Lists of remainder dealers may be found in Pub-lishers Weekly, Literary Market Place and American Book Trade Directory, all at your library. Write to a number of remainder dealers indicating the quantity, list price, title, hardbound or paperback, condition, location and whether they are prepackaged and if so, in what increments. Enclose a copy of the book and your sales materials. Establish a closing date and announce that you will accept the best offer for any quantity. Shipping is FOB your warehouse, terms are net 30 days and the books are not returnable. Once you have selected the highest bidder, call him and make sure you have a deal. You aren't making enough to ship the books two ways.

Your offers may be between 5 and 10% but don't be surprised at hearing 10¢ each. Since your name is on the book, it is worth your while to get it out to the field and onto peoples' shelves, rather than to throw them in the Dumpster. Even at 10¢, they are still "sold." Most remainder dealers will want 1,000 to 5,000 books, minimum, and they want your entire stock so as to have an exclusive. Some will take your slightly damaged stock—those scratched copies returned by bookstores. Hopefully, you won't have to deal in remainders.

DONATE DAMAGED RETURNS to a charity. You may deduct the value of the book at its original acquisition cost plus the postage out. Prisons, foreign libraries and church bazaars will be very happy to accept your books. By donating your scuffed books, you recover your original investment in them.

> *"Doing business without advertising is like winking at a girl in the dark. You know what you are doing but she doesn't."*

> *"Your book is a success when people who haven't read it pretend they have."*

Chapter Ten

DISTRIBUTION
GETTING YOUR BOOK TO MARKET

Distribution or "fulfillment" consists of invoicing, inventory storage, packaging and shipping. These routines involve opening the mail, sorting it, typing the invoices, wrapping the books, affixing the shipping label, applying postage to the package, making the trip to the Post Office and maintaining a record of the sale. Inventory management includes stock monitoring so you will know when to order another printing.

MAIL ORDER selling offers you the opportunity to run a high volume, worldwide business without a large cash investment in facilities. To compete with larger companies, all you need is a better ad or mailing piece. All you see are the sales, you never experience a "turn-down" like a regular salesperson. You deal with friends who keep coming back. The business continues to run even

> *"Books on money-making, self-improvement, weight-reduction and recipes are staple mail order sellers."*

when you take a few days off. You are only limited by the quality of your advertising copy and the amount of money you are willing to invest. Dealing direct with the customer, you eliminate all the middlemen. Mail order is probably the best way to get started in book distribution.

"Mail order" businesses refer to those which deal with their customers at a distance, without face-to-face selling. The product may not be delivered by the Post Office; a large shipment might go by truck. Mail order is particularly appropriate for the distribution of books. In fact, over half of the business and professional books are shipped directly from the publisher to the final consumer.

The Maxwell Sroge company reports that $779-million worth of books were sold via mail order in 1975. Of course, most were through book clubs but not all. Sroge says the boom largely reflects the growing number of working wives. They find shopping from home more convenient and, with two incomes, they can afford it.

It should be noted that some books are designed to be marketed primarily by mail; the Association of American Publishers calls these "Mail Order Publications." Some books are aimed at other markets but may also have a small portion marketed through mail order. Many bookstores ship books and are, therefore, dealing through mail order. Incidentally if you see a book you like and are willing to order three or more, find the address of the publisher in Books in Print. Then simply order direct taking your 40% discount.

Smaller publishers are attracted to mail order selling because it is easier than getting into bookstores. They ship to wholesalers and stores but they don't spend the money on visiting them. In fact, there are many stories about books which have done poorly in the stores which when properly promoted sold well through mail order.

Mail order buyers probably do not frequent bookstores and it is likely they do not even think of themselves as book buyers. They are probably more interested in the subject than in reading. If they go to a bookstore looking for a book on a particular subject and cannot find one, they consult the subject index of Books in Print. Then, finding a suitable title, they take the information home to order it themselves rather than ask the store to special order it. In a Publishers Weekly article on Bantam, it was noted that geographically, mail orders line up proportionately with population figures. Most orders come from the most populated states, California and New York, not from the states with fewer bookstores. Mail order purchasing is a habit. Many people prefer to buy informational books this way. Once they begin, they buy everything they can find on the subject.

THE FEDERAL TRADE COMMISSION (FTC) has some strict new rules for mail order operations. You must ship an order within 30 days unless you have clearly stated another date in your offer. If you cannot ship within the 30 day period, you must inform the customer of the delay, quote a new shipping date and offer to return their money if requested. If you miss the second announced date, you must automatically refund the money to all customers except those who have given explicit instructions to you to keep it. See the FTC pamphlets listed in the Appendix.

Orders should be shipped as soon as possible after receipt and there is no reason why they cannot go out the next day. This involves a trip to the Post Office once each day to pick up the mail and to deliver the wrapped books from orders received the previous day. The sooner the orders are processed, the sooner the money will be deposited; the best incentive for speedy fulfillment.

Customers want their book as soon as possible. A few who are not familiar with mail order will even write two days later looking for their package, but this is rare. When business is slow, Post Office runs may be made every other day, say Monday, Wednesday and Friday. And if you must be away from the business, you will find that only one or two inquiries will be received if you fail to ship up to 30 days. But, remember, the Federal Trade Commission (FTC) says you must send an explanatory post card if you can't ship within 30 days.

ORDER PROCESSING. Once your business grows to where you have numerous titles and several employees, you will require a more elaborate fulfillment system but initially you will do it all yourself so you can keep it simple. One way is to streamline the workload to avoid any duplication of effort. For example, typing up an invoice and then typing a separate label is a waste of time and money (cost of label, etc.) A number of pieces of information must be recorded to process an order. Through the use of carbon copies, all may be done at the single initial invoice typing. This "one-writing" also avoids transposition errors in figures and addresses.

To enable you to visualize the distribution system, the fulfillment process will be discussed in sequence.

Open the mail and check the contents but do not take the orders and checks out of their envelopes. Sort the stuffed envelopes into piles according to whether they are individual retail sales, book dealers (stores or distributors), libraries or special accounts such as associations, sport centers, etc. Make up a separate pile for inquiries--you will want to send them a brochure.

INDIVIDUAL ORDERS from retail customers who are sending cash or check with their order (CWO) are best handled with a sheet of 33-part address labels with pressure sensitive adhesive (e.g., Avery Label #5351). Make a carbon copy using carbon paper and ordinary typing or mimeo paper.

Type the date on the first label in the upper left hand corner of the sheet of labels. Going down the column, as you pull each order out of its individual envelope, type the check number, the amount of the check without a decimal ($16.95 becomes 1695), your code for the book being shipped and any special shipping instructions, if applicable. Then space down typing the customer's name and address.

A typed label might look like this:

```
1234   1695   spm   AIR
Dustbooks
Len Fulton
P.O. Box 100
Paradise, CA 95969
```

The check was #1234, the amount of the check was $16.95, the book was The Self-Publishing Manual and it is to be shipped via air instead of Book Rate.

The labels are easy to affix to the shipping bags. The carbon copy is your permanent record for tax and other management (planning) purposes. This system is much faster, simpler and cheaper than using individual invoices for each order. As you grow, you may install a personal computer with data base management software such as dBASE II. It will be easy to write a simple program to produce labels like the system mentioned here. However, with the computer you will be able to do much more with the collected information.

If you have another need for this individual order information (perhaps you are selling the mailing list), make another carbon or photocopy your file copy. If you want to send brochures out to past customers, photocopy the carbon sheet onto 33-part label stock.

Save the envelopes with their orders. At the end of each month, total up the responses to each address code and record the responses on a spread sheet (see Chapter Seven).

If a book is returned by the Post Office as undeliverable, check the label carbon to determine which month the shipment went out and then go through the envelopes to find the original order. The book may have been sent to the address on the check rather than the one on the envelope, numbers may have been transposed, etc. Keep the envelopes for at least six months.

When a retail order arrives without a check, make a note of the omission (such as "check not enclosed") on the envelope. Then send a brochure with a note requesting money in the correct amount. Occasionally, you will get a letter back saying that check was sent with the original order. But you will have your note on that envelope to confirm your suspicions and jog your memory. Make a photocopy of the envelope with the notation and request the sender to send you a photocopy of the cancelled check.

Small improper payments (high or low) are not worth haggling over. Just ship the book. When a customer sends too much, ship the book by air; they will be happy you used their money this way. If not quite enough, it is not worth trying to collect the difference.

Rick Hartbrodt read the previous paragraph in a library copy of the second edition of this book. Testing the author/publisher, he sent just $9.95; not enough for sales tax or shipping. Dr. Hartbrodt moved to Santa Barbara and went on to write and publish his first book. Later, he confirmed to the author that he had indeed received his book for just $9.95

Checks rarely bounce, and it is not worth the record keeping and loss of customer goodwill to delay shipments until a check clears the bank. When a check is returned, scan the label carbon to find the date the book was shipped and to identify the name with the check number. Send off a photocopy of the returned check and the bank notice that came with it. Write across the photocopy "Please send another check." Perhaps half of these "paper hangers" will make the bad check good. You may always include a short, direct letter but this photocopy technique is faster and simpler. It probably is not worth your time to expend more effort trying to collect these few, small debts.

Occasionally a customer will write complaining that he has not received his book. Check back through the label carbons to make sure you received the order, that the book was sent and when. Then write him stating the date it was shipped and that it was sent via slower but cheaper "book rate" which often takes some 30 days in the U.S. and 90 days to foreign addresses. Remind him the package had a returned address and mention that the parcel was not returned to you. Rarely does the Post Office lose books. Tell him if the book does not arrive in a couple weeks more "to return this letter and you will ship out another book." When you ship the second book, write the transaction up on an invoice and note on it that if he receives two books to "refuse delivery" of the second one. This way the Post Office will return the book to you with only postage due. If the customer accepts delivery, he may never get around to sending the book back and you are out a book. If he has already received a book the chances are very good he will refuse delivery of the second one.

Refunds should be handled promptly. "The customer is always right" or, at least, he must be treated as though he is. A cheerful, fast refund will let him know he can trust you and there is a good chance he will be back.

Complaints should be answered promptly. Even if the book has probably arrived by the time you get the complaint, you should answer. The customer will be waiting for the shipment and you must maintain credibility.

As you grow, you may investigate credit cards sales, accepting orders via toll-free (800) telephone numbers, etc. But initially, Postal and regular telephone communication will be sufficient. Remember that you are dealing with a low-priced product. Credit card sales mean more paperwork. Toll-free numbers probably will not increase your business enough to justify their expense.

DEALER ORDERS from commercial customers and those individual retail customers who must be billed are best handled with a multiple copy, carboned (or NCR) invoice. Initially, when your business is slow and you have to keep stationery investments small, you may use standard invoice forms with your address rubber stamped on them. Next you may wish to order a more attractive imprinted standard invoice form. And finally, you will graduate to your own custom designed invoice.

Invoices should be typed to insure clarity but, unfortunately, most standard invoices are not laid out for typewriter use; they require you to tab and index all over them to insert the necessary information. The most often needed information should be on the left-hand margin to eliminate tabbing.

All your commercial mail should focus on an individual. Personal contact is more effective than simply addressing a letter to a company. The people in the mail room may misdirect the letter or package if you have not included a specific person in the address.

Do not forget the customer's purchase order (P.O.) number; they want it on all invoices, packages, etc. Make sure you are sending the invoices and packages to the correct addresses; they may be different and the addresses are particularly hard to find on military and government purchase orders. Some purchase orders have three to five different addresses on them.

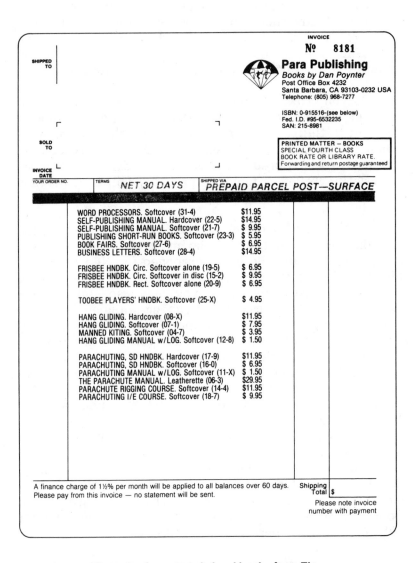

Example of a custom designed invoice form. The common information such as "shipped to," the terms and "shipped via" are light so they may be overtyped if the information is different.

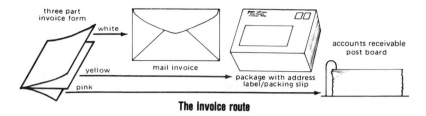

The Invoice route

Send the first (white invoice) copy via first class mail by simply folding and slipping it into a windowed #10 envelope. Include your brochure and other promotional information. The yellow second copy goes to your shipping area and the third (pink record) copy is stapled to the purchase order, hole punched and placed on your accounts receivable post board or three-ring binder in invoice number order.

If you have another need for all this invoice information, you may use a four-piece invoice. Occasionally, orders will be received with requests for "four copies of the original invoice." But suppliers often just send one with the thought that if the purchaser really needs more copies, he can use his own photocopy machine. Why spend your money for both photocopies and postage.

Invoices may be purchased with or without sequenced numbers. Some publishers like to add their own invoice numbers and work a code into them. On the other hand, others like the prenumbered forms as typing in numbers only takes valuable time.

The sales tax will have to be added onto the invoice on those retail sales made within your state. See the discussion in Chapter Three. The sales tax is on the merchandise only, not the shipping charges.

The bottom of the invoice may be used for any other pertinent information or even nice personal notes. Most publishers use a common code of abbreviations to cover the most frequent problems: "OS" (out of stock), "TOS" (temporarily out of stock), "OP" (out of print), "TOP" (temporarily out of print)., "NOP" (not our publication), "FP" (future publication, etc. On those titles you cannot ship right away, state an estimated shipping date or suggest an alternative title.

297

COMPLIMENTARY COPIES will be sent to certain reviewers, teachers who wish to inspect them for course texts and subsidiary rights buyers. "Comps" should be written up on an invoice and marked "no charge." This not only gives you a record of the freebees, helping you to keep track of the inventory, it is also more formal and lets them know they are receiving something of value.

You will have to decide on an individual basis who deserves a complimentary copy and who does not; it is a question of balancing the inexpensive publicity against the ripoff artist. Of course, many of your acquaintances will expect a special "friendship discount" (free) too and here you must draw the line. If they are really your friends, they will purchase the book. After all, you do not ask them for free carpentry or dental work. It is common practice to use slightly damaged books in these complimentary shipments. This saves you money as damaged books have little other value to you. See the discussion on book reviews in Chapter Seven.

BOOK STORAGE should not be taken lightly because books are not light. If your floor will not support a water bed, do not haul in a ton of books. The people downstairs will not like your books any better than the water. The best place to store your new product is in the garage along with the shipping table. This way, the books may be off-loaded in the driveway and stacked in the garage, wrapped as needed and placed back in the car for the Post Office run. All these operations will be with a minimum of carrying. Hauling books down steep steps into a cellar only to be wrapped and hauled back up gets old very soon and makes no sense at all. This is heavy work.

Store the books all in one place for the best inventory control. If you have them scattered around your place, at the printer's, with friends, etc. some will disappear and you will never know how many you have. If you do not have a garage or spare room, try renting warehouse space. Mini warehouses are quite common now, check the Yellow Pages.

Tell the printer you want the finished books shrink wrapped in stacks or packed in plastic bags and sealed in cardboard cartons. Each carton will weigh about 50 lbs. making them easier to stack and move. The plastic wrap will keep the books clean, dust free and the books will not rub on the carton.

Books must be kept in a cool, dry, dust-free place. Dampness may curl the pages, make them stick together and rust wire stitches (staples). It may be wise to stack the cartons on pallets so air can circulate under the stack. Sunlight will fade and yellow paper. Dust will scratch the covers and dirty the edges. Fire is always a problem and insuring the inventory in a non-commercial (hence non-fire-rated) area may be impossible.

If your books are damaged, slow or fast, you are out of business. Your inventory must be protected and this means starting by leaving the books in their protective cartons and bags and opening only one carton at a time as needed.

INVENTORY CONTROL is simpler if all the books are stored in a single place. Visual physical inspection is the easiest way to get stock information; it is faster than going through the invoices. If you quickly count the books on hand monthly, you will be able to plot a good sales chart. These figures will be a great help in your planning next year. Reorders must be scheduled so the reprints will arrive just before exhausting the previous supply. Having to report a delay in filling an order costs in paperwork, and time is money. Decisions to reprint will be determined by rate of sale, stock level, seasonal sales expectations (outdoor books sell better in the spring), the time required to print and, in some states, the date of the inventory tax.

If your state has an inventory tax, you can avoid most of the bite by careful ordering or by having your printing done in another state. Then, keeping an eye on the tax date, have the printer ship in a pallet of books as needed.

As noted above, the books should be bagged, boxed and sealed. Then the cartons should be palletized top and bottom, banded three ways and trucked to you as a unit. This keeps the books from shifting in the cartons which scratches the covers. Palletized and banded cartons are less likely to be broken open in-route but always expect at least one carton to be torn so that the spine of some books can be read. Books delivered to home addresses, as opposed to places of business, are often porno books. Of course, if you are publishing porno books, expect some to be missing from the shipment.

New titles may be shipped direct from the printer to your wholesale accounts. There is no reason to expend the time and money to route them through you.

Dun & Bradstreet reports that 9.5 percent of all business failures are due to excessive inventory. Keep the inventory under control.

THE SHIPPING AREA is where you do the picking, packing and posting. It should be arranged so as to require as little motion as possible; books, bags, cartons, etc. must all be within easy reach. Store hardcover and paperback editions of the same titles next to each other to make them easier to locate. Position the faster selling books closer to the shipping table.

PACKING involves the placing of the books in a protective wrapper so that your customer receives the clean, unmutilated goods he or she is paying for. Small wire stitched (stapled) paperbacks may be safely shipped in a heavy kraft envelope; make sure the size is correct. If the envelope is too large, the book will slide around inside scuffing the cover.

Hardcover and perfectbound (square-back) paperbacks require a padded bag. Standard padded bags are heavy, dirty and can only be stapled closed. The plastic bubble Mail-Lite bag, on the other hand, is clean, light and waterproof when heat sealed. Compared to other plastic-lined bags, the Mail-Lite is not as smooth inside making it difficult to stuff large books but they offer the best protection.

Mail-Lite bags cost more but you will save on postage. A standard 6 x 9 hardcover book measures a half inch wider and longer and is a quarter inch thicker than its paperback edition. Both fit the #1 Mail-Lite bag when they have less than 200 pages. The bags may be stapled closed or heat sealed; the sealing machines come in several sizes. Write to Sealed Air Corporation, Park 80 Plaza East, Saddle Brook, NJ 07662 for the name of the nearest Mail-Lite dealer and for their promotional deal on heat sealers. Mail-Lite bags may be stapled closed if you are not ready to invest in a heat sealer. Get the heavy hand grip type stapler. Your return address and other postal information may be printed on the bags though Sealed Air requires quite a large order; initially you will use a couple of rubber stamps.

Multiple book orders, up to three books, may be shipped in larger shipping bags. Greater quantities should be boxed. Check the Yellow Pages for a nearby office supply store and purchase standard 5½ x 8½ or 6 x 9 cartons of various depths which ordinarily come 25 to the bundle. While there, pick up some plastic bags. It is incredible how much protection plastic bags provide to the books in the carton. If you will standardize the size of all your books, you will minimize the carton and bag sizes you require. Incidentally, some states do not charge sales tax on shipping supplies, probably to encourage exports. Check on this with your office supply store.

To seal the cartons, the least expensive way is with 3" non-reinforced brown paper tape. The reinforced tape is strong but it is also dirty and hard to cut with inexpensive tape dispensers. Plastic sealing tape costs much more than paper and is harder to use. Fancy tape machines cost several hundred dollars--quite a shock--so look around for a used one. The water will flow into the paper tape easier if you add a little vinegar to the reservoir in the tape machine.

You will need ½" reinforced glass strapping tape for large cartons, so you should also use it on the small ones. Do not use twine; UPS does not allow it anymore. String takes too long to put on and it catches in mail handling machinery. You will also need some cellophane tape to seal the packing list/label envelope.

The machinery will include tape dispensers, knife, stapler or heat sealer and a 0-50 lbs. scale. Packages heavier than 50 lbs. do not protect their contents well and should not be used.

Single orders may be prepackaged and stacked to wait for a label. Done in front of the TV set, the time passes quickly. Do not overlook this opportunity to generate more sales. Always stuff in your brochure and consider inserting fliers for others. If you are shipping a hang gliding book, gather goodwill by inserting a membership application for the hang gliding association. Or, make a deal with another publisher whereby you stuff his brochures in your book and he stuffs yours in his. Once you have sold your customer a book, you have nothing left to sell, so why not stuff a competitor's brochure?

Once the bag is stuffed or the carton is wrapped, it is time to apply the commercial yellow packing list/shipping label. This copy of the invoice is simply folded and inserted into a large, pressure sensitive adhesive-backed clear envelope and placed on the bag or carton. If any other special insert is required, it should come with the packing slip and be included with it now. Now the person receiving the shipment will have exactly the same information as the person receiving the bill. Occasionally, the one receiving the bill will not want the one receiving the books to know the prices and terms (such as in a drop shipment.) In this case, simply use scissors to clip off the pricing information. When the "ship to" address is not the same as the invoiced address, cross out the latter and circle the former with a felt tip pen.

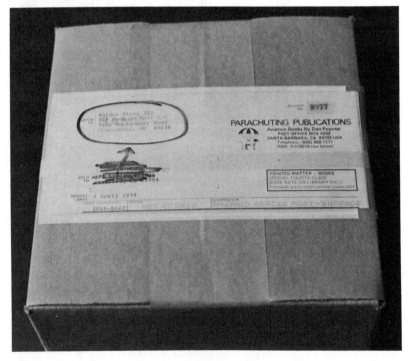

A wrapped carton with a different "ship to" address

PRINTED MATTER – BOOKS
SPECIAL FOURTH CLASS
BOOK RATE OR LIBRARY RATE
Forwarding & Return Postage Guaranteed

AIR MAIL

SPECIAL HANDLING

FIRST CLASS MAIL
THIRD CLASS MAIL

Even if you have shipping bags custom-printed, you will need rubber stamps for the cartons. Self-inking rubber stamps save time.

SHIPPING. Most books are shipped with the Post Office at the Special Fourth Class "Book Rate." To qualify, books must have at least 24 pages, 22 of which are printed, contain no advertising and be permanently bound. Book Rate is much cheaper than regular Parcel Post and there are no Postal zones to compute. The same low rate applies to any destination with a Zip Code from Guam to the Virgin Islands, including APO's and FPO's. Those packages going to libraries, schools and even bookstores associated with schools enjoy the even lower "Library Rate."

United Parcel Service (UPS) provides excellent service including daily pickup but due to zoning, their prices are competitive with the Post Office only in the first three zones and there is more paperwork. By way of comparison, a one pound parcel shipped coast to coast in the U.S. in 1984 would cost the following:

> POSTAL SERVICE
> Book rate (surface): 63¢
> Library Rate (surface: 35¢
> Parcel Post (surface): $2.48
> Priority mail (air): $2.58
>
> UNITED PARCEL SERVICE
> Surface: $1.59
> Second Day Air: $3.00
> Next Day Air: $11.50

The Postal service will accept parcels up to 70 lbs while the UPS limit is 50. Over 50 lbs., however, cartons become unmanageable and are more subject to damage.

Obtain both the domestic and international rate booklets from the Post Office and make up postal charts for both the invoicing and wrapping areas. Inflate the figures on the chart for the invoicing area to allow for the price of the shipping bag, invoice, tape, envelope, the first class postage of the invoice and self-insurance (because you will replace any books which are lost or damaged in transit.) It is cheaper to replace a lost book than to write a letter explaining why you won't.

International parcels of printed matter are limited to five kilograms (11 lbs.) Larger shipments must be broken down into 5 kg. increments or wrapped in a larger carton weighing over 15 lbs., inserted into a mail sack and shipped as "direct sack of prints" in "M" bags. Visit your Post Office for some sacks and to read section 225.953 of Publication 42, International Mail.

There is a slightly better Postal rate for Latin America which you should investigate if you are shipping a lot of orders south.

As long as the carton is plainly marked and it is obvious the contents are books, no customs forms are required. Few countries charge duty on books.

Weighed and stamped, you can drop the packages off at the loading dock at the rear of the Post Office. Just drop them into a wheeled bin. Do not wait in line at the counter. Most Postal employees do not know much about classes and rates (just quiz one about library rate or direct sacks.) Mail is usually sent from each Post Office to a centralized bulk mail facility before shipping it out of town. If you drop the packages at the bulk mail annex, they will move out faster and will be subjected to less handling. For these Postal addresses, consult your telephone directory. If you like the large ½" x 2" rubber bands used by the Postal Service, you can get a box free. Just stop by the bulk mail annex and tell them you are planning a large mailing. While there, pick up some mail trays and mail sacks.

POSTAGE METERS are nice but they cost extra time and money. It takes time to have them reloaded at the Post

Office, there is no discount on postage and they must be rented from the meter company. On the plus side, metered mail travels faster and is handled less. Stamped parcels are taken out of the bins, cancelled and thrown back in. A heavy carton may come down on some of your single book packets. Whereas the Postal clerks compare stamps with weight, they rarely return metered mail for more postage. Once your firm has grown and you are afraid some employees might be walking off with stamps, you might consider a meter. You can never stop employees from running a few personal letters through the machine but this is better than pinching a couple of one dollar stamps every day. Start out with stamps. Book rate postage will require three stamps (until the next rate change) but pasting them on won't take much longer than sticking a meter tape. If you have a lot of stamps to put on and don't like the taste, try an ice cube. Ice cubes never dry out and do not get gummed-up.

First Class Mail is best handled with a stamper machine filled with rolled stamps. Use the 100 stamp rolls, the rolls of 500 are too heavy to feed well. Stamper machines are less than $15 at most office supply stores.

PROCESSING RETURNS is not the best part of the book business. When a book comes back, make out a receiving slip. This does not have to be a fancy form, a note on a scratch pad or your notation on their packing slip will do but you will need a written record. Note the date received, the sender and the condition of the books. Determine whether any damage was caused in mailing or before shipping by the condition of the package.

Bookstore shipments almost always arrive damaged because they just will not pack the books correctly. Bookstores will dump the books in a carton without a protective plastic bag or cushioning material so they rattle around and become scuffed and bent.

On receipt, the good books should be returned to the storage area and the bad ones set aside in their box pending settling up with the dealer. Damaged books may be used as review copies, offered to acquaintances as "selected seconds" and donated to institutions.

When an individual retail order is returned by the Post Office marked "undeliverable," check the original order to verify the address. If it is wrong, slip the whole book and bag into another larger bag so the addressee will see what happened and what took so long. If address is correct, put the order and book aside and wait for his or her anxious letter or call.

Insuring books is a waste of money. Books lost or damaged in the mails should be replaced by the shipper. Your only alternative is to insure each parcel. It is far cheaper to "self-insure" and replace the occasional lost or damaged book. There will not be many lost books and the cost is small compared to insurance and the value of a happy customer.

JOINT REPRESENTATION is where a large publisher accepts a smaller one with like titles. Commonly, the big firm takes over all the marketing, distribution and billing functions as well. But the cost can be high, 20% or more of the net sale. Like the commission salesmen, the firm gets credit for all the sales no matter who generates them. Not only does the arrangement cost more than doing it yourself, you never learn the ropes. You become more dependent than ever. Since your efforts are creating the demand, most of the business will come your way with or without the middleman. Unless you simply do not have the time or the will to do your own marketing and fulfillment, joint representation should not be considered until you have operated long enough to make an educated decision.

FULFILLMENT HOUSES. If you are unable to spend the time picking, packing and posting, lack the necessary space, or would rather concentrate on writing or marketing, there are commercial fulfillment organizations which can do the job. Typically, they may charge 50¢ per order for packaging while you supply the postage and all packing materials. Additionally, they may charge $5 per month per skid of books for storage. Fulfillment firms advertise in the classified in Publishers Weekly and a large listing can be found in Literary Market Place; consult your library.

As your business grows, you may consider hiring someone to do the shipping, hiring someone to work part time out of their own home or dealing with a self-employed independent contractor. The independent contractor is usually better motivated providing better service and you avoid payroll taxes. Unless you already have other employees, hire a business not an individual for your shipping. Check the Yellow Pages and ask your printer about these independent contractors.

Whichever fulfillment choice you make, continually calculate the cost. As you grow, the figures will change and you may deem it wise to alter your procedure.

"You have all the ingredients for being a published author. This book is your recipe."

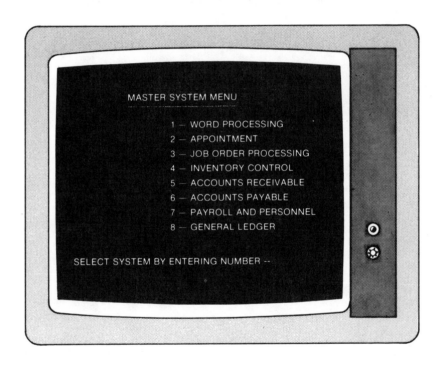

MASTER SYSTEM MENU

1 — WORD PROCESSING
2 — APPOINTMENT
3 — JOB ORDER PROCESSING
4 — INVENTORY CONTROL
5 — ACCOUNTS RECEIVABLE
6 — ACCOUNTS PAYABLE
7 — PAYROLL AND PERSONNEL
8 — GENERAL LEDGER

SELECT SYSTEM BY ENTERING NUMBER --

"A good test of the worth of a book is the number of times we can read it with profit."

Chapter Eleven

COMPUTERS AND BOOK PUBLISHING

This book has outlined manual methods of writing and publishing to provide an understanding of the systems. Now, since so many people have access to computers, we will describe their use in publishing.

The computer is making self-publishing a more attractive, affordable and competitive option in today's market. This one invention is prompting an explosion in the number of authors deciding to accept the risks and rewards of publishing themselves.

A word processor (or a personal computer with a word processing program) is an expensive typewriter but a very smart one. It is a typing system which allows instantaneous editing and it has an electronic memory capable of storing everything you type into it. The word processor saves time by eliminating both the retyping of previously approved text and redundant proofreading. The machine removes the possibility of human error inherent in retyping.

The author has been using a computer since 1980 and he feels it has increased his production 3-400 percent. Book writing is faster and easier with the mechanical cut and paste. News releases are not only easier to write, they can be individually tailored to each magazine. He maintains a list of over 1,500 magazines sorted by type to which he sends news releases and review copies. Order fulfillment and accounting are handled by machine. Contracts, policies and over 80 special letters are all stored in the machine requiring only editing for use. The author has even developed a way to set type with his computer. Setting his own type saves a couple of months and a few thousand dollars on each book. This book is a good example.

Many magazine editors agree that authors who use computers submit articles which are generally free of typos, misspellings and awkward constructions while being ahead of deadline. These writers can handle assignments on short notice and do not complain about revisions.

Computers can be asked to remember everything that has been typed into them. Correspondence, manuscripts, memos, proposals and other written material are kept in magnetic storage—usually on disks about the size of a 45 rpm record. This electronic file is not only more compact than rows of filing cabinets (some disks hold over 500 pages), the machine also has the ability to find the filed documents much faster. If a hard (printed) copy of a report is lost or destroyed, the printer can always type out a clean, new one from information that has been held in the magnetic storage.

Computer-produced work is more attractive and more professional: clean and balanced. With proportionally spaced type (the machine allows more space for a "W" than an "i") and right-hand justified margins (all lines exactly the same length) work resembling a professionally typeset effort can be produced by almost anyone.

WRITING. There is a lot of "electronic authoring" going on. Many writers are using personal computers with word processing programs to generate magazine articles and book manuscripts. In a Publishers Weekly article in 1982,

Jerome P. Frank noted that 40% of all authors already had access to word processing.

Computers improve writing immeasurably. There is a big difference between a manuscript written, edited and typed by hand, and one that has been worked over as many times as necessary to pull every last bit of creativity out of the prose and to wring out every redundant phrase or unnecessary word.

People who type original material on a computer usually find that their style improves. They can edit while they type, catching extra words, breaking up long sentences, and rewording for clarity.

Word processing reduces procrastination. Getting started on a big project is easier. Now random thoughts may be entered, and there is no need to be completely organized. Editing is easier than creating. What is tough is getting thoughts, anything, down on paper in the first place. The machine allows you to get something down on paper to be cleaned-up later.

Some word processors will mark the revised portions of a document in the margin to indicate which sections need a second look. Then on the final printout, the revision marks are deleted. This is especially useful in lengthy manuscripts.

Books are much easier to write on a word processor. Researched material and raw ideas may be typed into the computer almost randomly. The search feature may be used to locate the right place in the text for the filing of each note. As material is added to the middle of the manuscript, the text grows not from the end but in both directions from the center. Then the book may be written from these notes mostly by filling in the blanks and tying the ideas together. During the editing phase, sentences, whole paragraphs and even entire chapters will be moved as the text is organized and refined.

EDITING may be done on the computer screen before the manuscript is committed to paper. There are never any erasures or correction fluid blemishes. If even the smallest error is found, it is easy to make the change. Only when the document is ready does the printer put it on paper.

With a computer, a letter or manuscript is typed only once. The words are rearranged on the screen and then the machine takes over to automatically type out the revised, error-free document. If there are further changes, they are easily added to the copy residing in electronic storage. A final printout is made automatically and without the tedious retyping of previously proofread and approved copy.

With a conventional typewriter, a document is exposed to new errors every time it is retyped. With a word processor, duplicate proofreading is eliminated. Errors are caught and corrected during editing; and the machine keeps those phrases, paragraphs or pages error-free thereafter. Only corrections or additions need be proofed.

Some writers have sent their work to magazine and book publishers on a disk so that editing could be done on a screen rather than on paper. This author was the first to send a book to New York reviewers over telephone lines.

Many computers will help you correct spelling. One proofreading program will go through a 20-page document comparing it to its own 80,000-word dictionary in about five minutes. The program catches the misspelled words, transpositions and the narrow characters added or missing from the middle of long words that human proofreaders sometimes overlook. The value of a spelling program is easily demonstrated on old, conventionally produced documents. It is amazing how many typos the spelling program will locate in a report thought to be error-free.

The spelling correction feature not only produces better work, it may also save a great deal of time. The operator can type at rough draft speed without slowing to check spelling or worrying about transpositions.

"Search & Replace" is a time saver which promotes consistency. Say, for example, that "California" and "CA" were used interchangeably throughout a 50-page manuscript. By touching just a few keys, the machine will find the form not preferred each time it occurs and replace it with the one preferred. The machine will open the spaces for the inserted material, reformat (rearrange) the page and retype the final draft. Whereas a proofreader might miss a "CA" here and there, the computer will not. The changes can be made accurately, quickly and inexpensively.

Most word processors will allow the "programming" of words, sentences or paragraphs which are used repeatedly. For example, the term "self-publishing" is used over and over in this book. By telling the machine that an "s" means "self-publishing," it is only necessary to touch the program key and the "s" key; the machine will spell out the words. Another way to achieve the desired result is to use a code such as "sp." Then, when the manuscript is finished, make a search & replace and have the machine exchange the "sp" for "self-publishing" throughout the entire text.

PRODUCTION. Computerized typesetting has arrived and, ironically, the newer publishers with fewer titles are taking more effective advantage of the new technology than the big New York publishers. The savings in both time and money are enormous.

There are three ways to set type with a computer. The first is to draft and edit the text on a computer and then to communicate it to a typesetter over telephone lines. The result is regular photo-composition type. Typically this saves 30-40 percent in costs and cuts down the time to set a 150-page book from several weeks to a couple of days. Some typesetters can convert your media into type while others can also automatically paginate the material and scribe the trim marks in the corners. One company with advanced equipment is Data Graphics (2720 South Hardy Drive, Tempe, AZ 85282.) Call typesetters in your area and ask if they can set type from your disk.

The second way to set type is to communicate your text to a Xerox 9700 Electronic Printer. The 9700 looks like a big photocopy machine but it does not operate optically. The 9700 takes text from magnetic tape and prints it on paper. Coupled with the XICS (Xerox Integrated Composition System) software, a book may be laid out, paginated and indexed automatically--at the rate of two pages per second. This system is especially good for short run publications which must be updated frequently. Contact the Printing Systems Division of Xerox in El Segundo, California, for the address of the 9700 service bureau nearest you.

The third way to set type is to draft and edit the text on the computer and then set the type with the computer's own letter quality printer. The basic formula is to use a metal printwheel, a single-strike ribbon and clay-coated "repro" paper. The author has used this method to write, edit and typeset seven books so far.

With the proper software, most computers will produce proportionally spaced, right-justified, strike-on, camera-ready type similar to an IBM Composer.

One combination of machines and materials that has worked successfully is the IBM Personal Computer with Spellbinder word processing software driving a Diablo 630 daisywheel printer. The printer is fitted with a metal printwheel and a single strike ribbon, if available. Clay coated "repro" paper is used (IBM Photomaster #1136296.) A reversible template is used to scribe the trim marks in the corners of the typeset "board."

For a book, the savings may amount to five weeks of typesetting time, a lot of potentially frustrating and redundant proofreading, and some $2,000 in typesetting charges. With this saving of time and money, (not to mention the investment tax credits and depreciation) it is easy to see how an author/publisher can pay for a personal computer in a short time.

FULFILLMENT. Most personal computers will also run common business accounting programs. With the simple typing of an invoice, the computer will automatically subtract the items from inventory, issue packing slips and labels, then post the figures to accounts receivable and the general ledger. There is no need to re-post the information, no need to enter it twice. Accounting programs save time and avoid human error.

Another method of automating your fulfillment is to use a data base management program such as dBASE II. The data base management program (once programmed) will type out invoices and keep such financial records at your finger tips as how many books have been sold in any given period of time, what your accounts receivable should be, what the response has been to each address code, and generate mailing lists for different search categories that you have seen fit to track. Writing your own programs in dBASE may be easier and less time consuming than an accounting package for the self-published author with only a few titles, operating on a cash basis.

Writing your own accounting programs in a computer language such as BASIC is a nightmare of a job. Writing them using dBASE II is not so difficult. However, even with dBASE, most small publishers new to computing should hire a consultant.

Once you begin generating invoices with a computer, order continuous form invoices. Continuous forms save a lot of printer loading time.

PROMOTION. Perfectly phrased form letters incorporating all the key information can be stored in the machine. Correspondence is handled quickly, easily and precisely by calling a form letter to the screen; adding the date, address block and any customizing changes. Correspondence that used to take hours to compose and produce can be completed in a minute or two--including final typing. While the machine is printing out the letter, the operator can be stuffing the envelope with the enclosures.

Business Letters for Publishers is a collection of form letters useful in the book trade. It is available in hard copy, ready to be typed into any computing system as well as on disk ready to be inserted into your computer. See the appendix.

Correspondence always fits the letterhead when printed with a computer. If the letter is not perfectly balanced, the margins may be moved or the line spacing may be changed. The retyping is done by the machine.

Word processing programs are well known for producing repetitive "personalized" letters. The operator first types the letter leaving blanks for certain variables and then types the mailing list with the variables such as the amount owed and the date of the sale. The machine "merges" the two lists and the result is a letter to many addressees which incorporate a lot of personalized information. This feature is especially useful when querying magazines or doing research.

315

Computers are very useful in maintaining frequently revised documents. For example, many businesses must have current price lists; and during periods of high inflation the prices change quite often. As a result, the small changes are written in by hand. Soon the sheet is a mess and has to be retyped. This is no simple task given all the numbers and columnar work. No wonder the job is continually postponed. With a computer, it is not necessary to retype and reproof the whole page. The typist simply makes the individual changes, proofs only the corrections, and the machine types out the new, clean, error-free document. In just a few minutes, everyone has a current copy.

The computer may be asked to review the invoices for a list of all those people who have purchased a certain type of book from you. Then when you publish a second book on the same subject, it is a simple matter to send a brochure to all of them. Before computers you would have spent days going through your records and typing labels. With your computer the search can be accomplished in a matter of minutes and the labels or personalized letters can be generated while you eat dinner or walk to the mail box.

MARKET RESEARCH. By entering codes for address (magazine, etc.) and marketing (category of buyer: library, bookstore, etc.) with the orders, it is easy to find where your business is coming from. Once you know who is buying your books and through what promotion/advertising medium, you may plan on how to reach them cheaper and easier.

Again your data base management system comes in handy here. While you are generating the invoice for a sale you should keep track of what category of customer they are. Then you can go in and ask the computer how many books of a certain title were sold to wholesalers during a certain period. You may also be marketing your book through mail order. By asking the computer the same question for your mail order business during the same period a comparison of the two figures will help you to analyze whether you will spend more time and resources on getting reviews and placing ads or on your mail order business. Having this information at your finger tips helps you make the best management decisions for your business on a weekly or even daily basis.

FINANCIAL MANAGEMENT. In addition to typing and filing, computers will automate many other routine jobs. They can handle basic mathematical calculations such as totaling statistical columns and can sort alphabetical and numerical items such as mailing lists (e.g., by ZIP Code). Since word processors are simply computers set up for text editing, all they need for data (numbers) processing is a new program. Programs come on floppy disks which are inserted (loaded) into the machine by the operator.

Many small publishing firms are using data base management programs such as dBASE II to set up their own accounting and fulfillment systems. For most people it is probably more cost and time efficient to hire a computer consultant to design your own personalized system. They can then be available in the beginning for questions as you are learning your system.

For larger self-publishing operations you may want to consider purchasing a financial package to automate all your accounting procedures: general ledger, accounts receivable, accounts payable, inventory control and payroll. This takes a much larger commitment to automation and should be entered into with the full knowledge that a good background in traditional accounting methods is necessary as well as a love of the computer. For most small publishers a good data base management program will be enough to make the month-end accounting functions easy and correct.

THE NEXT MOVE. Computers take time to learn but even if you use them only for word processing, they do pay off. Start with word processing and consider other uses later. Once you do learn to use the machine, you will never go back to a typewriter.

Start by visiting a computer store for a demonstration of a newer, more sophisticated word processing program such as Spellbinder or Perfect Writer and a data base management program such as dBASE II. There are many, many programs available and some work better and/or faster than others. Have the store demonstrate the programs with your application. Take your work in and let them show you how their machine and software will run it. Your enthusiasm will grow once you see the capability of these machines.

For more information on writing and typesetting with a computer see Word Processors & Information Processing and the Computer Selection Guide both by Dan Poynter.

"The public believes three myths about authors: that a person who writes a book becomes rich immediately; that an author has an unlimited supply of free copies to hand around; and that there's a celebratory cocktail party for every book published." — William Cole in Publishers Weekly

Chapter Twelve

COPING WITH BEING A PUBLISHED AUTHOR
or
WHAT DO I DO NOW?

Once you become a published author, your life will change. Being in the limelight may not be as much fun as you used to dream. This chapter discusses some of the interesting problems you will encounter and will provide some suggestions on how to deal with them.

YOUR NEW STATUS. Your status will change from that private person the "writer" to a public person, the "expert." Your friends will treat you differently now that you are published. Some will be very happy for you and some will be jealous--jealous because they did not write the book. People new in your field will treat you like a god while those who have been around for years may be rather unkind.

Many new authors do not foresee their new popularity, their celebrity status. There is little you can do about your new treatment but to be prepared for it. Be nice and in a few years your reputation will be so strong that no one will take swipes at you anymore.

319

Gary Glenn spent 27 years working as a fire investigator. When he and his wife Peggy wrote DON'T GET BURNED! A Family Fire-Safety Guide, life at work changed. The new fire fighters put him on a pedestal while his contemporaries in the very status conscious fire fighting community were very cool. This was not the only change. Peggy was known as a successful author-publisher and Gary was not pleased at being referred to as "Mr. Peggy Glenn " at publishing functions. Now they were colleagues. The book project brought Gary and Peggy closer together while Gary's in-laws suddenly saw him in a new light.

Bob Johnson wrote a book on the Triathlon. While some of the other ironman athletes were jealous, he couldn't get rid of the groupies.

ARTICLES. Once your book is published and you become better known, editors will contact you for material. Usually they will ask you to write an article on your subject—something you probably will not have time to do. Additionally, once your book is in print, you will find new, pertinent information and will devise new, unique ways of explaining your program and methods. Your solution to these two problems is the "interview article."

As you think of an answer, draft it along with a question. Let these questions and answers build until you have several pages of them. Then when an editor calls, say you are too busy to generate an article but that you have this Q&A article with all the very latest information. Say they may select the Q&A's most likely to be of interest to their readers and to call if they have any more. They love this system and rarely can think of any more questions. Some editors run the Q&A's as is while some reporters use them to generate an original article. What is important is that you have supplied an interview with written, well thought-out answers. This system gets editors off your back, save you a lot of time, fulfills your obligation to the media and generates a lot of publicity for your book.

Another way to quickly handle these requests is to use a word processor to extract articles from your book.

Just extract a section, add an introduction and a conclusion and the article is complete.

Spin off is an important concept. Repackaging the same information for various markets will bring in more money while promoting the book. Magazine articles may be extracted from the book, book chapters may be used as a basis for conference workshops, a series of magazine articles may be combined into a book or the book may be rewritten and directed toward a new audience.

CONSULTING. Many authors consult on their area of expertise. This author consults as a technical expert in parachute and skydiving legal cases. If you decide to sell your time, set your fee schedule early so you will be ready with figures when you receive a call. Be advised that most beginning consultants price themselves too low.

SPEAKING. As a published author, you will be asked to address all sorts of groups. Make sure the gathering will be large enough to make the trip worth your while. Unless they can guarantee a large group where you may sell a number of books, you should require an honorarium. Insist on some quiet time before your speech so you can gather your thoughts.

PROMOTION. Once your book is out, you will have to switch gears and put on your promotion hat. Your creativity will be redirected to brochures, sales letters and advertising copy. When sales slow down, you will have time to write another book.

YOUR WILL. Your book is a valuable asset. Draw up a will or have your current will amended. You will die but you want your work to live on. Name an executor who understands publishing so that your books and papers will continue. The cost of a will is very little compared to the expense in taxes and litigation, the time and the heartache it could save your family and friends. See The Writer's Legal Guide by Tad Crawford.

STAY IN YOUR FIELD. It is nice to have your eggs in more than one basket but you may spread your talents too thin. You are an expert in one field. You can stay in that field and become a super expert or you can branch out into another field and run the risk of being unable to keep up with both fields adequately. The only problem with staying in one field is that it may change and leave you without a vocation. For example, if you were an expert on brewing beer and Prohibition were passed, you might have difficulty finding work.

PLACE YOUR BOOKS IN LOCAL STORES. Then when fans call up asking where they can purchase your book, you can send them to the store. This approach avoids the awkward situation where fans try to talk you into a free book and it limits their late-hour visits. A one-hour visit for one book sale is not very cost efficient. The store is a more objective sales rep. You don't have to try to talk the customer out of his or her money while they don't have to decide against the purchase with you standing there.

RESEARCHING FOR REVISIONS can bring a few surprises. Other books are liable to come out on the same subject after yours. In reading them, you will find many interesting, though familiar ideas. Many will be copied from your own work.

YOUR SECOND BOOK. Your big day arrives when someone calls for a book and you get to ask "which one?"

AFTERWORD. "We learn by doing" and your first book will be your hardest. "We learn by our mistakes" and, hopefully, through the use of this book your mistakes will be small ones. Learn the entire business by doing everything yourself before you begin to "farm out" some of the work. Doing it all yourself will provide you with a better understanding of publishing. I hope it introduces and guides you to a richer, more rewarding life.

The first step, the next one, is up to you. I hope you will take it. As you write, publish and market, refer to this manual. As you learn the business, make notes in it. Tell me your experiences. Let me know where this book may be improved. When you do get that first book into print, please send me a copy--autographed, of course.

APPENDIX
Your Book's Calendar

One of the biggest pitfalls in small publishing is the lack of sufficient planning, especially the first time around. You don't want to tie up funds by purchasing materials too soon and you don't want to miss out on some important publicity because you missed a filing date. This checklist will help to keep you on track. Follow this schedule for your first book. On your second, you will want to move some items up while skipping some others.

NOW

1. Send for five copyright forms. See Chapter Five.
2. Subscribe to Writer's Digest. See the Appendix.
3. Join COSMEP. See the Appendix.
4. Review the Appendix. Send for the books, magazines, brochures and catalogs which interest you. Join those associations which can help you.
5. Order some office supplies such as letterhead stationery and envelopes. See Chapter Three and the Appendix.
6. Write to Bowker for ABI information and forms. See Chapter Five.
7. Send to Delta Lithograph for their Publisher's Planning Kit. (14731-P Califa Street, Van Nuys, CA 91411). Normally $6.95, they will send it to you free if you order with the address as coded (-P) here.
8. Send to Bank of America, Marketing Publications #3120, P.O. Box 37000, San Francisco, CA 94137 and request both a Small Business Reporter publication index and a copy of Steps to Starting a Small Business.
9. Apply for a Post Office box.
10. Choose a company name. File a fictitious name statement if, applicable.

WHILE WRITING YOUR BOOK

1. Review Chapter Two.
2. Write the CIP Office for "Information for Participating Publishers" and some "Publisher Response" forms. Fill out a form and send it in 30 days before you deliver the manuscript to the printer.
3. Send to Bowker for ISBN information. See Chapter Five.
4. Subscribe to Publishers Weekly.

WHEN YOUR MANUSCRIPT IS NEARLY COMPLETE

1. Send ten Requests For Quotations to printers. See Chapter Four.
2. Send to Bowker for an ISBN log book sheet. See Chapter Five.
3. Design the book covers. Hire an artist.
4. Fill out the ABI form. See Chapter Five.
5. Send a photocopy of your ABI form to Baker & Taylor Co., Academic Library Services Selection Department, P. O. Box 4500, Somerville, NY 08876.
6. Send to Bowker for your own copy of Literary Market Place.

WHEN THE MANUSCRIPT IS READY TO BE DELIVERED TO THE TYPESETTER

1. Set the publication date. It will be at least five months in the future. See Chapter Seven.
2. Assign ISBN's. See Chapter Five.
3. Prepare a news release. See Chapter Seven.
4. Contact book clubs. See Chapter Eight.
5. Write the CIP Office for your CIP data and LCCC number. See Chapter Five.
6. Apply for a resale permit and, if applicable, a business license. See Chapter Three.

WHILE THE BOOK IS BEING TYPESET

1. Set up storage and shipping areas. See Chapter Ten.
2. Maintain a good proofreading schedule. Don't hold your typesetter and printer back.

3. Write Contemporary Authors for information. See Chapter Five.
4. Prepare mailing lists. See Chapter Nine.
5. Order shipping supplies and the rest of your office supplies. See Chapter Ten and the Appendix.
6. Send photocopies of the boards to certain review magazines. See "pre-publication reviews" in Chapter Seven.
7. Prepare ads for specialty magazines. See Chapter Nine.
8. Send a book announcement to all distributors.
9. Prepare brochure. See Chapter Nine.
10. Send inquiry to reviewers. See Chapter Seven.
11. Mail pre-publication offer. See Chapter Eight.
12. Print book review slips and order rubber stamps. See Chapter Seven.
13. Pursue subsidiary rights. See Chapter Eight.
14. Order reply post cards. See Chapter Seven.
15. Write to Book Publishers of the United States and Canada for an application form. See Chapter Five.
16. Write to Publisher's International Directory for an application form. See Chapter Five.
17. Write to the International Directory of Little Magazines and Small Presses for an application form. See Chapter Five.

WHEN BOOKS ARRIVE (3+ months prior to the official publication date)

1. Make promotional mailing. See "Copyrights, listings and early reviews" in Chapter Seven.
2. Photograph book and order prints.
3. Print brochure. See Chapter Nine.
4. Pursue dealer sales. You want the books to be in the stores when all the promotion hits on the publication date.
5. Draft magazine articles. See Chapter Seven.
6. File Copyright. See Chapter Five.
7. Pursue book reviews. See "Book reviews" in Chapter Seven.
8. Pursue promotional possibilities per Chapter Eight.
9. Send copy to CIP Office. See Chapter Seven.

PUBLICATION DATE

Ninety percent of your initial promotional effort will be done before your official publication date. Your consumer advertising should be concentrated in the first few weeks after the publication date.

1. Pursue consumer-oriented promotion such as autograph parties, talk shows, author tours, etc. See Chapter Seven.

2. Outline your continuing promotional program.

> *"Some people commit a crime and go to jail; others commit a crime, write a book, and get rich."*

APPENDIX
Resources

BOOKS

Most of the reference books may be found in your local library. In addition, there are many good books on writing, publishing, printing, marketing, distribution, etc. A few are listed here. Check the card file in your library, ask the Reference Librarian and visit a nearby bookstore. Write to the publishers for latest price and delivery information.

Be advised the R.R. Bowker Co. is a large firm with numerous functions, products and services. While they have several offices, most of them are at the same New York address. Each office should be treated separately.

BROCHURES ON BOOKS of interest to writers and publishers are available from:

R.R. Bowker Catalog, P.O. Box 1807, Ann Arbor, MI 48106
Direct Marketing Assn., 6 East 54rd Street, New York, NY 10017
Dustbooks, P.O. Box 100-P, Paradise, CA 95969
Gale Research Co., Book Tower, Detroit, MI 48226
Knowledge Industry Publications, 701 Westchester Avenue, White Plains, NY 10604
Ross Book Service, P.O. Box 12093-P, Seminary, Alexandria, VA 22304
Self-Publishing Book Review, John Kremer, Ad-Lib Publications, P.O. Box 1102-P, Fairfield, IA 52556
Self-Publishers Book Store, P.O. Box 2038-P, Vancouver, WA 98661
J. Whitaker & Sons Ltd., 12 Dyott Street, London WC1A 1DF, Great Britain. Covers publishing in the UK
The Writer, Inc., 8-P Arlington Street, Boston, MA 02116
Writer's Digest Books, 9933-P Alliance Road, Cincinnati, OH 45242

REFERENCE BOOKS AND DIRECTORIES may used and previewed at the reference desk in your local library. Write to the publishers for ordering details.

From: R.R. Bowker Company, P. O. Box 1807, Ann Arbor, MI 48106
Literary Market Place. Very important. Lists agents, artists, associations, book clubs, reviewers, exporters, magazines, newspapers, news services, radio & T.V., and many other services. Annual.
International Literary Market Place. Lists publishers, agents, suppliers, etc. in 160 countries outside the U.S. and Canada.
Publishers' Trade List Annual. A compilation of publishers' catalogs.
Publishers Of The United States: A Directory.
Ulrich's International Periodicals Directory.
Translation and Translators: An International Directory and Guide.
International Book Trade Directory. Lists 30,000 booksellers in 170 countries which handle U.S. publications.
Magazines for Libraries. Lists 6,500 magazines of interest from over 60,000 available.
American Book Trade Directory. Lists booksellers, book clubs, etc.
American Library Directory. Lists 30,000 U.S. and Canadian libraries.

International Publishers, Imprints, Agents and Distributors Directory.
Books in Print. Lists all books currently available by subject, title and author.
Annual.
> Paperbound Books in Print. Lists all softcover books currently available
> by subject, title and author as well as addresses of publishers.
> Subject Guide to Forthcoming Books. A preview. Bimonthly. Non-
> fiction.

From: K.G. Saur Publishing, Inc., 175 Fifth Avenue, NYC, NY 10010
American Publishers Directory.
International Books In Print.
International Directory of Booksellers
World Guide To Libraries.

From: B. Klein Publications, P. O. Box 8503, Coral Springs, FL 33065
Guide to American Directories. Lists 5,900 mail order and catalog houses.
Mail Order Business Directory. When you run out of leads, use this list of all
the other directories.
Directory of College Stores.
Directory of Mailing List Houses.

From: Dustbooks, P. O. Box 100-P, Paradise, CA 95969
International Directory of Magazines and Small Presses. A comprehensive
listing of small publishers.
Small Press Record of Books In Print.
Directory of Small Magazine/ Press Editors and Publishers International
Yearbook. Lists newspaper personnel, ad agencies, etc.

From: Gale Research Co., Book Tower, Detroit, MI 48226
Book Publishers of the United States and Canada.
Contemporary Authors. Lists biographical information on authors.
Encyclopedia of Associations. Lists over 13,000 national organizations.
Media Personnel Directory.

From: Editor and Publisher, 575 Lexington Avenue, NYC, NY 10022
Market Guide.
International Yearbook
Directory of Syndicated Features.

From: Association of American Publishers, One Park Avenue, NYC, NY 10016
Exhibits Directory. Lists book fairs and exhibits.
Educational Directory.

From: Writer's Digest, 9933 Alliance Road, Cincinatti, OH 45242
Writer's Market. Lists over 5,000 paying markets for writing, etc.
Writer's Yearbook. Information on writing, markets, etc.
Writer's Digest also publishes market directories for photographers, artists,
song writers and craft workers.

From other sources:

Ayer Directory of Publications, 210 West Washington Square, Philadelphia, PA
19106. Publication circulation, rates, etc.
Book Buyers Handbook, American Booksellers Assn., 122 East 42nd Street,
New York, NY 10017
Broadcasting Yearbook, 1735 DeSales St. N.W., Washington, DC 20036

The Dewey Decimal Classification and Relative Index, Forest Press, Inc., 85
Watervliet Avenue, Albany, NY 12206
Directory of Publishing, Bradford Mt. Book Ent., 125 East 23rd Street #300,
New York, NY 10010, Covers the UK and Commonwealth
The Foundation Directory, Columbia University Press, 562 West 113th St.,
New York, NY 10025
The Free Stock Photography Directory Infosource Business Publications, 1600-
P Lehigh Parkway East, Allentown, PA 18103
Larimi Media Guides, Communications Associates, Inc., 151 East 50th Street,
New York, NY 10022, Radio & TV show contacts.
Les Livres Disponibles, Cercle de la Librairie, 925 Larkin Street, San Fran-
cisco, CA 94109, French Books in Print
Membership Directory, American Library Association, 50 East Huron Street,
Chicago, IL 60611. Lists the names and addresses of over 30,000
members
National Trade and Professional Associations of the U.S. and Canada,
Columbia Books, Inc., 777 14th Street NW #236, Washington, DC 20005.
A directory of organizations.
National Union Catalog, Library of Congress. Available in your local library.
Standard Rate & Data Service, 5201 Old Orchard Road, Skokie, IL 60076. A
series of directories covering all types of advertising media and mailing
lists.
Vinebrook Documents, P. O. Box UP, Bedford, MA 01730. Huenefeld's forms
for publisher planning, control, etc.
Working Press of the Nation. National Research Bureau, 310 South Michigan
Avenue, Chicago, IL 60604. Lists newspapers, magazines, T.V./radio,
feature writers and internal publications. Includes (old) Gebbie House
Magazine Directory.
Writer's Handbook. The Writer, Inc., 8 Arlington Street, Boston, MA 02116.
Lists over 2,000 places to sell manuscripts, etc. Annual.

BOOKS ON WRITING, PRINTING, PUBLISHING, MARKETING, DISTRIBUTION, ETC.

Publisher addresses may be found in Books in Print. Order through your
bookstore or from the publisher. Write to the publishers for descriptive
brochures.

Allen, Herb. The Bread Game. Explains how to get grants.
Anna, James W. How to Write Your Life Story.
Appelbaum, Judith and Evans, Nancy. How to Get Happily Published.
Aronson, Charles. The Writer Publisher.
Assoc. Am. Univ. Presses. One Book/Five Ways.
Author Aid/Research Associates Int'l. Literary Agents Marketplace.
Balkin, Richard. A Writer's Guide to Book Publishing.
Barnes, J.E. How to Make Money Writing & Selling Simple Information.
Bjorkman, David. Write, Publish & Sell It Yourself.
Blackey. Publicizing Your Self-Published Book.
Bodian, Nat. Book Marketing Handbook: Tips & Techniques
    Book Marketing Handbook: Volume Two
Bohne, Harold and Van Ierssel, Harry. Publishing: The Creative Business.
Bowker. The Business of Publishing.
Bradshaw & Hahn. World Photography Sources.
Brohaugh, William. The Writer's Resource Guide.
Buell & Heyel. Handbook of Modern Marketing.
Bunnin & Beren. Author Law & Strategies.

329

Burgett, Gordon. (P.O. Box 706-P, Carpinteria, CA 93013)
    How to Sell 75% of Your Freelance Writing.
    The Query Book.
    Ten Sales from One Article Idea.
Burke, Clifford. Printing It.
Cain, Michael Scott. Book Marketing A Guide to Intelligent Distribution.
    The Co-op Publishing Handbook.
Caples, John. Tested Advertising Methods.
Case, Patricia Ann. How to Write Your Autobiography
Chesman, Joan & Andrea. Guide to Women's Publishing.
Chickadel, Charles. Publish it Yourself
Coaching Assn. of Canada. Publishing a Manual.
Copyright Office. General Guide to the Copyright Act of 1976.
Coser, Kadushin & Powell. Books, The Culture & Commerce of Publishing.
Crawford, Tad. The Writer's Legal Guide.
Curtis, Richard. How to be Your Own Literary Agent.
Dalton, Bill. Printing in Asia.
Daniel, Lois. How to Write Your Own Life Story.
Day, Robert A. How to Write & Publish a Scientific Paper.
Dessauer, John. Book Publishing: What It Is, What It Does.
Dible, Donald M. How to Write, Publish, and Market Your Own Book.
Doyle, Thomas F. Jr. How to Write a Book About Your Specialty.
Durst, Sanford J. Copyright Practice and Procedure.
Erbe & Earle. The Fifty Billion Dollar Directory—Mail Order Companies.
Geisler, Ross & Tejeda. How to Make a Book.
Goodman, Evelyn. Writing Television & Motion Picture Scripts That Sell.
Goodman, Joseph. How to Publish, Promote and Sell Your Book.
Goulart, Frances Sheridan. How to Write a Cookbook and Sell It.
Graham, Walter. Complete Guide to Pasteup.
Grannis, Chandler B. What Happens in Book Publishing.
Greenfield, Howard. Books: From Writer to Reader.
Grimm, Susan J. How to Write Computer Manuals for Users.
Gross, Edmund J. 101 Ways to Save Money on All Your Printing.
Gross, Ronald. Independent Scholar's Handbook. Turn Your Interest in Any
Subject into Expertise.
Halpern, Francis. Writer's Guide to West Coast Publishing.
Hasselstrom, Linda. The Book Book.
Hawes, Gene R. To Advance Knowledge: A Handbook on American University
Press Publishing.
Henderson, Bill. The Publish-It-Yourself Handbook.
Hill, M. & Cochran, W. Into Print.
Hoge, Cecil. Mail Order Moonlighting.
Holt, Robert. Publishing for Schools, Small Presses & Entrepreneurs.
Huenefeld, John. The Huenefeld Guide to Book Publishing.
Joffe, Gerardo. Make at Least $1 Million (But Probably Much, Much More) in
the Mail Order Business.
Johnson & Straayer. A Book of One's Own. Guide to Self-Publishing.
Kamoroff, Bernard, CPA. Small Time Operator. How to start a small
business, keep records and stay out of trouble.
Kelly, Kate. The Publicity Manual.
Kephart. Mail Order Writing Made Easy.
Kleper, Michael. Typesetting by Microcomputer.
Kremer, John. (P.O. Box 1102-P, Fairfield, IA 52556.)
    Directory of Short-Run Book Printers
    Self-Publishing Book Review
    FormAides for Successful Book Publishing
    FormAides for Direct Response Marketing.

Lee, Marshall. Bookmaking: The Illustrated Guide to Design and Production.
Lowery, Marilyn M. How to Write Romance Novels That Sell.
McHugh, John B. (92-P Hartford St., Framingham, MA 01701.)
    Introduction to Marketing, Publicity and Bookfairs.
    Advertising: Selling to the Trade and other sales.
    Direct Mail Marketing for Book Publishers
    The College Market
    Self-Publishing
    Independent Contractors and Publishers
    Product Repackaging and Book Publishers
    Audio Tape Cassettes and Book Publishers.
Mayer, Debby. Literary Agents.
Meyer, Carol. Writer's Survival Guide
Mueller, L.W. How to Publish Your Own Book.
Nicholas, Ted. How to Self-Publish and Make It a Best Seller.
Owens, Bill. Publish Your Photo Book.
Ploman & Hamilton. Copyright.
Poynter, Dan. (P.O. Box 4232-P, Santa Barbara, CA 93103-0232.)
    The Self-Publishing Manual. How to write, print & sell your own book.
    Publishing Short-Run Books
    Business Letters for Publishers
    Book Fairs.
    Publishing Forms
    Word Processors & Information Processing
    Computer Selection Guide
Rehmel, Judy. So, Your Want to Write a Cookbook!
Rice, Stanley. Book Design: Systematic Aspects.
Rice, Stanley. Book Design: Text Format Models.
Ross, Marilyn & Tom. The Encyclopedia of Self-Publishing.
Shaffer, Susan E. Guide to Book Publishing Courses.
Shinn, Duane. How to Publish Your Own Book, Song (etc.).
Simon, Julian. How to Start and Operate a Mail Order Business.
Stern, Al. How Mail Order Fortunes Are Made.
Stevenson, T. How to Start Publishing Newsletters.
Stone, Bob. Successful Direct Marketing Methods.
Strong, William S. The Copyright Book.
Strunk, W. & White, E.B. The Elements of Style.
Tattan, L.A. Publish Yourself Without Killing Yourself.
Tebbel, John. Opportunities In Publishing Careers.
University of Chicago Press. A Manual of Style.
Vandeventer & Vineyard. How to Publish a Directory.
Venolia, Jan.
    Better Letters.
    Write Right! A Desk Drawer Digest of Punctuation, Grammar & Style.
Webber, Earlynne. Your Life Story. How to Write, Print, Publish & sell it
Yourself.
Weber, Olga S. Literary and Library Prizes.
West, Celeste. Where Have All The Publishers Gone?
West, Celeste and Wheat, Valerie. The Passionate Perils of Publishing.
Weiner, Richard. Syndicated Columnists.
Wilbur, L. Perry. How to Write Books That Sell.
Wilson, Adrain. The Design of Books.
Young, Jordan. How to Become a Successful Freelance Writer.

And you will want Roget's Thesaurus, Bartlett's Familiar Quotations, a good
dictionary and a ZIP code directory. Try a used book store.

MAGAZINES FOR AUTHOR-PUBLISHERS
Write for a sample copy and current subscription rates.

ALA Booklist (book reviews)
50 East Huron Street
Chicago, IL 60611

American Bookseller
122 East 42nd Street
New York, NY 10017

American Libraries (Library news)
50 East Huron Street
Chicago, IL 60611

Canadian Author & Bookman
P.O. Box 120
Niagara-On-The-Lake, Ont.
Canada LOS IJO

Choice
100-P Riverview Cen.
Middletown, CT 06457
(undergraduate library market)

The College Store Journal
528 East Lorain Street
Oberlin, OH 44074

Directions Magazine
Baker & Taylor
1515 Broadway
New York, NY 10036

Forecast Magazine
Baker & Taylor
1515 Broadway
New York, NY 10036

The Horn Book Magazine
Park Square Bldg.
31 St. James Street
Boston, MA 02116
Books for children and young adults.

Kirkus Reviews
200 Park Avenue South
New York, NY 10033

Library Journal
R.R. Bowker Co.
P.O. Box 67
Whitinsville, MA 01588

Publishers Weekly
R.R. Bowker Co.
P.O. Box 67
Whitinsville, MA 01588
This is the magazine of
the publishing industry.

Reference Service Review
P.O. Box 1808
Ann Arbor, MI 48106
For reference librarians

San Francisco Review of Books
1111-P Kearny Street
San Francisco, CA 94133

School Library Journal
R.R. Bowker Co.
P.O. Box 67
Whitinsville, MA 01588

Small Press Magazine
205 East 42nd Street
New York, NY 10036

Small Press Review
P.O. Box 100-P
Paradise, CA 95969
Len Fulton's magazine for
authors and publishers.

West Coast Review of Books
6565-P Sunset Blvd
Hollywood, CA 90028

The Writer
8 Arlington Street
Boston, MA 02116

Writer's Digest
9933 Alliance Road
Cincinnatti, OH 45242
Inspiring reading for writers.

NEWSLETTERS FOR AUTHORS AND PUBLISHERS
Write for a sample copy and current subscription rates.

Author's Newsletter
P.O. Box 32008-P
Phoenix, AZ 85064

Editorial Eye
5905-P Pratt Street
Alexandria, VA 22310

The Huenefeld Report
P.O. Box UP
Bedford, MA 01730

Information Age Letter
Jerry Buchanan
P.O. Box 2038-P
Vancouver, WA 98668

Inkling
P.O. Box 128-P
Alexandria, MN 56308

LJ-SLJ Hotline
R.R. Bowker Co.
P.O.Box 67
Whitinsvile, MA 01588

Mail Order Connection
Galen Stilson
P.O. Box 2505-P
Bonita Springs, FL 33923

Memo To Mailers (free)
P.O. Box 1
Linwood, NJ 08221-0001

Output Mode
P.O. Box 1275-P
San Luis Obispo, CA 93406

Selling To Libraries
American Library Association
50-P East Huron Street
Chicago, IL 60611

Spotlight
Linda Meyer
18409-P 90th Avenue West
Edmonds, WA 98020

Towers Club USA Newsletter
Jerry Buchanan
P.O. Box 2038-P
Vancouver, WA 98668

PAMPHLETS AND REPORTS OF INTEREST TO AUTHORS AND PUBLISHERS. Write for latest prices.

Dustbooks
P.O. Box 100-P
Paradise, CA 95969
1.   Book Publishing Agreement by Richard Balkin. 60¢

Federal Trade Commission
Washington, DC 20580
1.   Shopping By Mail? You're Protected!
2.   FTC Buyer's Guide No. 2
3.   Consumer Alert - The Vanity Press News release dated 19 July 1959
4.   Vanity Press Findings. Dockets 7005 and 7489.

Popular Mechanics
224 West 57th Street
New York, NY 10019
1.   Profits from Classified Ads. $1.00.

Superintendent of Documents
U.S. Government Printing Office
Washington, DC 20402
1.   Domestic Mail Manual.
2.   Postal Bulletin.

3. International Mail.
4. U.S. Government Purchasing and Sales Directory.
5. Selling to the Military.
6. Starting & Managing a Small Business of Your Own (SBA 1.15:1/4)

P.E.N. American Center
47 Fifth Avenue
New York, NY 10003
1. Grants and Awards Available to American Writers. $2.25

Literature Program
National Endowment for the Arts
2401 E Street NW
Washington, DC 20506
1. Assistance, fellowships and residencies for writers.

Poets & Writers, Inc.
201 West 54th Street
New York, NY 10019
1. Awards List. $2.50
2. The Sponsors List. $2.50
3. Literary Bookstores in the U.S.
4. Writers Guide to Copyright.

Departments of the Army and Air Force
Hqs. Army and Air Force Exchange Service
Dallas, TX 75222
1. Contract Terms and Conditions (AAFES Form 4200-13/19)

Bank of America
P.O. Box 37000, Dept. 3120,
San Francisco, CA 94137 $1.00
Small Business Reporter Series
1. Steps to Starting a Business
2. Bookstores
3. Financing Small Business
4. General Job Printing
5. Mail Order Enterprises

Chicago Advertising Agency
28 East Jackson Blvd.
Chicago, IL 60604
1. Ad Guide

The Copyright Office
Office of Public Affairs
Library of Congress
Washington, DC 20559
1. General Guide to the Copyright Act of 1976

Writer's Digest Books
9933-P Alliance Road
Cincinnati, OH 45242
1. Getting Started in Writing
2. Jobs & Opportunities For Writers

PROFESSIONAL ORGANIZATIONS

Write for an application and inquire about benefits and dues. Many associations publish a magazine or newsletter.

American Booksellers Association
122 East 42nd Street
New York, NY 10017

American Library Association
50 East Huron Street
Chicago, IL 60611

The Association of American
Publishers, Inc.
One Park Avenue
New York, NY 10016

The Association of American
University Presses
One Park Avenue
New York, NY 10016

Association of Canadian Publishers
70 The Esplanade, 3rd Floor
Toronto, ON M5E 1R2

The Authors Guild
234 West 44th Street
New York, NY 10036

Aviation/Space Writers Association
1725 K Street NW #1412
Washington, DC 20006

Book Industry Study Group
P.O. Box 2062
Darien, CT 06820

Book Publicists of Southern California
9255 Sunset Blvd. #625-P
West Hollywood, CA 90069

Bookbuilders of Southern California
5225 Wilshire Blvd. #316-P
Los Angeles, CA 90036

Bookbuilders West
170-P Ninth Street
San Francisco, CA 94103

The Christian Booksellers Assn.
P.O. Box 200
Colorado Springs, CO 80901

COSMEP (Committee of Small
Magazine Editors and Publishers)
P.O. Box 703-P
San Francisco, CA 94101
This is the international association
of independent publishers

Coordinating Council
of Literary Magazines
1133 Broadway
New York, NY 10010

Independent Publishers Guild
52 Chepstow Road
London W2
Great Britain

Marin Self-Publishers Assn
P.O. Box 343-P
Ross, CA 94957

National Assn of Book Manufacturers
1730 North Lynn Street
Arlington, VA 2209

The National Assn. of College Stores
528 East Lorain Street
Oberlin, OH 44074

The National Writers Club
1450 South Havana #620-P
Aurora, CO 80012

Poets & Writers, Inc.
201 West 54th Street
New York, NY 10019

Publishers Assn of Southern California
500 South Sepulveda #215-P
Manhattan Beach, CA 90266

For a list of writers' associations, see Writer's Market.

> *"The book 'How to Beat Inflation' has just gone from $9.95 to $14.95.*

335

BOOK WHOLESALERS AND DISTRIBUTORS

For more wholesalers, see the American Book Trade Directory and Literary Market Place available in your local library. The most important are listed here.

Academic Book Center
2424 NE 52nd Avenue
Portland, OR 97213

Airlift Books
Beth Grossman
12 Market Road, #5-P
London N7 9PW
Great Britain

Angel Book Distribution Center
Andre D'Angelo
561 Tyler Street
Monterey, CA 93940

The Baker & Taylor Co.
Attn: Maureen Gordon
6 Kirby Avenue
Somerville, NY 08876

Ballen Booksellers Int'l.
66 Austin Blvd.
Commack, NY 11725

Blackwell North America
1001 Fries Mill Road
Blackwood, NJ 08012

Blackwell North America
6024 SW Jean Road
Lake Oswego, OR 97034

Bookazine Co.
William Epstein
303 West 10th Street
New York, NY 10017

Book Bus Distribution
892 South Clinton AVenue
Rochester, NY 14620

Book House, Inc
208 West Chicago Street
Jonesville, MI 49250

Booklink Distributors
P.O. Box 1275-P
San Luis Obispo, CA 93406

Bookpeople, Inc.
2929-P Fifth Street
Berkeley, CA 94710

Bookslinger
P.O. Box 16251
St. Paul, MN 55116

Carrier Pigeon
75 Kneeland St. #309-P
Boston, MA 02111

Coutts Library Service
736-738 Cayuga Street
Lewiston, NY 14092

The Distributors
702 South Michigan
South Bend, IN 46601

Eastern Book Co.
131 Middle Street
Portland, ME 04112

EBS Book Service
290 Broadway
Lynbrook, NY 11563

Emery-Pratt Co.
1966 West Main Street
Owosso, MI 48867

Gordon's Books
5450 North Valley Highway
Denver, CO 80216

Ingram Book Co.
347 Reedwood Drive
Nashville, TN 37217

Inland Book Company
P.O. Box 261
East Haven, CT 06512

"Read a good book . . . before Hollywood ruins it."

336

International Service Co.
333 Fourth Ave.
Indialantic, FL 32903

Key Book Service
425 Asylum Street
Bridgeport, CT 06610

Midwest Library Service
11443 Charles Rock Road
Bridgeton, MO 63044

New England Mobile Book Fair
82 Needham Street
Newton Highlands, MA 02161

New Leaf Distributing Co.
1020 White Street, SW
Atlanta, GA 30310

Pacific Pipeline
Michael Brasky
19215 66th Avenue South
Kent, WA 98031

Publishers Group/West
Charlie Winton
5855-P Beaudry St.
Emeryville, CA 94608

Quality Books
Tom Drewes
400-P Anthony Trail
Northbrook, IL 60062

Second Back Row Press
P.O. Box 43
Leura, NSW 2781
Australia

Scholarly Book Center
3828 Hawthorn Court
Waukegan, IL 60087

Small Press Distribution
1784 Shattuck Avenue
Berkeley, CA 94709

Yankee Book Peddler
Maple Street
Contoocook, NH 03229

CHAIN BOOKSTORES

For a complete list, see Literary Market Place and The American Book Trade Directory in your local public library. Direct your letter to the "Small Press Buyer" or the "Paperback Buyer."

B. Dalton/Pickwick
9340 James Avenue
Minneapolis, MN 55341

Walden Book Co.
201 High Ridge Rd.
Stamford, CT 06904

U.S. GOVERNMENT PROCUREMENT OFFICES.

See the "Selling to the Government" discussion in Chapter Eight.

The Adjutant General, Department of the Army
Attn: DAAG-REL
Washington, DC 20314

Acquisitions Librarian
Chief of Naval Education and Training Support
General Library Services Branch, N32
Pensacola, FL 32509

Acquisitions Librarian
Air Force Libraries Section
AFPMPPB-3
USAF Military Personal Center
Randolph Air Force Base, TX 78148

Veteran's Administration Library
810 Vermont Ave., NW
Room 976
Washington, DC 20420

International Communications Agency
Attn: Acquisitions Librarian
1750 Pennsylvania Avenue
Washington, DC 20547
or:
    Paul Steere
    ECA/FL
    International Communications Agency
    1717 H Street #756
    Washington, DC 20006

Army and Air Force Exchange Service
Attn: MR-G
Dallas, TX 75222

Co. Comm., Navy Resale Systems Office
Third & 29th Streets
Brooklyn, NY 11232

U.S. Coast Guard
Code G, FER-1/72
Washington, DC 20590

U.S. Marine Corps
Headquarters, Marine Corps
LFE
Washington, DC 20380

For the addresses of other government offices, call the local office of your congressperson. Look up the name in your telephone directory.

EXPORTERS
For a complete list, see Literary Market Place in your local public library. See the discussion of international markets in Chapter Eight.

ADCO Int'l Co.
80-00 Cooper Ave #3
Glendale, NY 11227

Kaiman & Polon Inc.
2175 Lemoine Avenue
Fort Lee, NJ 07024

Feffer & Simon, Inc.
100 Park Avenue
New York, NY 10017

Worldwide Media Service
286 Park Avenue South
New York, NY 10016

REVIEWERS
For a complete list of book reviewers and book review syndicates, see Literary Market Place in your local public library. The "Media" section in Publishers Weekly lists a couple of new reviewers almost every week. Also see the discussion and listings in Chapter Seven. Here are a few more.

John Barkham Reviews
27 East 65th Street
New York, NY 10021

Jan Frazer
P.O. Box 368-P
Naples, FL 33939

Best-In-Books
Forest Wallace Cato
205 Moonshadow Court
Roswell, GA 30075

DeKalb Book Review
Community Services Office
College of Continuing Education
Northern Illinois University
DeKalb, IL 60115

Los Angeles Times
Art Seidenbaum, Books
Times Mirror Square
Los Angeles, CA 90053

Herald Examiner
Frances Halpern, "Bookings"
P.O. Box 1976-P
Studio City, CA 91604

King Features Syndicate
235 East 45th Street
New York, NY 10017

The Madison Review of Books
1121 University Avenue
Madison, WI 53715

Albert F. Nussbaum
P.O. Box 746-P
Tarzana, CA 91365

Patrician Productions
WGCH
145 West 58th Street
New York, NY 10019

San Francisco Chronicle
Patricia Holt
901-P Mission Street
San Francisco, CA 94103

San Francisco Examiner
P.O. Box 31000
San Francisco, CA 94119

George H. Tweney
16660 Marine View Drive SW
Seattle, WA 98166

United Features Syndicate
200 Park Avenue
New York, NY 10166

United Press International
220 East 42nd Street
New York, NY 10017

BOOK PRINTERS

These printers specialize in manufacturing books. For more, see the listings in Literary Market Place and the advertisements in Writer's Digest Magazine. Those printers marked with an asterisk (*) provide extensive brochures on printing or "planning kits."

*Adams Press
30-P West Washington St.
Chicago, IL 60602

American Offset Printers, Inc.
3600-P South Hill Street
Los Angeles, CA 90007

George Banta Co.
Menasha, WI 54942

Book Press
Putney Road
Brattleboro, VT 05301

BookCrafters, Inc.
P.O. Box 370-P
Chelsea, MI 48118

BookMasters
P.O. Box 159
Ashland, OH 44805

*Braun-Brumfield
100-P North Staebler Rd.
Ann Arbor, MI 48106

Budget Book Printing
Harry Paul Publishing
1939 Grand Avenue
San Diego, CA 92109

*Champion Printing Co.
1677-P Central Parkway
Cincinnati, OH 45214

Day and Night Graphics
217-P West Gutierrez Street
Santa Barbara, CA 93101

*Delta Lithograph Co.
Ken Hoffmann
14731-P Califa St.
Van Nuys, CA 91401

*Dinner & Klein
600 South Spokane Street
Seattle, WA 98124

R.R. Donnelly & Sons
2223 Martin Luther King Dr.
Chicago, IL 60616

Edwards Bros., Inc.
2500-P South State Street
Ann Arbor, MI 48104

Graham Printing & Lithograph Co
1751 Floradale Avenue
South El Monte, CA 91733

Harlo Press
50-P Victor Avenue
Detroit, MI 48203

Inter-Collegiate Press
P.O. Box 10
Shawnee Mission, KS 66201

Interstate Book Manufacturers, Inc
2115 East Kansas City Road
Olathe, KS 66061

KNI, Inc.
1240-P South State College Blvd
Anaheim, CA 92806

Kimberly Press
Bill McNally
5390-P Overpass Road
Santa Barbara, CA 93111

Lorell Press
Industrial Park, #P
Avon, MA 02322

*Maverick Publications
P.O. Box 243-P
Bend, OR 97701

*McNaughton & Gunn, Inc.
P.O. Box M-2060-P
Ann Arbor, MI 48106

Frank Gaynor
64-P Golden Hind Passage
Corte Madera, CA 94925

*Morgan Printing & Publishing
900 Old Koenig Lane #135
Austin, TX 78756

*Multiprint, Inc.
28 West 23rd Street
New York, NY 10010

Murray Printing Company
Westford, MA 01886
Richard Palmer
9560-P Black Mt. Rd #120
San Diego, CA 92126

*Prinit Press
P.O. Box 65
Dublin, IN 47335

Publishers Press
Bert Price
1900-P West 2300 South
Salt Lake City, UT 84119

Rose Printing Company, Inc.
P.O. Box 5078
Tallahassee, FL 32301

Sprlman Printing
1801 9th Street
Sacramento, CA 95814

Thomson-Shore, Inc
7300-P West Joy Street
Dexter, MI 48130-0305

GRAPHICS AND PRINTING SUPPLIES

A.H. Gaebel, Inc.
P.O. Box 5-P
East Syracuse, NY 13057
Catalog

Artmaster
550 North Claremont Blvd.
Claremont, CA 91711
Clip art

The Bettmann Archive
136 East 75th Street
New York, NY 10022

Photos

Dot Pasteup Supplies
1612-P California Street
Omaha, NE 68102
Catalog

Dynamic Graphics
6707 North Sheridan Road
Peoria, IL 61614
Clip art

Forward Graphics
7031-P University Avenue
Des Moines, IA 50311
Clip Art

Graphics Master
Dean Lem Associates
P.O. Box 46086
Los Angeles, CA 90046
Graphics kit

Hartco Products Co.
226 West Pearl Street
West Jefferson, OH 43162
Graphic supplies catalog

Letraset USA
40 Eisenhower Place
Paramus, NY 07652
Press type

Midwest Publishers Supply Co.
4640 North Olcott Avenue
Chicago, IL 60656
Catalog

The Printers Shopper
111-P Press Lane
Chula Vista, CA 92010
Catalog

Volk Corporation
1401 North Main Street
Pleasantville, NY 08232
Clip art.

Zipatone, Inc.
150 Fencl Lane
Hillside, IL 60162
Press type

OFFICE SUPPLIES

To obtain the business forms described in this book, order from the following firms:

Business Envelope Manufacturers
900 Grand Blvd.
Deer Park, NY 11729
Envelopes.

Grayarc
P.O. Box 2944
Hartford, CT 06104
Invoices and clear packing slip envelopes.

The Drawing Board
P. O. Box 220505
Dallas, TX 75222
Memo letters ML-5-N72

Robbins Container Corp.
222 Conover Street
Brooklyn, NY 11231
Clear packing slip envelopes

MAILING LISTS

For mailing list brokers and mailing services, see the Yellow Pages of your local telephone directory. Brokers may also be found listed in Direct Mail Lists Rates and Data, Direct Marketing Magazine and Literary Market Place. Ask for them at the reference desk of your local public library. See the discussion in Chapter Nine.

If you don't mind hand addressing, go to your library and look up Bowker's American Library Directory which lists libraries and the American Book Trade Directory which lists bookstores.

For lists outside the book field, consult Direct Mail Lists Rates and Data, published by Standard Rate and Data Service available in your library. Another source is Bulletin No. 29 published and available from the Small Business Administration.

R.R. Bowker Co.
Attn: Sal Vicidomini
205 East 42nd Street
New York City, NY 10036
Bookstores, libraries, etc.

Dustbooks Lists
P.O. Box 100-P
Paradise, CA 95969

Service
P.O. Box 29214-P, Presidio
San Francisco, CA 94129
The COSMEP and Dustbooks lists

Market Data Retrieval
Ketchem Place
Westport, CT 06880
Lists of elementary and high school
   teachers, broken down many ways.

Curriculum Information Center
Ross Bldg.
1726 Champa Street
Denver, CO 80202
Elementary and high school teachers

College Marketing Group
6 Winchester Terrace
Winchester, MA 01890
College faculty broken down many ways.

The Educational Directory
One Park Avenue
New York City NY 10016
College faculty broken down many ways.

IBIS Information Services, Inc.
51 East 42nd Street
New York, NY 10017
(Foreign lists and mailing services)

American Library Assn.
50 East Huron Street
Chicago, IL 60611
Libraries and booksellers.

Hugo Dunhill Mailing Lists
630 Third Avenue
New York City, NY 10017

Ed Burnett Consultants
Two Park Avenue
New York City, NY 10016

BOOK PUBLICISTS

These professionals will schedule you for T.V. appearances, write your news releases and introduce you to their media contacts (see Chapter Seven for details.) For an expanded listing, see Literary Market Place.

Alice Allen, Inc.
Alice Allen
515-P Madison Avenue
New York, NY 10022

Deuel Purposes
Pam Deuel
P.O. Box 338-P
Santa Barbara CA, 93102

Frank Promotion Company
Ben G. Frank
60 East 42nd Street #757
New York, NY 10017

Judy Hilsinger, Inc.
Judy Hilsinger
824 North Robertson Blvd
Los Angeles, CA 90069

Susan Hirsch Publishers Services
Susan Hirsch Schwartz
500 North Michigan Avenue, #1940
Chicago, IL 60611

The Kelly Company
Paul Kelly
220 Main Street, #3
Nevada City, CA 95959

Media Tours West
Cyndy Cordova-Jensen
P.O. Box 7, Northgate
Seattle, WA 98125

Planned Television Arts
Richard Frishman
25 West 43rd Street
New York, NY 10036

PR Aids
Richard Toohey
330 West 34th Street
New York, NY 10001

Richard H. Roffman Associates
697 West End Avenue, 6A
New York, NY 10025

Promotion in Motion
Irwin Zucker
6430-P Sunset Blvd.
Hollywood, CA 90028

BOOK FAIR EXHIBITING SERVICES
If you cannot attend the fair yourself, you might hire an exhibiting service to represent you. For a complete list, consult Literary Market Place. See the discussion in Chapter Nine.

The Combined Book Exhibit
100 Providence Highway
Westwood, MA 02090

Publishers Exposition Displays
235 Park Avenue South
New York, NY 10003

The Conference Book Service
P.O. Box 298
Alexandria, VA 22314

Publishers Book Exhibit
86 Millwood Road
Millwood, NY 10546

COSMEP Exhibit Service
P.O. Box 703-P
San Francisco, CA 94101

COURSES, CONFERENCES AND SEMINARS
There are many educational programs of interest to authors and publishers. For conferences, see the list published in Writer's Market. Course for the book trade are listed in Literary Market Place. Many courses are listed in the Calendar section of Publishers Weekly and The Guide to Book Publishing Courses by Susan Shaffer and published by Peterson's Guides. Write to the addresses listed below for brochures.

Huenefeld Seminars
P.O. Box UP
Bedford, MA 01730

Stanford Conference on Book Publishing
Stanford Alumni Assn.
Bowman Alumni House
Stanford, CA 94305

Lachlan P. MacDonald
P.O. Box 1275-P
San Luis Obispo, CA 93406

UC Berkeley Extension
University of California
Berkeley, CA 94720

Publishing Institute
University of Denver
Denver, CO 80208

School of Graphic Art Pasteup
Walter B. Graham
1612-P California Street
Omaha, NE 68102
Workshop and home study course.

INDEX

COLOPHON

This book was completely produced with computer-ized equipment. The author used his computer and word processor for gathering and filing information as well as for writing, editing and even setting the type. This book is an example of typesetting with a computer.

PRODUCTION NOTES

Composition
    Input,
        IBM Personal Computer XT
        Xerox model 860 word processor
    Output,
        Diablo printer, single-strike ribbon and repro paper
    Typestyle,
        Bold PS metal printwheel
    Photocomposition type for headlines and quotes
        Fournier & Fraser, Goleta, California
    Cover art
        Robert Howard

Paper
    Text, 50# white offset book
    Cover, 12 pt. C1S white

Ink
    Text, standard black
    Cover, four colors with film lamination

Printing
    Offset, McNaughton & Gunn, Ann Arbor, Michigan

Binding
    Perfect (adhesive)

Edition
    Third edition: 10,000

FOR MORE INFORMATION

Writing, publishing, computing, and word processing books by Dan Poynter.

The Self-Publishing Manual, How to Write, Print & Sell Your Own Book. The faster, surer, more profitable way to becoming a published author. A manual on book promotion.

Publishing Forms. A collection of the most needed forms for publishing books. Everything from copyright forms to distributor new book submission applications. Why send to dozens of different places for all the forms mentioned in this book (and some not mentioned) when you can get a complete supply from a single source?

Business Letters For Publishers. A collection of 75 form-type letters conforming to the pecularities of the publishing industry. Letters cover sales, promotion, collections and other daily problems. A real time-saver. Also available on disk, write for details.

Book Fairs. An exhibiting guide for publishers with everything you need to select, arrange and operate a booth. Don't leave for a book fair without it.

Publishing Short-Run Books, How to Pasteup and Reproduce Books Instantly Using Your Quick Print Shop. A complete graphic arts book from pasteup to printing.

Word Processors & Information Processing, A Basic Manual on What They Are and How to Buy. Includes using a computer to write articles and books.

Computer Selection Guide, Choosing the Right Hardware and Software: Business-Professional-Personal. Contains a special bonus chapter on how to use a computer to set type.

Send for FREE descriptive brochure.

ORDER FORM

Para Publishing
Post Office Box 4232-P
Santa Barbara, CA 93103-0232 USA
Telephone (805) 968-7277

Please send me the following books by Dan Poynter:

_____copies of The Self-Publishing Manual @ $14.95 each.

_____copies of Publishing Forms   @ $9.95 each.

_____copies of Publishing Short-run Books @ $5.95 each.

_____copies of Book Fairs   @ $6.95 each.

_____copies of Business Letters For Pubrs @ $14.95 each.

_____copies of Computer Selection Guide @ $11.95 each.

_____copies of Word Processors   @ $11.95 each.

I understand that I may return any book for a full refund
if not satisfied.

Name:_____

Address:_____

_____ ZIP:_____

Californians: Please add 6% sales tax.

Shipping: $1 for the first book and 25¢ for each additional
book.

___ I can't wait 3-4 weeks for Book Rate. Here is $2.50
per book for Air Mail.

___ Please add my name to the Self-Publishing Grapevine
by circulating my address to other people in publishing.